THE ALLAN FAMILY

THE ALLAN FAMILY

Scottish/Canadian Shipowners

"They left the world a better place"

MAUREEN BORLAND

First Published in 2013 by
Maureen Borland
4 Shanter Place
Kilmarnock KA3 7JB

A catalogue entry is available from the British Library.

ISBN 978-0-9552714-2-7

Typesetting by Graham Lumsden, Norfolk
Printed and bound by ClaroPrint.co.uk

Contents

PART ONE

1750 – 1869

To see her is to love her,
And love but her for ever;
For Nature made her what she is,
And never made anither.

ROBERT BURNS
Saw Ye Bonnie Lesley (1792)

Chapter 1

Old Rome

The history of Scotland, going back many centuries, is one of migration to new lands and new adventures. These hardy men took with them new ways to travel, to farm the barren land, to export goods and merchandise. They introduced banking and commerce. They were guided always by their Scottish Presbyterian Faith, which they knew would see them through whatever dangers lay ahead.

The Allan family, from Ayrshire, were among these formidable early pioneers, who in the nineteenth century saw a challenge and accepted it with dogged determination to succeed. Failure was not a word that passed their lips. Born in to humble surrounding of rural Dundonald, in the latter end of the eighteenth century, Alexander (Sandy) Allan, deserves a special place among the heroes of Scotland and Canada.

The Allan Family, they left the world a better place, is the story of how Sandy Allan became, with the help of his five sons, the friend of royalty, of parliamentarians, of merchants, industrialists and bankers; how they created a great shipping line; and how this changed the lives of their children, grandchildren and their descendants.

The men of the Allan family were joined by a very formidable band of Allan women, Victorian by birth but very much the pioneers of women's movement and the right of every women to live without fear or favour and ever ready to help the poor, the dispossessed and the hungry.

The story begins with the arrival at Fairlie Estate of William Burns [Burnes], the father of Robert Burns the poet. Burns senior served as a gardener before moving two years later to Alloway. While at Fairlie, he could have met John Allan, an estate worker, who a son named James, who later became related through marriage to William Burns. James was born in 1750 and baptized in Dundonald.

3

Jean was a half sister to Robert Burns's mother Agnes, the wife of William. Jean's father and the father of Agnes and Jannet, was Gilbert [Broun] Brown; Agnes was baptized on 26 March 1732, Jannet on 24 February 1734, and Jean on 10 January 1750. All three girls were baptized in Kirkoswald and Kilmarnock. The mother of the first two girls was Agnes Rainie, she married Gilbert on 3 July 1731, while Jean's mother was Margaret Blain, whom Gilbert married on 26 June 1744.

In 1775 the following entry appears in the Dundonald Kirk Session Register of Baptism and Marriage.

> James Allan in Old Rome and Jean Broun in Irvine after having their purpose of marriage three several Sabbaths proclaimed in this congregation were married at Old Rome on 21 April 1775 years by Mr Walker.

James and Jean were to have four sons and three daughters: James born August 1776, Andrew born April 1778, Alexander born March 1780, and John born 1782. There has been considerable argument over the centuries as to exactly where Alexander was born. His birth place has been claimed by Saltcoats and Ardrossan, but the Parish Records of Dundonald are in no doubt about the place of his birth. Alexander himself confirmed the location in the Census of 1851. The three daughters were Margaret born 1784, Janet Frances born 1786 and Fairlie Cunningham, born 1790. The naming of the youngest daughter is interesting, she bears the name of the family her father worked for; much later a descendant of the Cunningham line, who died in Australia in the 1930s, bore a second Christian name of Allan.

The Allan home at Old Rome Ford was a welcome refuge to Robert Burns on several occasions when he needed a safe haven from, among others, the wrath of James Armour, the father of Jane, who at the time was expecting illegitimate twins. This was in July 1786, as he was said to be correcting proofs of his poems for what became known as the Kilmarnock Edition. Jane's babies were born early in September. Earlier in the year he had accepted a three-year post as overseer and account for Dr Patrick Douglas, in Jamaica. As James Armour pursued him Burns was ready to flee to escape his wrath. According to legend, he was about to leave on an Allan ship for the West Indies. It is very doubtful that it would be an Allan ship; the first voyage of an Allan ship was not made until 1802!

As things turned out, with the success of the publication of his poems, Robert Burns made other plans. It would be interesting to know what Jean

4

made of the behaviour of her errant nephew; in late July 1786, she was heavily pregnant with her sixth child, born just a week after the birth of Jean Armour's twins.

In trying to record exactly where James and Jean lived during their marriage, it has been a matter of trying to resolve again the differences between a cottage on the Fairlie Estate, the village of Old Rome, and Romford (Old Rome Ford). The spelling of Old Rome has at least three interpretations: Old Rome Ford, Roomfoord, Rumford; but it would, perhaps, be convenient to stick to the modern spelling of Old Rome Ford. It is perhaps worth mentioning that where a child was born was frequently not the same place as where they were baptized.

For more than two hundred years a controversy has continued as to where exactly James and Jean Allan lived.

Therefore, it should make an end to the arguments to quote the following paragraph.

> By Burns's time, it would appear, the hamlet of Old Rome also existed, for it was to it, some three years after Burns's took refuge with her, that his aunt moved with her seven children when her husband died in 1789 [*he died in 1790*]. Their former house, according to one of Jean Allan's grandsons "where Burns spent some of his evenings", was "an isolated cottage" which was "outside the village and within the policies of the Fairlie estate. The description is very precise. The policies, like the village, are distinguished as a separate area within the Fairlie estate, which implies that the Allan cottage stood within the proximity of the original mansion, as 'policies' [*is a Scots word for an enclosed ground of a large house or the part of an estate*]. The village, however, was some distance from the mansion".[1]

After fourteen years of marriage James Allan died on 23 June 1790, at Old Rome Ford, according to the Old Parish Register. Less than a month after James died, his father John died on 23 June 1790, again at Old Rome Ford, which appears from all the evidence to have been his usual home. When Burns stayed with the Allans in July 1886, he gave his address as Old Rome Ford, so it must be safe to assume that James and Jean moved from the Fairlie Estate to be closer to his father, who was then in his mid-seventies.

A gracious tribute to the character of James came from his employer on the Fairlie Estate, Sir William Cunningham Fairlie. *As for you James Allan, I never found you idle and you must do as you like.*[2]

James's death left Jean with a family of seven, all under the age of fourteen, to bring up alone. According to James's nephew Andrew Jack, in a very detailed letter written in 1886, Jean and her little family removed to a cottage at the village of Old Rome. Jean was determined that her sons would have a good education at the local school followed by an apprenticeship, fitting them for a rewarding career, and that her three daughters would find "good" hard-working husbands. Jean was true to her word.

James was apprenticed as a joiner, later becoming a wright and in February 1797 he married Jean White but he died shortly after his wedding.

Andrew served his apprenticeship as a weaver, and moved to Loudoun. In 1798 he married Anne Morton, and they had three daughters that can be identified, Anne born 1800, Janet born 1811 and Isabella born 1814. There may have been other children between 1800 and 1811 but they could have died in childbirth and their births and deaths not registered. The mortality rate of stillbirths has always been high but actual numbers are difficult to access. Andrew and Anne by 1811 had moved to Greenholm, in Galston.

John, like Andrew, became a muslin weaver. In 1803 he married Janet Richmond, and they set up home in Newmilns in the parish of Loudoun. There were five sons, James, Andrew, John, Alexander, and William, all born between 1804 and 1824. Their only daughter Janet was born in 1819.

Of James and Jean's three daughters, Margaret married Hugh Jack in August 1803 and there were, according to their son Andrew, another five sons and four daughters. Identified by a 1841 Census, their sons were, James, Richard, Alexander, Hugh, and their daughters were Elizabeth and Margaret. Unfortunately, only two of Margaret Jack's children were baptized in the parish church, but may have been baptized in an Antiburgher church or a similar Nonconformist one.

Janet Frances married James Stevenson, a mason, in 1814 in Kilmarnock. According to the Old Parish Records there were nine children; their sons were James, John, James, Andrew and Alexander. Their daughters were Mary Jean and another Mary; all the children were born between 1825 and 1832. It would appear that Janet's first two children died.

Fairlie Cunningham married James Findlay, a coal miner in Gargieston, Kilmarnock. It has been difficult to confirm the marriage and births of her children, but from a monumental inscription it possible to say she had, at least six children. Jean died in 1824 at the age of five weeks, Andrew died in 1832 aged eleven, Margaret died 1841, the wife of William Garven, she was twenty-eight years old; John died in 1848 aged nineteen, which left just Hugh and Alexander.

If Jean had ambitions for her sons, then surely Alexander more than fulfilled her wishes. There is a beautiful poem by Thomas Lovell Beddoes, a nineteenth-century poet and physiologist, that best sums up Jean's gift to her son Alexander: "*If there were dreams to sell, What would you buy?*"[3] Jean bought him a dream, and with it the courage, the wisdom and the means to succeed beyond even that which she would have wished.

Alexander began his apprenticeship as a shoemaker with James Cunninghame, of College Wynd, Kilmarnock, walking the three miles each morning and night to his home at Old Rome. When he completed his apprenticeship he began work as a wright with James Nisbet in Loudoun. The Loudoun connection is important, his brothers John and Andrew were already there working as weavers. There can be no doubt that Jean's family continued to have close links with each other.

If Jean gave considerable support and encouragement to her children, then it is surely possible that when she heard in July 1796 that her nephew Robert Burns had died she must have wept for his short life. He was thirty-seven years old, but in the ten short years since he had been at Old Rome Ford, correcting the proofs of his first anthology, he had produced a vast collection of poems, songs and letters. He may have led a life of infidelity but he lived it to the full. His enduring legacy, though, would be his written words, not his misdemeanours. The anniversary of his birth each January, would be celebrated throughout the world where there are Scottish descendants, and he is now rightly regarded as a great Scottish poet.

Jean Allan, after being a widow for fifteen years, and having fulfilled her intention of seeing her family settled and able to live independent and purposeful lives, married again. On 11 March 1805 she married Adam Baird, at Riccarton, Kilmarnock, a union that would comfort her as she grew older and her family became less dependant on her.

There is a story for young people, told in 1874 in the *Porcupine,* a Liverpool paper, of four little boys with four little boats, who sailed them on the pond at Newham Park. It was not long before their activities came to the notice of other children playing in the park. It soon occurred to the four boys that in order to extend their play, they began to send their little boats across the pond filled with sweets. Not content with that, they filled the boats with tiny dolls, and called them passengers. It was then their entrepreneurial spirit crept into their play: realizing their little boats cost money to buy and money to keep them in pristine condition, they began to charge for the transfer of sweets and dolls.

For four little boys, read five, and so began the story of the Allan Line.

It was around 1804 that Alexander moved from the Irvine Valley to the small but bustling port of Saltcoats. He had been unwell during the last few months in Galston; there are some conflicting stories about the nature of the illness, some said he injured his leg, while others said he injured his arm. Whatever the truth of the injury, Alexander's move to the bracing and invigorating air of the Clyde coast quickly restored the young man to full health. It also gave him his first glimpse of a busy seafaring life that would dominate him for more than five decades.

His apprenticeship years as a shoemaker behind him, and with the carpentry skill inherited from his father, it was not long before Capt Sandy (as he was known for the rest of his life) attracted the attention of shipowners, always on the look-out for promising young men. He was taken on as a ship's boy, although he was older than most boys, but he did not care, he had knowledge of various trades that were much in demand and his long association with the sea began. As with all things in life, he was in the right place at the right time, and had the added advantage of having the right character to be trusted by shipowners and military officials.

Saltcoats had other attractions as well; it was not long before his attention was drawn to a young lass, Jean Crawford [Craufurd]; when he came ashore after a voyage, it was to her family home in Windmill Street that he sought warmth and company. In November 1806 he and Jean were married.

Chapter 2

New Horizon

Capt Sandy would have been the first to admit he had enjoyed the thrill of the war, but now he looked for a different challenge. He turned his thoughts to a new and unexplored continent; he had strong connections with other like-minded men of Ayrshire: Alexander Harvey, James Gilkison, Samuel Paterson and John Wilson. The five men commissioned the building of a wooden brigantine from the shipbuilders Gilkison, Thomson & Co of Irvine. The Gilkison involvement with the Allan family extended for many decades. James was the shipbuilder, his brother Robert a merchant in Port Glasgow, their father was David and their mother Mary Walker.

The launch of the *Jean*, named after Capt Sandy's wife and mother, was held at Ardrossan in the spring of 1819; it would be, as all future launches of an Allan ship, an occasion for much celebration. Little did those watching that day know that the launch of *Jean* would be the beginning of a great new adventure for Capt Sandy and his sons, James aged ten, Hugh aged eight, and the twins Bryce and Alexander. The sight of the new ship, as she slipped into the waters of the Clyde, must have filled them with wonder and pride.

Capt Sandy took the ship around the Clyde coast to Greenock, which would become her home port. There was, however, much work for her master to do before embarking on his first voyage in the *Jean*. A crew had to be picked, cargo assembled and passengers signed up, and agents appointed to handle the arrangements for the first voyage to Montreal. In March 1819 there was an announcement in the *Glasgow Herald* that would be the first of many such announcements.

Notice to Shippers and Passengers for Montreal, Alex Allan, master *The Jean*, now at Greenock, will clear on Saturday 1 April, and proceed to sea first favourable opportunity there after. As Friday the 31 current is a

holiday at the Customs House, goods ought to be on board by Thursday.
John Parker, Wallace Court.[1]

Today, it is hard to comprehend the dangers the North Atlantic Ocean
posed in the days of the sailing ships as they took their much needed cargo
of dry goods to the settlers in the New World. The season for sailing from
Scotland to the St Lawrence River was short, from late April to November,
and even then storms, gales and ice floes could wreck a voyage and bring
death to her crew and her passengers.

The men who first conquered, yet did not tame the Atlantic Ocean,
were a very special breed of man. If the men sailing the ships with their
precious cargo were a special breed, then it was also true, that the settlers
in the harsh empty wilderness of Canada were made of the same grim
determination to succeed, in spite of the dangers. On the outward voyage
Capt Sandy would load dry goods, and on the return voyage he would fill
the hold with timber.

The life of a logger in the Canadian wilderness was as hard as that of
a sailor at sea: the isolation of the camps, the ever threat from the native
Indians, hungry maundering bears and other wild life made the arrival of
shipments from Scotland a welcome distraction.

> Such were the problems of trade in Canada with which [*Capt Sandy*]
> and other shipowners had to contend when they started their merchant
> business ... Another difficulty, and a danger to navigation, was the ice.[2]

Capt Sandy was lucky, he was able to make two round trips in 1819,
each trip taking almost two months. On his second trip that year he
took a few passengers; this would be a forerunner of the hundred and
thousands of passengers the Allan Line would carry over the next hundred
years.

Jean Allan did not live long enough to see and understand the success
that her sons were making of their lives, she died in 1821, aged sixty-
nine years. She had enjoyed a loving and companionable relationship with
Adam Baird for sixteen years. Less than eight days later, after attending her
funeral in Dundonald Church Yard, Adam died. In 1790 when her first

husband James died, he left her £20; Jean's Estate at her death showed that the whole amount was still in her bank account. It was to be divided between her remaining six children, but Capt Sandy refused his share saying he was certainly not in need of the legacy.

Expansion of his ambition meant that by 1822/1823 Capt Sandy, perhaps reluctantly, since he had so obviously enjoyed the little port of Ardrossan/ Saltcoats, decided that he need to move his business and his family up the Clyde to Greenock. James by now was fifteen and already familiar with ships and ship life; he probably made his first crossing of the Atlantic as a thirteen year old, on his father's ship. Hugh was thirteen, and had been educated at the local school, but by 1823 he had joined the accounting house of his father's agent, Alan Kerr & Co; this move was to prove a real apprenticeship for the rest of his commercial life. Bryce and his twin brother Alexander were just twelve, but as in so many instances when everything seems to be going well, tragedy struck the Allan family. Alexander died on 14 November 1824; whatever the sadness and despair Capt Sandy and Jean experienced, it was lessened by the knowledge that Jean was again pregnant. Her sixth son arrived in May 1825 and was named after his dead brother. In the fullness of time Alexander would pick up the baton of the family and honour not only his parents' memory but also that of his dead brother.

By 1826, three of Capt Sandy's sons were playing their part in the expansion and future of the Allan Line. James and Bryce both learnt their seafaring skills from their father and, as was the custom in those days, all the essentials of ship management both at sea and in port. They would both command their own ships with great success, and would from then on be known as Capt James and Capt Bryce.

Hugh made his first voyage to Canada in 1826 when he was sixteen and had already spent a couple of years working for Alan Kerr. That first voyage to Montreal on the *Favourite*, commanded by his father and crewed by Bryce, would have lasting implications for the young man. He had impressed one of his fellow passengers William Kerr with his knowledge of ship life and commercial acumen. Shortly after the ship docked, Kerr offered him a post as a clerk in his Canadian operation: a more accurate term would be financial accountant. Hugh always had a head for figures and knew the value and prestige that wealth would bring him.

The Canada that greeted Hugh that day was, even then, an alien world from the one he had left behind. The dockside at Montreal was a teaming mass of men loading and unloading cargoes, in what to Hugh seemed disorganized chaos. They spoke in a language he had not heard before: in 1826 most the people spoke only French. While the *Favourite* cargo was being discharged, and taking on a return load, Hugh had time to wander away from the frenetic scenes and dangers of the dockside. He must have thought of the quiet, green beauty of his Ayrshire home with its wide expanse of river, the towering hills of Arran in the distance, and the green meadows he had explored as a child. The sight of the Notre Dame Cathedral and a few fine houses did not sit comfortably with the slums and the small streams used as sewers. The stench, on a warm May day, must have been overpowering.

In spite of these unpleasant memories Hugh became devoted to Canada, and particularly the expansion of Canadian commerce and transportation; this dominated him for the rest of his life. He returned to Scotland when *Favourite* was ready to set sail, he watched from the deck as the ship weighed anchor, with mixed emotions, but he knew in his heart that Canada would be his future home.

He was, though, in those early days, restless for new adventures, and before making his future safe, he embarked on a "tourist" journey to the great untamed New World of North America. Not for Hugh the Grand Tour of European cities of Paris, Vienna, Florence and Rome with their art, literature and music; he wanted to experience the life of a settler. In 1830, after four years in Montreal, he returned to Scotland to see his family and to discuss his decision to return to Montreal and become his own master of the Allan Line.

The spirit of adventure was part of the lives of all five of the Allan sons, and something of what they experienced can be seen in the log books kept by Bryce. In meticulous detail, in a beautiful copperplate handwriting, a product of his education in Ayrshire, he records voyages, both sailing under his father as master, and later in his own right. He records longitudes, latitudes, weather and sailing times, with a precision that for the time was remarkable for a boy with only a very basic education.

In June 1829, Capt Bryce records a trip from Quebec to Greenock which took twenty-nine days; they left again in August, but the journey back to Canada took thirty-eight days, even though Capt Bryce says the weather conditions were fine.

In a log written in 1834, there is a fascinating account of exactly what he and his fellow mariners encountered every time they set sail:

> got underway and beat down to Grosse Isle, *Tam o'Shanter* in company, hove up again with a light air from the westward. Wind east, beating above the Bird Rocks. At noon off Brandy Pots. Strong breeze from N.E. carrying double-reefed topsails.[3]

As Capt Sandy's small fleet of ships expanded, there were, fortunately, some voyages that were trouble-free; but crossing and re-crossing the Atlantic, getting into fog and out of it, getting into ice and then into clear water, were a constant hazard. Simple words cannot hope to give more than a glimpse into the conflicting worlds of sailing on a ocean of azure blue with the sun high in the noon sky, and the raging wind-lashed ocean under a storm of such ferocity that all those on board the little ship must have wondered if they would ever see land again.

The life of a seafarer was hard, but for the women left at home, without the benefit of modern communications, the wait for the safe arrival of their men folk must have only added an extra burden to their everyday life. Jean, with three of her men folk away on the high seas and Hugh alone in a foreign land, must have worried constantly about them. In Greenock, alone except for the company of Alexander, who was still only a child, and three teenage daughters, to watch over and care for, she would have longed for the day when Captains Sandy, James and Bryce were home safe, before leaving on their next voyage.

The marriage of her three daughters would have occupied her thoughts as it had done for her mother-in-law. They had both wanted their daughters to marry well and enjoy the strong lasting relationships that they had enjoyed. It is to be hoped that Capt Sandy was back in Greenock on

13 December 1836, for the marriage of his middle daughter, Janet. She was twenty when she became the wife of Thomas Service, nine years her senior. Thomas was the son of William Service and Janet Workman, of Stevenson, a successful cloth manufacturer; Thomas joined his father in the business.

It is difficult to be certain how much contact Capt Sandy had with his brothers, John and Andrew, or his sisters, Margaret, Janet Frances and Fairlie Cunningham. That there was some contact cannot be denied: in 1831 when Margaret's husband, Hugh Jack, died, her son Andrew, then a small boy, remembers his cousins Hugh and Bryce coming down to see his mother. Andrew's tribute to his grandparents and his mother was perhaps echoed by many of the Allan sons:

> Peace to the ashes, and pleasant be our memories of worthy James Allan and Jean Brown ... of the present remaining memories of the Allan family, but sweeter and more tender still because far nearer to me, be the memory of their eldest daughter Margaret Allan, my dear departed mother to whom I owe more than I care to or can express.[4]

John and Andrew, weavers in Newmilns, were not as so often thought the "poor relations", but the life of a handloom weaver was not without its difficulties. In the second half of the nineteenth century the handloom was being overtaken by the power loom and the beginning of industrialization was taking a heavy toll on the small family owned looms.

Social, political, and religious unrest began to sweep the country. Prominent was the rise of the Chartist Movement, with its six demands: (1) Universal suffrage for men, (2) Equal electoral districts; (3) Abolition of the property qualifications for Parliamentary candidates; (4) Payments for MPs; (5) Annual Parliaments (6) a secret ballot. In the original charter there was no talk of trade unionism, but as the coal masters and factory owners tried to reduce wages and did nothing to improve working or living condition for the poor, the mood of the working men changed.

In many ways the success of the shipowners in opening up new routes and new trade opportunities should have lessened the worries of the weavers. Regrettably, as one new employment door opened, another closed. In many Scottish towns and villages, and in the Welsh valleys, protests by miners and the starving peasants were quelled by the militia. Violence and transportation were the natural consequences of such action. The Government, as all Governments have done since, set up a commission to look into the working conditions and the pay of the weavers, but, as always, it was the women and children who suffered.

Fairlie, the wife of a miner, was only too aware of the terrible working conditions which her husband endured day in and day out. The conditions for grown men were bad, but the implications for children as young as five or six working underground are impossible to comprehend. The terrible conditions of the mining industry in the nineteenth century can best be illustrated by the following passage:

> miners were often under pressure to work longer darg [Scots word for a day's work] for their pay while the wages themselves fluctuated wildly, reflecting the price received for the pig iron by their ironmasters, also the dominant owners of the coal mines. Their power was such that they could raise and cut wages at will.[5]

Strikes were the miners' only available response to such demands, and in the early 1840s these strikes were common. No work meant no pay, and the miners turned to raiding farms for food to feed their families: the militia and the local police exacted a terrible revenge on them, including the miners of Old Rome. Interestingly, two members of the Ayrshire Yeomanry were Majors James Fairlie and Cunningham of Caprington: a harsh world when former employers' children turned on the children of their former employees. The miners of Caprington where James Findlay worked tried to defend their pit against attack. The reason for this may not just have been to help their employers but, as reported at the time,

> An entry in the Dundonald parish records suggests why the miners at Old Rome might have had particular reason to be interested in the agitation. It noted that from June to September 1842, Old Rome had suffered from unemployment and fever, and the minister is allowed £2 for distribution.[6]
> [Ayrshire Notes 37 Spring 2009]

Capt Sandy, aware of the problems that were facing his brothers and sisters, was always ready to give them financial help. The Irvine Valley of Newmilns, Galston and Darvel, was not only involved with strikes, disease and political conflicts, it also became the centre for religious discontent. John Allan told a story of how his mother, Janet Richmond, ran into trouble with the Burghers' Church and the Antiburghers' Church. The dispute between the two churches had been raging for decades; the Antiburghers had split from the Burghers as far back as 1747. The Antiburghers eventually became members of the United Presbyterian Church, a Church that all the Allan family attended. Disputes between the two churches were common, but Janet Richmond, as her son later recalled, was a strong-minded woman who had no time for such nonsense.

> His aunt gave birth to a child, but her health would not permit the carrying of it to Galston for baptism. His uncle came to see if his mother would carry the child, which she did. Afterwards an elder of the Burgher Church came to see her to ask if she had done this, which she admitted. A meeting of the Session was held, before which she was called, but her answer was, "Go back and tell the Session that I did it, and should the like occur I will do it again".[7]

Janet Richmond, as so many of the Allan women, whether born Allan or Allan by marriage, stood up for what they believed right, and had no hesitation in telling the men who did not show an ounce of Christian or human kindness that they were wrong. The problems between the two churches were the least of Janet Richmond's worries, Newmilns, Galston and Darvel were experiencing a wave of illness that were taking the lives of their children. Scarlet fever, whooping cough and measles were rife, but what the women feared most was cholera and typhoid. Infectious diseases on land were one thing, but to Capt Sandy and the other seafarers, an outbreak of cholera or typhoid on a voyage was disastrous. The ship would not be allowed into port, and would have to lay-off until the disease had run its course. As migration became a large part of the Allan Line service, the harrowing concern for steerage passengers was whether they would reach their destination in good health, even allowing for the constant threat of *mal de mer* caused by a cruel and turbulent ocean.

Chapter 3

A Long Voyage

As the decade of the 1830s gave way to the 1840s, Capt Sandy was approaching his sixtieth birthday. He had all but retired from the sea, and was prepared to leave the shipping line in the hands of his five sons. Even his youngest son, Alexander, was about to take his rightful place among his four brothers. He had not, as Capt James and Capt Bryce, served his apprenticeship on a ship, though he was an accomplished administrator. Nor had he shown any inclination to join Hugh in Canada.

Andrew, Old Andrew as he was to be known for the rest of his life, did however join Hugh in Montreal in 1840. The previous year had been significant for Hugh, as his business partner William Edmonstone died, which then allowed him to reorganize the company, and it became known as Edmonstone, Allan & Company. But there is little doubt that by 1840, Hugh was the leading director of the new company, and they were regarded as the largest shipping company in Montreal.

The five brothers were then divided into three groups, Capt James and Bryce, Hugh and Old Andrew, and Alexander, and as happens with most youngest brothers, it was his role to try and placate the brothers when conflicts arose. And arise they did; Capt James and Bryce were first and foremost seafarers, Hugh, with Old Andrew tugging along, was a hard-headed, frequently ruthless businessman. He was not content to be second best, he wanted to be the best, and he would strive to get his way what ever it cost. In the early 1840s, to prove that he was a Canadian, he had a number of new ships built in Montreal, raising some of the capital costs locally from merchants who had traded with his father, but also getting a good deal of financial assistance from Capt Sandy and his brothers in Scotland. They may have mistrusted some of Hugh's business dealings, but they never doubted he would succeed.

The future looked secure for all the brothers, and it was then that their thoughts turned to romance; Captain James had spent almost sixteen years at sea, and at the age of thirty-four he was ready to settle down. In June 1841 he married the twenty-one-year-old Eleanora Blair Gilkison, the daughter of Robert Gilkison, a ship owner, and Eleanora Brown, of Greenock. Robert was the son of David Gilkison and Mary Walker, shipbuilders, from Irvine, Ayrshire.

As with so many Victorian marriages, Capt James and Eleanora had a large family by today's standards.

There were five sons: Alexander, Robert Gilkison, James Hugh, Richard Gilkison and Bryce. Their four daughters were Eleanora Brown, Jane Crawford, Mary Gilkison, and Janet Charlotte, all born between 1842 and 1859. Alexander and Robert Gilkison were born in Greenock, but the remaining children were registered in the Barony Parish of Glasgow. With the registration of Eleanora in Glasgow in 1846, it would be reasonably safe to assume that Capt James and his family left Greenock between 1843 and 1846, which would indicate that it was then that he made his last voyage as a commander of one of his father's ships. Capt James and his parents both sought houses in the West end of Glasgow; Capt Sandy purchased an elegant villa in Newton Place; James and Eleanora's first home was at Garnethill. By early 1850 they were in the elegant Park Circus area, among many of Glasgow's wealthy merchant families.

Eighteen months after Capt James's marriage, in January 1844, Capt Bryce married Janet Blair, the daughter of Robert, a sugar refiner and the grandson of George Blair, another Greenock merchant and shipowner. Bryce and Janet had just one son, Alexander, who became Alexander of Aros.

Nine months later, in September of that year, Montreal witnessed the marriage of Hugh Allan to Matilda Caroline, the daughter of John Smith, a Montreal dry-goods merchant. Matilda was a very young bride: the exact date of her birth is not known, but according to various census records, she was either fifteen or seventeen years Hugh's junior. Hugh brought his young bride to Scotland for their honeymoon, travelling from Montreal on the company's ship *Caledonia*, commanded by Capt Bryce. They were welcomed in Glasgow by Capt Sandy and Jean, who must have been delighted that three of their five sons were now safely married. Hugh and Matilda visited London and Paris before returning home in 1846. The couple had thirteen children including five sons: Alexander Rae, Hugh Montagu, Bryce James, John Smith and Arthur Edward. They named the first child, a son, Alexander Rae, the name of Rae coming from another of Hugh's business associates. Their eight daughters were, Jane [or Jean] Crawford, Phoebe Mary, Matilda Jane, Elizabeth, Florence Adelaide, Margaret MacFie, Edith Maud, and Mabel Gertrude. All the children were born between 1845 and 1871. To have thirteen births in a little over twenty-six years was not untypical of a family in the nineteenth century. What was surely a measure of Hugh's wealth, and his ability to care for his chldren was that only one of their sons, John Smith, died within a year of his birth.

Capt Sandy and Jean must have given themselves moments of anxiety when trying to decide which of their three grandsons named Alexander belonged to which of their sons.

Two years after Hugh's marriage, his brother, Andrew, married Isabella Ann, the elder sister of Hugh's wife, Matilda. The couple would have eight children: five sons, John Smith, Hugh Andrew, Andrew Alexander, James Bryce, William Rae, and three daughters, Jean Crawford, Elizabeth Rae and Isabella Brenda.

The 1840s, in many ways, were unique for the Allan family; before the end of the decade seven of Capt Sandy and Jean's children would be married. In September 1846, Capt Sandy's sister, Margaret, married Claud MacFie, like Robert Blair a member of a wealthy sugar refinery family. Claud was the son of William MacFie and Janet Marshall, a family that could trace their ancestral roots back to Robert MacFie of Langhouse, Inverkip. Claud's elder brother, Robert, would provide another couple of links to the Allan family. In 1851, while sailing his yacht *La Belle Anglaise* around the west coast of Scotland, Robert sailed into Airds Bay, Port Appin, and instantly fell in love with Airds House, and such was his wealth that a few weeks later he bought the whole estate for twenty-six thousand pounds.

The last marriage of one of Capt Sandy's daughters took place in Glasgow in July 1848: his eldest daughter, Jane, married Alexander

Greenhorne. Yet again, Jane was following a custom set by her sisters: Greenhorne was a ship's master and a shipowner from Greenock, and had been a business colleague of Capt Sandy's. The wedding took place at the United Presbyterian Church, Wellington Street, the minister officiating being Dr John Robson, a connection that would remain in the Allan family for decades. Jane and Greenhorne had two daughters, Jane Crawford and Lizzie Kincaid. Both were born in London, which became their home until they themselves married.

If the decade was all about weddings and births, that did not mean that the business of the family was neglected. Hugh was not about to let family social occasions interfere with his ambitions for the expansion of trade between Canada and Scotland. He was, though, back in Scotland in 1848, when he and Capt Bryce were witnesses to the baptism of their niece Jane Crawford. The Allan fleet now numbered more than eight ships, and most were regarded as being of a superior quality to any other ship plying their trade between the old country and the new world. They could also claim that they were a lucky company: in the early years of trading they lost very few vessels. The *Blonde* and the *Brunette,* part-owned by Hugh, were lost, but Capt Sandy and his two seafaring sons, Capt James and Capt Bryce were extremely lucky, not that their voyages were always free of hazards.

Capt Bryce, as master of the *Albion,* left Glasgow on 25 March 1847 bound for Montreal. The ship was only two years old, and was in every way the finest ship of her type. He had no reason to believe they would not have a trouble-free journey, indeed, they were sixteen days into the trip, when he had written to his family a few days earlier to say that so far he had encountered no problems. Then things changed dramatically:

> The *Albion* entered the ice on Saturday, April 10. When I was writing to you a few days ago everything was going on smoothly, but what a change since then! My prognostications about the ice have proved correct, and this is the third day we have been in it. For two days we continued boring through it with a fair wind, but last night a gale of east wind, springing up with snow, caused us to lay the ship and to furl the sail. To-day the wind is right ahead, blowing a gale, and we are still drifting in the ice without

a stitch of canvas set. We are heartily sick of it, and would be thankful for a glimpse of clear water.[1]

The *Albion* was not alone. Three other ships had entered the pack ice before her: *Great Britain, Eromanga* and *St Andrew. Great Britain,* belonged to the Ellmann & Hall Line, the other two were not Allan vessels, although they did have a *Saint Andrew* in 1861. Capt Bryce admitted, even after a few hours, he was already heartily sick of the ice and prayed they would soon see clear water. He then added another heart felt plea:

I hope, if we get all out safe, this will be a warning to the ship owners not to despatch the ships so early in the spring.[2]

Four days later he wrote a telling passage in his letter of how he came to be in the terrible situation that he and the others ships found themselves:

This voyage hitherto has been one full of adventure. On Monday night we succeeded in getting the good ship into clear water. About 40 miles from Cape Ray we found a clear passage of 30 miles between the ice and Newfoundland, but as we approached the Cape the passage became narrower until I found scarcely room to work the ship and, had last night not been calm, I do not know what we would have done, as the land being white with snow it is very difficult to ascertain our distance off at night. We therefore came here, Port-au-Basque where we now lie at anchor. I this afternoon, went up to the top of the high hill, and found with the aid of good glasses, that there was nothing to be seen but ice, ice, as far as the eye could reach.[3]

On the fifth day, Capt Bryce, admitted that he was tired of the ice and wished with all his might that he was able to weigh anchor. But, as he admitted, there was slight damage to the ship and he did not want to inflict more damage by barging a way through the ice. He knew that was not possible; he told his family in the letter that up to that moment he thought the Great God had been kind to him, but prayed that he would even yet show him a way of getting out of his difficulties and take him and his ship safely to their destination. On the last day of April, having spent nearly three weeks trapped in the ice, Capt Bryce wrote:

We were all day yesterday within a mile of being into clear water, but the wind was blowing upon the shore which caused the ice to pack up so thick we can walk for miles and miles upon it. The passengers walked to the *Bellisle* yesterday, which is a full mile from us and came back in less

than two hours after spending some time aboard her. We were cheered a
little yesterday by a visit from two men from a sealing schooner which was
in the edge of the ice. They informed us they had come from Cape Breton
and that the gulf is quite clear of ice.[4]

This is the first time in his letter that Capt Bryce mentioned *Bellisle*; she was
the *Belle Isle,* a barque out of the Clyde and owned by Kirkwood, and like
Albion, bound for Montreal. As with the *Eromange,* an error in transcribing
has occurred, she was the barque *Erromange,* out of Greenock and owned
by J Kelso. The Masters of the two ships were Capt Reid of the *Belle Isle* and
Capt Ramsay of the *Erromange*.

April turned into May and still Capt Bryce was stuck in the ice. His
thoughts turned to those at home in Scotland who would be enjoying a
May Day; he prayed that his God would grant him escape from his icy
tomb, but as he sadly admitted there was very little to remind him of May
day. His description of the hazards they encountered are graphic indeed,
hunger not being the least of them. The captain of the *Belle Isle* sent a crew
member to Capt Bryce to beg for provisions, as he and his crew were on
the point of starvation. He gave the crew man a hundred pounds of beef,
but was saddened that he could not spare more. He and his own crew were
already on short rations. The unimaginable cold, the fear of disease, and
the barren wilderness without a sign of human habitation were taking a
terrible toll of their spirits. As in such situations when only death seems a
likely outcome, Capt Bryce and his crew are given comfort from a visit from
a Free Church Minister, who was a passenger on one of the other stranded
ships. Capt Bryce voices his appreciation of the visit, but added somewhat
wistfully:

> we were all much refreshed [*by the Minister's prayers*]. I think they were
> very rash in attempting to come; as the ice was so bad they had difficulty
> in reaching us, when they were returning, the ice gave way, and I was
> obliged to launch my lifeboat and get them safely on board, for which
> they were grateful.[5]

It was not the only time during the long ordeal that Capt Bryce thought
he would have to take off her crew and passengers. As the ice moved and
they were drawn along by the flow, there was the ever-present danger
they would hit a sunken rock that lay a mile off shore. If that happened
they would have to abandon ship and take their chances on the barren
coast. He was both lucky and unlucky: they did not sink but it was

not until the third week of May that *Erromanga* finally escaped from the ice. *Belle Isle* escaped two days later, then a gale blew up and all hopes Capt Bryce had of following them into clear water faded. On 21 May, after twenty-one days he, his crew and passengers were still stuck in the ice.

> My heart almost failed me this morning when I saw the ice as firm as ever, and it is snowing and freezing, more like January than ... May. I feel very dull since the other two ships got clear, left alone in this place, far from the track of ships and our provisions going down so fast. It is a dull prospect with [*nineteen*] cabin passengers mostly females. ... Oh! that God would deliver us from this ice.[6]

Finally, after being stranded for forty-six days, the *Albion*, her gallant captain, crew and passengers were free of the ice and could make their slow progress to the port. News reached Glasgow on 28 June that the ship, her captain, crew and passengers were safe. They arrived back in Greenock in early July. The welcome home must have indeed been a moment of great celebration, and the last words Capt Bryce wrote in his long letter only added to his sense of achievement: *We are all thank God in perfect health.*[7]

Capt Bryce was right to thank his God: emigrants, passengers, and crew members from many of the others ships that had been stranded during that terrible spring of 1847 had not been so lucky, hundreds had died of disease or hunger.

In 1843, a thirteen-year-old Campbeltown boy entered the service of the Allan Line, initially as clerk to George Gillespie, agents for the Allan Line. Five years later he joined the Allan Line. Whether this was one of Capt Sandy's last acts as head of the family firm, or whether it was the first by Capt James and Alexander, it was an inspired decision. Nathaniel Dunlop, born in 1830, was the eldest of four sons of Archibald Dunlop, a hosier, and Jean Smith. He had been educated at Campbeltown Grammar School, leaving at the age of thirteen. Some time between 1841 and 1847 the whole family left Campbeltown and moved to Glasgow. In 1841 Archibald was a widower. By 1851 Nathaniel was a Canadian Merchants' Clerk, his brother Matthew was a Commission Merchants' Clerk, and James was a student at

Glasgow University where he was studying medicine. The youngest, John, was still at school. The family home was in Hospital Street, Gorbals.

It was very soon obvious to both Capt James and Alexander that Dunlop was a young man with energy, business aptitude, and with a burning passion to succeed; and, from their point of view, a good foil to Hugh's rather aggressive nature in wanting to ride rough-shod over his brothers. As later became clear, Dunlop was a man of exceptional charm and courtesy in dealing with passengers and their various concerns. He had an elegant, easy-going nature that belied his deep-seated concern that everything should be done right.

Chapter 4

Shipping Disasters

The early years of the 1850s were a time of expansion for the Allan brothers; Hugh in Montreal was looking very much to the future expansion of his business. The deepening of the St Lawrence Seaway would have delighted Capt Bryce, but it was emigration that was responsible for the increase in passenger numbers. These came partly from the Highland Clearances of the eighteenth and early nineteenth centuries, when crofters were forcibly removed from the land in order that absentee landlords could replace them with sheep and later deer, which they believed would be more profitable. Many of the poor and dispossessed peasants had little alternative but to emigrate to North America. In the 1850s the crofters were followed by the handloom weavers and others, ruined by the increasing use of mechanization. Sad as all this was for the Allan family, taking migrants to Canada became a large part of their trade.

The voyage to Canada for cabin passengers was probably just about bearable in a fair wind: for steerage passengers it was a very different experience. Complaints among emigrants were, however, not common as most accepted the hazards of the journey knowing that they had no other option. There is a warning given in a letter from a migrant on board the J & J Cooke vessel, *Nubia*, going out to Canada, that the would-be emigrants would be wise, if they wished to be at all comfortable during their voyage, to take their own bed, and not rely on those *miserable apologies* supplied by the Cooke Line.

Such criticisms of the comforts on Allan ships were never voiced, indeed, Capt James and Alexander were among subscribers and supporters of the Glasgow Unemployed Handloom Weavers' Emigration Fund. When the *St Andrew* left for Canada in June 1864, the emigrants were selected and mustered on board, where they were addressed by the secretary of the

Fund, the Rev Dr McTaggart; he was followed by James Watson with a few words of advice and encouragement to the emigrants as they started out on their new adventure. As the welcome committee were about to leave, one of the emigrants, Robert Richardson, stepped forward to express

> in a simple but feeling manner, the gratitude of the handloom weavers for the liberality and labours of the subscribers and committee ... The arrangements for the comfort of the emigrants were highly creditable.[1]

The safe and secure world for the Allan sons ended in March 1854, when Capt Sandy died at his Glasgow home, in Newton Terrace. He was seventy-four years old, and the world into which he had been born had changed beyond all recognition. He had seen his small shipping operations at Saltcoats become one of the major players in the cross-ocean shipping traffic. If he made a mistake, it was his opposing, in 1853, the desire of his sons and their Canadian partners to raise the finance to build five steam ships. Capt Sandy was a sail man and did not believe that steam would ever replace sail.

Capt Sandy died a wealthy and generous man. His Will gives a glimpse into his true nature: he may have been wedded to the past, but his thoughts were always on the future of his extended family. He added a codicil which ensured that his niece, Janet Morton, would have an annuity so that she could continue to look after her father, Capt Sandy's brother John. The shares in the shipping line he left equally to his sons, and to his three daughters he gave each a share, ensuring that they would always have an interest in the future prosperity of the Allan Line. His house in Newton Terrace and all its contents he left to his wife, as well as enough financial security to enable her to live well. It is also worth noting that at the time of his death he still owned the little cottage in Hamilton Street, Saltcoats, that had been their first home.

The death of their father left his sons with the usual dilemma of who should inherit the senior position in the company. The problem urgently needed resolving, as there were, by 1854, three major branches of the fleet: Hugh and Andrew in Montreal, Capt Bryce in Liverpool, and Capt James and Alexander in Glasgow. Capt James and Alexander were more cautious in their attitude to expansion, Capt Bryce, was if anything neither on one side or the other, Hugh, however, had no doubt about what he wanted to do; in 1854 he launched the Montreal Ocean Steamship Company as part of the Allan Line. Capt Bryce called his end of the operation "Allan & Brothers"; in Glasgow, Capt James and Alexander became "J & A Allan", but they were all still collectively known as the Allan Line.

It was Hugh's intention to go ahead with the building of steam ships; the first Allan steam ship was appropriately named the *Canadian,* built by Denny & Co. Hugh had plans for the ship, even before his fleet of superior and fast ships were ready, as he sincerely expected he would soon be able to offer the Canadian and British Governments a fast reliable service in return for a substantial subsidy.

It was less than three months after Capt Sandy's death that the youngest of his five sons married in June 1854. In choosing Jane Smith as his bride Alexander was marrying into yet another shipping family. Jane was the only daughter of Robert Smith and Eliza Service; Eliza was herself the daughter of William Service and Jane Workman, and was, therefore, a cousin to Alexander. Robert and his younger brother George owned and ran the City Line of Calcutta; they were born in Saltcoats at about the same time as Capt Sandy first set foot there.

Alexander and Jane were to have nine children, seven sons and two daughters. The eldest son, Alexander, died within three days of his birth, their third son, George William, born at Knockderry Castle, Cove, died in infancy. Robert Smith, James Alexander, Charles Edward, Henry and Claud Andrew, lived full lives. Their two daughters were Eliza [Elsie] and Jane [Janie]; all the nine children were born between 1855 and 1871.

Since Alexander married into the Smith family, with its close links to the wider Allan family, it is perhaps wise to give a reasonably full picture of the Smith brothers and their ancestry. George Smith, the father of Robert and George, was a weaver by trade and a small shipowner; he had married

Margaret Workman in 1798; there was a third son, James, born to the couple in 1799, but little is known about him.

George senior, his wife and his sons went to Belfast in 1810 where he established a textile business with the financial assistance of a bounty from the British Government. He was followed by other Ayrshire men, including members of the Workman and Clark families, all seeking Government bounties to start their businesses. George's business in Ireland was financially very successful, but when Margaret died he became lonely and depressed so he returned to Glasgow, and his enthusiasm for business never returned. He remained as nominal head but left the day-to-day running of the business to Robert and George. In 1837 he did find a measure of happiness when he married again, one Marion Watt.

George junior's life very much followed a similar pattern to that of his father; in 1830 he had married Margaret Richardson, but she died shortly after giving birth to a son, George Richardson, in 1832. In 1837, the same year of his father's second marriage, he married his sister-in-law, Ellen Service. There were to be five children, one son and four daughters, George, Jane, Margaret, Ellen and Eliza, all born between 1837 and 1847.

Robert and George junior shared much of their working life in a happy and fruitful partnership, and although they were similar in their attitudes and beliefs, there were differences in their characters. Robert was

> specially distinguished by a calmness and dignity of demeanour and a kindliness of disposition that nothing could disturb.[2]

George in contrast was more curt, and quick to take offence, yet he had a powerful intellect which masked his underlying kindness and consideration. Where other men may have lagged after an arduous day's work, George could, and often did the work of three men, rarely with a moment's complaint. George, as with all members of the Smith/Workman/ Service families, was a devout and active member of the Congregational Church. In politics he was not a member of any party, but did hold liberal views. He was not often actively engaged in public affairs, but when called upon to take part in shipping and railway investigations, he used his astute business mind to seek the truth before coming to a decision. When the integrity and the honesty of the directors of the Caledonian Railway Company was questioned by its shareholders, George took on the task of proving or disproving the allegations, and came out on the side of the company, to the dismay of the disgruntled shareholders. After the decision, he became the largest shareholder of the ordinary stock. Had he not bought the shares the Caledonian Railway would have closed, and Scotland would have lost its foremost railway.

The early years after Capt Sandy's death were a turbulent time for his sons; he had been a very competent seafarer who during his long years at sea had suffered the loss of very few of his sailing ships; and, in spite of the extreme weather conditions, few of his passengers had died at sea. Hugh's decision to introduce steamships looked for a few years as if his Midas touch and his luck had deserted him; during the years between 1857 and 1864 the Allan Line suffered the lost of nine steamships.

Did Hugh make a tragic mistake in commissioning a fleet of steamships too quickly? Did he employ masters and crews with insufficient knowledge and experience of steamships? Did he ensure that his captains had accurate charts and a good understanding of navigation? These are just a few questions which must have gone through the minds of Hugh's more cautious brothers. He and they were to pay a very high price for his reckless ambition to be the largest and most successful steamship owner in Canada.

In November 1859, the *Indian* was wrecked off Cape Race with the loss of twenty-seven lives. Three months later, in February 1860, the *Hungarian* was wrecked off Cape Sable with the loss of 237 lives. The loss of two ships in such a short space of time was a tragedy for the passengers who died, but it was also a disaster for the Montreal Ocean Steamship Company and the Allan family. They would have agreed wholeheartedly with the sentiments expressed by a Canadian correspondent to *The Scotsman*:

> The loss of the *Hungarian* is to Canada not only a great commercial calamity, but a serious national disaster. Much of the progress and prosperity of the country depended on the continued efficiency of the Montreal Ocean Steamship Company, and in the *Hungarian* that company has lost its "flagship" ... This tells heavily, against the line in contrast to the uniform success and safety of the Cunard steamers ... yet it is impossible to blame the company or their employees, we can only say they are signally unfortunate.[3]

Hugh's rage at some of the comments would not have been pleasant to witness: to be compared with Samuel Cunard was bad enough, to be thought that he ran a dangerous and inferior shipping line would have been more than he could bear. He knew that none of the losses were attributed to the ships being sub-standard, nor were his captains and crews ill-trained and negligent; there had never been a suggestion that the loss of the ships were caused by anything other than adverse weather. And over that, neither he or his brothers had any control.

Unfortunately, the losses continued, and Hugh and his family had to endure another four years of disasters.

The *Canadian* was the second of the Montreal/Allan Line to carry that name, replacing the first *Canadian* that was lost near Quebec just three years after being built. There was, in this instance, no loss of life. Her namesake was not so lucky, nor was her captain as fortunate as Capt Bryce had been aboard the *Albion* when he had been stranded for forty-six days in 1847:

> The *Canadian* was lost about noon on ... [4 June 1861] about five miles off Belleisle. The weather at the time was thick, and a short sea on. The ship was going "dead slow" when she struck a large piece of sunken ice, the top of which was flush with the water, and which appears to have ripped up the bottom of the vessel to a large extent.[4]

In spite of the efforts of Capt Graham, thirty-four passengers and crew died; that so many were saved is testament to the work of Graham and his crew that day in launching the lifeboats and getting his frightened passengers aboard. There were three French fishing boats in the vicinity and the passengers and some crew members were quickly transferred and taken to Quirpon Bay. Graham then chartered the largest of the French boats to take the survivors to St John's, Newfoundland. He left the two officers at the site of the wreck with instructions to intercept the *North Briton* and order her to follow the barque to St John's. The two officers and the rest of the crew managed to board the *North Briton* and sail up to Point Armour.

> The latter attempted to force her way down to St John's, but owing to the dense fogs and impenetrable ice, she was compelled to abandon the attempt and steer away for England, after a detention of seventy hours ... It was expected that the barque would reach St John's in time to telegraph to Montreal for the *Hibernian*, leaving Quebec on the 15 June, to call at St John's, and pick up survivors.[5]

It was not unusual for rumours to spread such as that Capt Graham had been negligent and derelict in his duty to his passengers and crew, and it was left to his Chief Officer, Alex Kelly, to put matters right. Writing from Liverpool on his return he stated:

> An impression having gone aboard that the ... *Canadian* was coming home by the Straits of Belleisle [sic] at an unusually early period of the year, and the loss of the ship is attributed to her having taken a passage, I beg to inform you that the Straits are frequently clear of ice by the end of April, and generally by the middle of May. It has been stated that the navigation is intricate and dangerous, but the captains of all steamers trading to Canada consider it much safer than the route south of Newfoundland, which is proved by the fact that no accident has ever happened to a steamer in the Straits of Belleisle.[sic][6]

Capt Bryce, aboard the *Albion* fourteen years earlier, would have been only too aware of the dangers a ship could encounter in the waters around Newfoundland in early April. He had warned at the time that it was not possible to say with any degree of certainty that the Straits of Belle Isle would be free of ice in late spring or even in early summer. Weather, in and around Newfoundland, Nova Scotia and the entrance to the St Lawrence Seaway was, as he knew only too well, not something that could be predicted with any degree of accuracy.

The heavy toll of losses increased with the wreck of the *Anglo-Saxon* in May 1863, 250 died, again the accident occurred off Cape Race. She was at the time considered to be the finest of the Montreal Ocean Steamship Company, and as a report in the *New York Journals,* and later repeated in *The Scotsman,* the fate of the ship was not the result of errors by her owners or crew:

> The terrible disaster to the *Anglo-Saxon* would most undoubtedly have been avoided but for the unaccountable refusal of the British Government to follow the Associated Press, the New York underwriters, the Transatlantic Steam Companies, and other parties in New York, to place one of Daboll's powerful air trumpets at Cape Race, which could be distinctly heard in foggy weather from six to ten miles at sea, and would save millions of property and hundreds of lives.[7]

There was a damning condemnation of the actions of some of the crew of the *Anglo-Saxon* by the barrister at the Board of Trade Inquiry. He said the

33

officers deserved the highest praise for their efforts to save the passengers after the vessel hit the rocks, but he had heard on good authority that

> the conduct of the crew was dastardly and foul in the extreme, and contrasted strongly with the general characteristics of British seamen. The crew appeared, during the trying scenes which occurred at the time of the wreck, to think of nothing but their own safety, and five of them succeeded in carrying away a boat which would have held at least forty persons.[8]

It seemed inevitable that in holding the BoT Inquiry, they would try to lay the blame on the captain and the crew. Capt Burgess had served the Allan Line well, and was a skilful officer; unfortunately, he was among those who perished in the wreck and could not refute the allegations against his crew. John A Allan, the third officer, however, gave a very detailed and honest appraisal of the events of that terrible day, and in particular the courageous part played by Capt Burgess and his crew.

Hugh in Montreal, Bryce in Liverpool, and James and Alexander in Glasgow, must have begun to wonder if there would ever come a day when they could look back on the loss of so many of their ships, their passengers and their crews, and so be able to plan for the future. There would be one final tragedy before that day came; in late February 1864, the *Bohemian* struck Alden's Rock, four miles outside Cape Elizabeth. She sank within an hour just off the shore of Richmond's Island; she carried nineteen cabin passengers, 199 steerage passengers, mainly migrants, and a crew of about ninety-nine. The local people from Cape Elizabeth rushed to the scene of the disaster, the first lifeboat to come ashore had a man and a child, both were dead. Teams were sent from Ocean House and the fishing house to help the survivors. The rescuers were helped by the Captain, Robert Borland, and his crew who managed to launch all the life-boats, all of which, with the exception of one that was swamped, managed to get to the shore. Nineteen passengers did not make it, but the rescuers did manage to salvage the mail. Captain Borland blamed himself, and as he said later he thought

> he was four miles further off than he was. The haze had mis-led him as to the true position of the lights. He had been looking for the pilot, and throwing up rockets and blue lights for half-an-hour, and was going at the rate of a mile and a half-an-hour when the vessel struck. Half-an-hour before he got soundings in forty-fathoms of water, with a soft bottom.[9]

The Board of Trade Inquiry, held in April 1864, was scathing in their condemnation of Capt Borland's actions leading up to the wreck of his ship:

> The Court having carefully weighed the evidence in this case, and given due consideration to the statement of the master, feels constrained to pronounce that the *Bohemian* was lost by the default of Captain Robert Borland ... The Court has to regret that the prudence and caution which Captain Borland evinced in using his lead while approaching the land seems to have deserted him at the most critical time.[10]

The Court's judgement against a captain who hitherto had had an exemplary record of service to the Allan Line was devastating. They removed his Certificate to sail, and suspended him for twelve months. It was too much for Capt Borland, he went home to his wife, three young sons and daughter, a broken man. He died in November 1870, of disease of the brain.

The loss of the *Bohemian* was the last of the ships the Montreal Ocean Steamship Company and the Allan Line suffered during those dark, terrible days from 1859 to 1864. The next decades would be a time of expansion, and they would regain their reputation for safety and competence.

Chapter 5

Bird & Dunlop

The death of a child is always a matter of regret, but the death of a wife can never have been a matter of easy acceptance. Capt James and Eleanora had been married for twenty-seven years, when she died at Claverhouse, Hunters Quay, Dunoon, in July 1868. She had not lived long enough to see her children marry, and indeed when she died three of her children, Mary and RichardG were in their early teens and Bryce was only nine. It is not difficult to appreciate just what a shock her death caused her husband and family. She had been ill for nine months with epilepsy, a condition for which in 1868 there was no treatment available. RobertG, her second son, was with her in Claverhouse when she died and was the informant of her death.

It was not unusual for the Allan Line to have to refute wrong information which had appeared in the press, and in June 1866 they wrote to *The Scotsman* denying the rumour that there had been an outbreak of cholera among the passengers of their ship, the *Peruvian,* which had recently left Liverpool for New York:

> [she] was a steamer formerly engaged in the New Orleans trade, and was, we believe, engaged to carry out to New York a portion of the German emigrants who were detained some time in Liverpool on account of the prevalence of cholera on board the *Helvetia.*
>
> The *Peruvian* of the Canadian mail line of steamers sailed eight days ago, from Liverpool to Quebec, and so far all the passengers by that line this season have reached their destination *in safety and in good health.*[1]

The *Helvetia* was owned by the National Steam Navigation Line, and once an infectious disease is confirmed aboard a ship it was not unusual for another Line to offer passengers a berth once they had been cleared of the disease and were no longer thought to be carriers.

Emigration in the middle of the 1860s was still very much a source of income for most of the ships going to the Americas, to Australia and New Zealand. It was the welfare of migrants that brought an English-born woman, Isabella Bird, to the notice of the Allan family and in the first instance to Nathaniel Dunlop. Isabella was born in 1831, the daughter of a wealthy clergyman, but as with her mother, Dora Lawson, she had a deep caring and compassionate nature, and a determination to spread the word of God to the poor of all lands. Concerned at the plight of the Highland crofters, she set about arranging for a number of them to travel to Canada where she would ensure they and their families would have a better life. Dunlop remembered vividly the first time Isabella came into the offices of the Allan Line to arrange the transport arrangements for her Hebridean crofters. At that time, due to government regulations, she was not allowed to help emigrants from the mainland of Scotland:

> The impression left … is of my great desire to serve the singularly gifted young lady well [*she was only a year older than Dunlop*]. She astonished me by her energy and her capacity in making arrangements for the conveyance of the emigrants … When all was settled and her people were about to embark, she was amongst them, seeing to their every want.[2]

Dunlop went on to say that for him, those early days of her involvement with emigrants was such that he and the Allan family were willing to help in every way they could. On the evening of the ship's sailing, Isabella was with the emigrants and she stayed with them all night until the ship left port. Never one to make just a token gesture, Isabella had provided the Highlanders and their family with

> new garments for all of them. Her mother, Dora, and Isabella's younger sister [*Henrietta*], and her loyal and ever charitable friends brought her cloth for gowns, coats, and kilts, calico and flannel, and such necessaries as brushes, combs, shawls, bags and hold-alls.[3]

It was to be hoped that the "Highland laddies" were better equipped after their first winter in Canada; before leaving their native Scotland, they had had little previous experience of the kilt and putting them on was remembered with amusement by a watcher on the eve of sailing: "*struggling with those twisted and uneasy skirts have never been forgotten*". The sight of those young Hebridean men struggling with the elegant modern version of the kilt would have been amusing, but to see them trying to don the kilt in its original form would have caused much amusement. The origin of the kilt was a piece of cloth, usually tartan, two yards wide and between four and six yards in length. To dress himself, the wearer

> put his leather belt on the ground and then placed the material lengthways over it. This he then methodically plaited it in the middle ... over the belt until he had gathered along its length leaving as much at each end as would cover the front of his body ... laying down on the belt, he would then fold these ends – overlapping each other.[4]

In 1866, Isabella arranged for another group of emigrants to go out to Canada, and recalling the incident much later, Dunlop wrote:

> One man alone of those who shared with myself in the shipping part of the work remains, and when I asked him if he recollected Isabella Bird and her Highlanders, – "Yes," he cried, "I mind her well, a grand woman she was. She went out with us on the *St David* in 1866, to Portland, Maine, when I was an officer in the ship. She went out to visit the people she had helped to settle in Canada." I have every reason to believe that she was instrumental in founding a prosperous settlement.[5]

Isabella Bird's emigrants were among the most fortunate of thousands and thousand of migrants that travelled the high seas in the nineteenth century. Conditions on some of the ships were intolerable, and it was not unknown for emigrants to be sent out on unseaworthy vessels with the very minimum of comforts.

Though he gave her help and assistance, Isabella Bird was not the only young woman in Nathaniel Dunlop's thoughts in 1866. He had marriage on his mind, but there does not appear to have been any hint of romance in his relationship with Isabella. He had "set his cap" at another young lady. She was Ellen Smith, the daughter of George Smith, and therefore also the niece of Jane Smith, wife of Alexander Allan, who was Dunlop's employer.

There is always a certain amount of misgiving on the part of fathers, who are notoriously reluctant to part with their female offspring. This was certainly true of Ellen Smith when she married Dunlop on the 13 June 1866. That she was eleven years younger than him may have been an added reason for George to be reluctant to give his blessing.

There is a story that when Dunlop asked George for the hand of his daughter George is reported to have been very reluctant to grant the request to a shipping clerk with not much prospects of advancement. Dunlop must have had a quiet smile when he replied that he had just been made a director of J & A Allan. To rise to the heights of a director in nineteen years and to consider marrying into the Allan/Smith/Service family must have impressed George: he gave his consent. The wedding took place at the bride's palatial home of Mount Blow.

Hindsight is a wonderful thing. But one is left to ask, would George have been so ready with his consent, if he had known that less than sixteen months later his daughter would be the mother of a baby girl, and less than a month after the birth, Ellen would be dead. According to her death certificate, she had suffered from rheumatic fever for ten days, and bleeding in the brain, which killed her in half an hour. Her brother-in-law, Dr James Dunlop, a witness at her wedding, had administered to her, but all to no avail. Dunlop, like his father-in-law, was to learn that money, position and the best medical care that was available could not buy the life of their young wives.

RobertG, was now twenty-three years old; he had for some time been working with his father Capt James and his uncle Alexander in the Glasgow office. The two senior directors probably thought the time had come to broaden the young man's experience. Bryce was running the Liverpool office, and RobertG went to join his Uncle Bryce and his cousin Alexander. In Glasgow, under the tutelage of his father and uncle, he had displayed an aptitude for commercial life and having an easy-going nature he very quickly became a welcome addition to the Liverpool operation. He combined his duties for the Allan Line with his work as a member of the Mersey Docks and Harbour Board, and he was one of the original directors of the International Marine Insurance Company.

In the spring of 1867 RobertG married Margaret Williamson Bennett, the daughter of William Bennett, a merchant, and Janet Findlater. Margaret had been born in Barony, in 1846, but by 1851 her mother was dead. Her father was in his mid-fifties with four children under the age of eleven to bring up without a mother.

Perhaps the only disappointment to the marriage of RobertG and Margaret is that it would remain childless.

A couple of months before RobertG's marriage, his elder sister, Jane Crawford, married; and not for the first time or the last this involved an Allan marrying a MacFie. Her husband was William, the son of Robert MacFie of Airds and Agnes Fairrie. William worked for the family sugar refinery business, and in 1861 he was in Birkenhead as a lodger with the Rev James Towers, a United Presbyterian Minister. In 1864, he married Agnes Hamilton the Rev Towers' eldest daughter, but shortly after the wedding, Agnes died, aged twenty-four. William's marriage to Jane Crawford Allan in 1867 lasted rather longer than a few months; they were to have six children, three sons, Robert, James Allan and Claud, and three daughters, Eleanora Gilkison, Mona Graham, and Jane Crawford Allan. Not only did the families inter-marry but they continued to give their children the surnames of their grandparents, parents and of their sibling's partners.

In less than three decades since Capts James and Bryce had sailed two, or at most times three times, a year to Canada, during the spring and summer seasons, by 1869, the Allan Line was sailing two or three times a month and not just to the St Lawrence Seaway. No voyage, however, was without risk as the company had learned in the late 1850s and early 1860s, but by 1868 conditions at sea for passengers, both cabin and steerage, and for their crews were improving beyond anything Capt Sandy ever experienced when he fist set sail. He would also have been shocked at the level to which the fares had risen in half a century. Cabin passengers were charged between thirteen and fifteen guineas, steerage passengers would pay around seven guineas. It was also now possible to book tickets in Great Britain from three major Allan offices: J & A Allan at 70 Great Clyde Street, Glasgow, Allan Bros & Co, Weaver Building, Brunswick Street, Liverpool, and Montgomery and Greenhorne, 17 Gracechurch Street, London. The Greenhorn connection is another reminder of just how inter-linked the family was, and how much they relied on those well-established connections to run their successful businesses.

If the ships and fares had changed, then so too had the level of service offered to the passengers, as Isabella Bird had discovered. The happy emigrant was worth the little bit of pampering: the passengers paying high fares wanted better conditions on their voyages.

As sail gave way to steam, major changes in the services the Allan ships could offer would not seem out of place in the floating hotels which now take thousands upon thousands on cruises around the world. In 1861 the Allan Line commissioned Denny of Dumbarton to build them a new liner. The *Hibernian,* when she went into service from Liverpool to Quebec, was among those ships to offer her passengers a daily report of their progress across the Atlantic Ocean. A remarkable document survives from a voyage which began early in April 1868; the *Hibernian's* first Master was Capt Smith who had recently joined the Allan Line after being Master with the Glasgow Line. The document, *the Hibernian News*, was the work of Thomas Rudd, the Saloon Steward. The first daily report written by Rudd showed that he had a very dry sense of humour. Writing under a sub-heading of "General Intelligence" he reported:

> It may not be out of place to remark that The Company for whose benefit this illustrious literary work is written, is not totally deficient in it-we may even add, above par-but as for those who would scorn to appreciate our efforts, the less we say about their intelligence the better.[6]

Rudd's first report gave the reason why the first *Newsletter* had only just appeared:

> We beg to apologize to our numerous subscribers for our non-appearance since the 16th instant. We had the misfortune to be deeply in debt of Father Neptune, for which he cruelly stuck us "in Limbo". We are happy to inform you that, through *indefatigable exertion*, we have at last succeeded in *raising* the needful *"de profundis"*, and have paid our debit in full, interest, though we must confess that the payment has left our pocket empty, and, therefore, contributions, however small, will be thankfully received.[7]

The *Newsletter* was not the only form of entertainment, they played parlour games, including a version of horse racing usually with four to six players. It was played on a board, with paper horses and a dice. The races were named after the Classics, including the Derby, and the 2,000 Guineas. Even in 1868, betting was allowed, and must have had Capt Smith's full approval as he was prepared to take an active part in the proceedings. On one occasion, at least, his horse won. They also held concert nights: Capt Smith was again in the forefront of the entertainment with a poem, "The Sea-Sick passengers", but this, as Thomas Rudd later wrote:

> was too much for us: it was too cruel of him to choose this subject, to remind us of our reduced circumstances. Had he read it badly, we might have forgiven him.[8]

Capt Smith, was also encouraged to sing "England the Pride of the Ocean", although, perhaps that should have been Scotland. Whatever he sang, it was in true naval style. The passengers so obviously enjoyed Rudd's newsletter, that one was able to write for publication:

> An excellent bill of fare is presented for dinner to-day, so all are expected to appear with good appetites and clean faces, to do justice to the good grub.[9]

Entertainment and good food were only a part of the joys of that voyage, but as always it was the weather that was frequently the main topic of conversation in all parts of the ship and in many of Thomas Rudd's editorial musings.

On Monday morning, 27 April, an unnamed passenger penned his impressions of that day, and there is much in his story that would have been well-known to Capt Bryce:

> Yesterday morning shortly after breakfast, the cry was heard, "Ice ahead," and on returning on deck after an excellent breakfast, we found that the ship was surrounded by large pathohes [*sic*] of ice, but the openings were quite large enough for us to get through without contact with the masses. It was one of these lovely mornings that we read of in novels, the golden sun rising majestically out of the eastern ocean, an ocean of burnished silver, studded with islands, islets and rocks of frosted silver, the whole far eclipsing any scene in the "Arabian Nights", or Eastern tale ... *Land ahead* on the starboard bow, caused a rush to that side, and all the glasses were in requisition; it was made visible to the naked eye, and every one

saw it quite distinctly. Immediately after receiving recognition from the officer of the watch, it vanished as if only waiting for official recognition. Those who took most credit for the first discovery, vanished as suddenly as the land from the landscape. It was a remarkable specimen of a fog mountain.[10]

The fog cleared and they were able to see that they were just off the little French fishing settlement of St Pierre et Miquelon. Later that day they saw a schooner ahead of them that had been held in the ice for thirty-four days. Capt Smith did not leave the bridge on that Sunday morning and the church service was cancelled and held later in the evening, but even then Capt Smith did not, as usual, conduct the service. The service when it was held in the late evenings was conducted by the doctor who stood in for the captain. The doctor was named Malloch. This is the first time that evidence has been found of Allan steamships now carrying qualified members of the medical profession. As the number of passengers increased, so did the need for professional care. In the *Hibernian Newsletter*, Thomas Rudd reported that during the voyage there had been a number of accidents, three to legs, five to arms and a fractured skull, and all had been treated by Malloch successfully.

In assessing the difference that the ice made to Capt Smith's voyage, it is only necessary to look at the log that Rudd had produced: after leaving Liverpool on 16 April, they had averaged 200 miles a day; for three days between 27 and 29 April they covered just 127 miles. The skill of her captain and his crew was outstanding, and the passengers were able to show their gratitude to Lieut W R Smith RNR, Captain of the Royal Mail Steamship *Hibernian*:

> Your saloon passengers, desirous to appreciate your excellent management of the good ship "Hibernian" during the present voyage from Liverpool, and more particularly your unwearied attention while jammed in by heavy ice off the Newfoundland, have had a meeting, at which their acknowledgement of your service and ability in having successfully extricated the ship from her difficulties and having carried her to safety ...[11]

The money raised was to be used for the purchase of a silver tankard or another piece of Sheffield silver. After the disasters of the previous few years, the reputation and service given by the Allan Line to her passengers, her cargo clients and her crews was again where it had been in Capt Sandy's time.

PART TWO

1870 – 1893

A few seem favourites of Fate,
In Pleasure's lap carest;
Yet, think not all the Rich and Great
 Are likewise truly blest.

ROBERT BURNS
Man was Made to Mourn (1784)

Chapter 6

Capt Bryce & Aros

T he end of the previous decade had been a bad time for Hugh Allan; the difficulties encountered by his ships in St Lawrence Seaway convinced him that things had to change. He made his views known to the port authorities that it was urgent, and necessary, to deepen the Seaway otherwise Montreal would never be a first class port for his larger ships. The Montreal Harbour Commission wanted to assist, but were not sure that they could, or should, do all that Hugh wanted. He was not always very popular, and his popularity did not improve when he was knighted in 1871; there were those who thought he had not earned the honour. A newspaper report later in the year spelt out the problems that he was facing

> there is a rumour that Sir Hugh Allan had formed the intention of making Quebec the terminus of the Allan line of steamers, owing to the difficulty experienced this summer by steamers of large draught, such as the *Sarmatian*, proceeding from Quebec to Montreal without being first lightened, and the crowded state of the harbour on their arrival. Several vessels have also been grounded in the St Peter channel, owing to the unprecedented lowness of the St Lawrence. This channel must be thoroughly dredged, if Montreal wishes to compete with Quebec and maintain her standing as the head of tide, or ocean, navigation.[1]

In his discussions with the Montreal Harbour Commission, Hugh could well have stated that in Glasgow, the Clyde Trust had already begun to make significant progress in dredging the River Clyde to allow for larger vessels to dock in Glasgow. In 1871, Capt James was chairman of the Clyde Trust, and at one meeting in April 1871 he was able to announce a large increase in the revenue the Trust had received that year.

As with all successful businesses and the men that ran them, accusations of wrongdoing were often made against Sir Hugh and the Allan Line. The truth is that rarely, if ever, were these accusations substantiated; it is true that Sir Hugh was an aggressive and often arrogant man, but he was always ready to help when called upon. If carrying goods and passengers were the currency of the Allan Line, then occasionally they were asked to carry unconventional cargo. One such occasion was caused by the sudden death, in 1871, at St John's, New Brunswick, of James Renforth, a world champion sculler.

Renforth had accepted a challenge from the Canadians to race over six miles on the Kennebecasis River. Renforth's crew that day was made up of Kelly, Chambers and Percy. After less than two hundred yards, to those watching from the river bank, something was sadly amiss with the British boat. Renforth was swaying side to side and seemed unable to control his movements, or his oar. Kelly urged Renforth to make a greater effort, but it was to no avail, it was obvious that he was very ill. They rowed back to Appleby's Wharf and carried Renforth ashore, where he was immediately taken to Claremont House, their training quarters. Medical attention was urgently sought, but Renforth sadly died. Rumours again circulated that the great sculler had been poisoned, but an inquest determined that the likely cause of death was an epileptic fit.

It was agreed by Renforth's friends that his body should be returned to Newcastle, his home town. His body would be cased in three coffins and preserved.

> From the experience in this art which the Americans gained in the late civil war, there is little fear but the body will be manipulated in the most skilled manner ... it will be despatched to England by one of the Allan line of steamers, which sails for Liverpool on Saturday, Kelly, Oldham and George Watson propose to accompany the body home.[2]

Religion played a very important part in the life of both Alexander and Jane, they shared the same beliefs and ideals. A part of their strong partnership was that they believed they were put on this earth not just to serve the needs of themselves and their immediate family, but to help the poor and needy. They were both members of the United Presbyterian Church; Alexander was an Elder, and attended the Synod gatherings in Edinburgh.

Alexander's beliefs may have been strong, but that did not prevent him from having an open mind when it came to the teaching of others. He and

Jane were Evangelical in their thinking; the Evangelical Movement began in the eighteenth century, a religious movement that laid much emphasis on personal conversion and salvation by faith as prescribed in the Atonement, the bringing about of a reconciliation between man and God.

In 1872, Dwight L Moody, an American Evangelist from Massachusetts, arrived in England, to bring his message to a country that was still trying to come to terms with the industrial revolution, turning simple farming folk into factory workers. Poverty and drunkenness was seen in every town and city. When Moody visited Scotland he met Alexander; the date of this meeting cannot be confirmed, but with Alexander's strong beliefs but open mind it would have been natural for him to attend one of Moody's gatherings. He later dined with Alexander and Jane at their home at 1 Park Gardens. The conversation after dinner would have given the two men the opportunity to discuss the true meaning of the "Evangelical Faith", and no doubt the Plymouth Brethren evangelist and the traditional Presbyterian had much to discuss!

Alexander would have had a compelling answer to many of Moody's arguments. This is best illustrated by another churchman, Andrew Aird, who in 1894 published a book, *Glimpses of Old Glasgow*, p. 399, in which he wrote:

> I often met with Mr Allan on church business. On these occasions I found him animated with a sincere desire to advance the interests of the congregation and the denomination to which he was very deeply attached. He was not, however, a religious partisan, but heartily co-operated with brethren of other evangelical churches.[3]

It was the death of Jane's father, Robert Smith, in July 1873, at Hafton House, that seemed to be the start of another decade of change. A new generation took over from their seniors, but in many ways the moral philosophy that they were taught as children they continued to practise.

A little of the character of the Robert Smith can be judged from his obituary:

> He was a partner of the well-known Messrs George Smith & Sons, and until within about a year ago was actively engaged in the practical

management of its affairs. He was an upright and able man of business, shrewd, active, and energetic in everything which he undertook.[4]

Robert and his brother George, as with Capt Sandy and his sons, had seen by their joint efforts the expansion and growing prosperity of the port of Glasgow since they and the Allans first arrived in the city from their native Ardrossan. There can be no doubt that the little ports of Ardrossan, Saltcoats and Irvine, at the turn of the nineteenth century, produced some exceptional hard-working and enterprising folk.

Robert Smith was a very wealthy man when he died, and although he was still married to Eliza Service, he left the bulk of his fortune to his only child, Jane. Eliza lived for another ten years, and died at Hafton House, Sandbank. Her grandson, CharlesE, was with her at the time. Robert had made provision for his widow, but he also made sizable donations to his various charities, and benevolent interests. Chief among these was his passion for the Scottish Temperance League, which he had joined at its formation in 1844. For a little over twenty years Robert was President of the League. A conciliator, rather than an aggressor, Robert could always make his point in a quiet controlled manner.

> For a good few years in succession, the annual meetings ... were clouded and convulsed by ... nitrogenized strifes. The thoughts of many minds were revealed; and in the freedom of our preventative constitution ... these thoughts were not always vented in Parliamentary language. But no regrettable language ever escaped the President's lips. He could be, and often was, inflexibly firm but it was invariably in the direction of order and fair play. Amid the crimination and debate, never a word fell from any, so far as we ever heard, implying the least reflection on the procedure of the President.[5]

The other great passion in Robert's life was his membership of the United Presbyterian Church, where he was an Elder and a frequent benefactor. He was a man of conviction and compassion who left his mark on his adopted city, and left the world a sadder place with his death.

As happens so frequently in life, a sad occasion was followed by a joyous one. In 1873, Capt James's twenty-one-year-old daughter, Mary, married at her family home in Park Terrace, her husband being John Graham, eight years her senior, and a sugar refiner. A few months earlier, her father had written to his son RobertG to find out what he thought of the union between his daughter and Graham. RobertG's reply must have allayed any fears that Capt James had. He told his father that JamesH had already informed him that for some months Graham had been paying the young Mary more attention than that of a casual friend. RobertG says that Graham is a man from a good family, and would assuredly give Mary a secure and loving future.

In the closing paragraph of his letter, RobertG says that as Graham is a partner in the firm of MacFie and Sons, and since his brother-in-law William MacFie was a senior partner, Graham was already in a sense a member of the family. He believed that if there was a reason why Mary and John Graham should not marry he would have informed her father. Mary and John had two sons, John and Allan James, and two daughters, Eleanora Allan and Mary Allan.

There has been much written over the years about the building of the Canadian Pacific Railway, and in particular about the so called "Pacific Scandal". It would be boring to repeat the whole story, but Sir Hugh's involvement with it was the last great challenge in his life. He saw the building of a railway from Halifax to Vancouver for what it would become: one of the greatest industrial enterprises of the nineteenth century. It was his misfortune that the contract for the new railway coincided with a General Election in Canada. Sir John McDonald, a fellow Scot, was up for re-election as Premier, and as always in these matters, he needed money to fund his campaign. Sir Hugh, a previous generous benefactor to Sir John, responded to the request. There the matter should have ended. Unfortunately, Sir John sent a telegram asking for a further donation, but the telegram fell into the hands of Lucius Seth Huntingdon, a Liberal and Parliamentary opponent of Sir John's, who immediately saw a way of not just damaging Sir John's chances of re-election, but destroying the reputation of Sir Hugh. It is always easy to make accusations of improper influence, and it is always hard to refute such accusations. Sir Hugh was by any standards a very wealthy man who could fund such donations from his own resources; however, to raise sufficient capital to build the railway, he needed other influential backers. He hoped to form a new company in conjunction with the Americans. He knew they were more than willing to support the project, and Sir Hugh knew he could find further sponsors in Great Britain.

It should have been an easy contractual arrangement to obtain the contract to build the great Canadian Pacific Railway. Regrettably, politics and Government contracts are rarely without opposition. Sir Hugh was accused of bribery, corruption and all manner of underhand deals. His reputation was tarnished for many years, even after his death, by politically motivated allegations. Opponents of the railway scheme saw it as a waste of public money; the Separatists and Annexationists saw it as a way for the Americans to gain supremacy over Canada. Truth would forever be the casualty of the squabble.

The opponents of the railway scheme won the first round; Sir John was forced to resign his position in late 1873, and he lost the 1874 election to Alexander MacKenzie. He was back in power by 1878, due mainly to the lack-lustre performance of the MacKenzie Government, despite the backing of a powerful group of Montreal manufacturers.

At a Royal Commission Inquiry, held in late October 1873, evidence was taken from all sides, and the more Sir Hugh's detractors tried to implicate him, the more they lost the argument. In his evidence, Sir Hugh made a typical robust reply to the allegations:

> [he]denied in the most positive terms the existence of any agreement between him and the Government prior to the granting of the charter to the present company. [He gave his reasons for] contributing to the election fund [as] his strong approbation to the commercial policy of the [The Reform Party] Government, particularly in relation to railways, canals, lighthouses and emigration.[6]

He reiterated that he was bound in all he did to ensure the general prosperity of the country he loved, and did not deny that his own interests in that prosperity were substantial. He declared that he had at least six millions of capital invested in national works. He admitted also that he had invested a great deal of money in promoting the extension of the Canadian Pacific Railway, which the Reform Party had always refused to support, and by supporting the re-election of the Conservative Party under Sir John MacDonald he passionately believed it was to the good of every Canadian.

He denied emphatically that by supporting them he had been promised the charter to build the extension of the railway. He agreed that the railway company had received money from their American backers, but this money had been returned when it became clear there would be no Canadian/American agreement.

In concluding his evidence Sir Hugh said

> he never got any advantage from the Government, not even their influence in his election as President of the Chartered Company.[7]

Sir Hugh was found not guilty, but this did not appease his enemies. The rumours persisted but it should be noted that his detractors did not profit from their vicious smears.

The findings of the Royal Commission, though, proved to Sir Hugh that he should leave the building of the Canadian Pacific Railway to others. In the early days of the negotiations he had been warned by his physician that his heart was not in a good state, and his desire for more excitement and more challenge would not be beneficial to him.

Sir Hugh should have listened to the advice of his physician, and he might have spent the last decade of his life in contented retirement. He lived well at Ravenscrag, the house he had built in 1864 in the beautiful surroundings of Mount Royal; he had wealth beyond his wildest dreams, and an army of family and friends to entertain him. He would have been able to look back with pride on all he had achieved since he had left his humble home in Saltcoats. He had played a prominent part in seeing the land of his adoption turned from an unexplored wilderness into a thriving, prosperous and beautiful country.

The last word on the whole saga should be given to Andrew Jack, the son of Sir Hugh's Aunt Margaret. Writing in the *Glasgow Herald,* under the nom de plume of "One Who Knows" he paid a well deserved and staunch defence of his uncle's reputation:

> and had the opposition succeeded, what would have been the consequences? Why, Sir, the country would have been reduced to anarchy; for the opponents of the men in power were Annexationists, Independents, Nationalists and Rogues! I do not seek to justify bribery in any form, but is there no bribery here? It was an election against a host of enemies that sums of money were given and spent ... You in Glasgow know what Sir Hugh has done. He did more to found a new Glasgow in Canada than any man in it, and perhaps the spirit of

commercial jealousy has as much, to-day, to do with the Pacific scandal
cry as anything else.[8]

Sir Hugh did not contemplate retirement, but Capt Bryce had begun to
make plans for his own future; in 1874 he purchased the Estate of Aros, at
Tobermory on the Isle of Mull. It was an impressive acquisition, comprising
a mansion house with extensive gardens, with three miles of shore frontage,
and six hundred acres of forests and tenant farms. The boundaries of the
Estate included the western half of Tobermory. It is hard to imagine a more
beautiful place for Capt Bryce and Janet to spend the rest of their lives
together; however, the dream was never to happen. He died suddenly at
the end of May 1874; according to reports at the time, he had appeared
to be in good health. On that fateful morning, he took his usual place at
the breakfast table, at his home in Holly Road, Fairfield, where he suffered
the bursting of a blood vessel, and he fell to the floor and was dead before
medical help could be sought. His life span was a little over sixty-years
but it had been full of adventure and achievement and surprisingly his
obituaries did not concentrate on his sailing but on the more private nature
of the man.

> But when the man who leads a private life is animated by zeal for the
> public good, and does more service to the world in seclusion than others
> do who occupy a front place on the stage, his modesty is a crowning
> merit, and cannot but be reckoned a most winning trait in a solid and
> noble character. ... He did good by stealth as far as it was possible, for
> a retired life was essential to his simple tastes, but he would have done
> the good all the same if it had compelled him to take a prominent public
> position, for he had a conscience in philanthropy, and the sight of evil
> and suffering which he could check and soothe would have pierced him
> constantly if he had left it alone.[9]

Capt Bryce knew from an early age, the dangers of the sea and seafaring, and
he was one of the first to support the Seaman's Orphanage, in Liverpool.
He gave them not just generous donations: that would have been easy, but
he put his substantial administrative skills at the disposal of the staff of the
Orphanage. He had no time for people with pretensions or lofty ideals, but
always managed the business of the Orphanage in a spirit of geniality and
kindness.

Unlike his brother Alexander he did not join the Temperance League, but he was a life-long abstainer from the demon drink. He believed, passionately, that he could achieve more by example than by forcing his views on his fellow men and women.

Capt Bryce's death left a void in the Liverpool operation of the Allan Line, and an even greater problem of what should be done with the Aros Estate which he had left to his only son Alexander. He was a still a relatively young man, but he decided he wanted to become, as his father had hoped to be on his retirement, the "Laird of Aros".

Alexander had married Juliana Elizabeth McEwan in Edinburgh in September 1866. She was just nineteen; her parents Alexander McEwan, a sugar refiner, and Jane Thomson were both dead. At the time of her marriage Juliana was staying with Claud and Margaret MacFie, a sister of Capt James. Juliana may have been another reason why Alexander wanted to go to Aros: her father had died in 1860 at Sunderland House, Isle of Islay, so Juliana would have appreciated, even though she was only thirteen when he father died, exactly what it meant to live on a beautiful but isolated island like Mull.

Juliana had gone to West Derby with Alexander after their marriage, but their son Bryce was not born there until June 1874, just a few days before Capt Bryce died. Janet also went to Aros with her son and daughter-in-law and lived there for the rest of her life.

The decision to find a replacement for Alexander of Aros (as he was now to be known) was not that difficult. Alexander of Glasgow's five sons were too young, ranging in ages from seventeen to just four. Capt James, however, had five sons: RobertG had been part of the Liverpool office since 1866, and it seemed only right that he should be joined by his brother James Hugh (JamesH): like RobertG he had experience of working in the Glasgow office, and may have relished the chance of being closer to Yorkshire.

It was around 1875/1876 that another young man and woman came on to the scene; in April 1876, Janet Charlotte, JamesH's young sister, married William Stead, the son of Charles Stead and his wife, Mary Ann Wood, from Baildon, Yorkshire. Charles Stead was a wealthy woollen manufacturer with a large Victorian family.

Janet and William were to have two daughters, Eleanora and Marjorie Allan, and in 1881 they were living at Fern Hill House, Moorhead Lane, where Janet's sister Eleanora was staying as a guest.

Perhaps it was inevitable that at the wedding, JamesH should meet and become fascinated with Clara, William's twenty-year-old sister. The fascination developed and they married a year after Janet. They had two daughters, Hilda Mary and Doris, and in the fullness of time another link would be forged between the Liverpool family and Aros.

Chapter 7

Arise Sir Hugh

As the second generation of Capt Sandy's sons entered into old age, it would have been gratifying to the old sailor to know that his grandchildren were embarking on new lives of their own. James Henry and Janet Charlotte, Capt James and Eleanor's son and daughter, could well have surprised the inner circle of neighbours around their Glasgow home of Park Terrace by marrying "foreigners", the English siblings William and Clara Stead. Capt James, however, had no such worries especially when James Henry agreed to go to Liverpool to join his brother RobertG who had been there for some time. The Glasgow operation under Alexander would be, eventually, in the capable hands of his sons.

In Montreal changes were also taking place. Hugh had built himself a palatial mansion, Ravenscrag, named after that outcrop of rock off the coast at Ardrossan. The expansion of the business had been such that he and his family were regarded as members of the "Golden Square Mile" of West Montreal. The wealthy merchant families there maintained a close link with each other, though there were moments when the cosy relationship could be shattered. Hugh had a reputation of being a strong-minded man who demanded of others the same standard he expected of himself. He certainly did not suffer fools and knaves. It is true that accusations of corruption and wrong-doing were often laid at his door; however, none were ever proved to the satisfaction of his enemies. Like most successful Canadian businessmen at that time, he used his position and his wealth to change Parliamentary business when it suited him to do so. Canada was a new and expanding country which did not receive dominion status until 1867 (a couple more provinces joined in 1873). Until then the government was in the hands of the provinces. It was easy for the detractors to find fault with the system that existed.

In July 1871 Hugh's detractors might have been silenced for good, when the *Montreal Gazette* announced:

> We mentioned yesterday a rumour to the effect that Mr Hugh Allan had been honoured by the Queen [*Victoria*] in having had conferred on him a Baronetcy ... That his eminent services in connection with ocean steam navigation have been thus recognized is matter for sincere congratulations among all classes of the people in Canada ... No Knight ... has more worthily won his spurs.[1]

It is always easy to denigrate a man's worth with the benefit of hindsight. Conditions for factory workers and for immigrants that apply in the twenty-first century are very different from those of the early pioneering days in Canada. The Allan Line were in the forefront of the shipping business of transporting assisted emigrants in the 1850–1860s. Conditions for these migrant passengers were not comfortable; they travelled steerage class, and had to provide their own food.

> The firm's promotional literature noted that indigent passengers would receive free Grand Trunk rail passes from the government and assured immigrants that "Canada is a cheap place to live in" where even the poorest could have "the confident hope" of becoming a landowner.[2]

Hugh had shown by dint of his own abilities that what the company's literature said was more than possible.

There was a strict separation between the sexes on all ships, with stewardesses appointed to make sure the female passengers were not harassed in any way. Passengers were also asked to buy a "steerage passenger kit", which included a patent "life-preserving pillow". That very obviously was before the advent of the issue of regulation life-jackets and life-boats. That deaths did occur on the voyages was again an inevitable occurrence of ocean travel, in the middle of the nineteenth century.

The early immigrants had a hard and dangerous fight to establish themselves in their new home land. Farming was at the mercy of the weather, summers were short, winters unbelievably long and hazardous. The conditions of the textile/cotton factory workers would not stand scrutiny under today's employment legislation. It would be unfair to condemn Hugh Allan because he imposed on his workers conditions that would not be allowed today. A claim was made that Hugh cared more for profit than for the welfare of his workers. But such a claim could be made against every textile factory owner, mine owner, plantation owner, across the globe. Complaints against working conditions, wages, industrial accidents and child labour could be levelled at all employers in the middle of the nineteenth century and, indeed, are still being made today in the twenty-first century.

A ten-year-old child worked incredibly long hours, an adult mill worker earned a little more than $5 a day. It is impossible with the passing of time to understand how such conditions existed, but they did, and it is pointless to say now, with hindsight, that something should have been done. It should have, but to blame Hugh for not doing it is to deny him the many, many good things that he did to bring prosperity to the people of his adopted country.

Yes, he was a hard man; he had to be. It could be said that carving a path from a desolate wilderness made him a hard man. He was often called obtuse but that is nonsense; he was not stupid, though he was obdurate, unwilling to listen, proud, and arrogant. The seeds of his success had been sown in his upbringing in the land of his birth.

The children of the Golden Square Mile were the recipients of the industrial pioneers, of whom Hugh was a leading exponent. Their children were educated at the same schools, and later they would marry within the square mile of wealthy, powerful families. If one family was temporarily in financial problems, the rest would rally to support them. Inevitably, though, changes were taking place within the families as they looked farther afield for their spouses.

Phoebe Mary, Hugh's eldest daughter, married in March 1877 Captain George Lauderdale Houstoun-Boswall, the son of Colonel Sir George Augustus Houstoun-Boswall, of Blackadder, Edrom, Berwickshire. The wedding took place at the Church of St James the Apostle, and not as one would have expected St Andrew's Church, where Sir Hugh and his family had worshipped for years. According to a report of the marriage in the *Montreal Star* on 1 March, Houstoun-Boswall had requested that the marriage be solemnized according to the rites of the High Anglican Church which he and his family recognized.

The report also made reference to the fact that the wedding was not the lavish occasion one would have expected of Sir Hugh's daughter: because the family were still in mourning following the death of Phoebe's uncle in London they had thought it more appropriate to keep the arrangements private. The report may have been in error: Phoebe did have two uncles who had recently died. Bryce in 1874, but not in London as reported but in Liverpool. Alexander Greenhorne, her uncle by marriage, died in 1877 but again not in London but in San Remo, Italy.

Be that as it may, the church was still crowded with the pretty daughters of Montreal's leading citizens. As Phoebe had seven sisters and three cousins, it is not at all surprising the congregation was made up of pretty and elegantly dressed young women. As the report managed to get the spelling of Houstoun-Boswall wrong, so getting the date and location of the death of her uncles is just another journalistic error.

Phoebe and Sir George left Quebec shortly after their marriage to return to Scotland to the splendid Kelloe Mansion in Edrom, Berwickshire, and an elegant townhouse in St Andrew's Square, Edinburgh. There were three children of the marriage, George Reginald born 1877, Thomas Randolph born 1882 and a daughter Evelyn Mary Alice. George inherited the Baronetcy in 1886 on the death of his father, and Blackadder became Phoebe's Scottish home.

Phoebe had every reason to celebrate her marriage into the Houstoun-Boswall family. However, while she was celebrating, her cousin Jean Crawford, the daughter of Old Andrew, was causing her father a good deal of grief.

In 1868, at the tender age of seventeen, Jean had married William Ellice McKenzie, four years her senior. He was the son of John Gordon MacKenzie and the widower of Seraphina Gale. The Allan and McKenzie families had long been acquainted; John Gordon McKenzie had been a financial backer of Hugh as early as 1852, when he was raising funds to deepen the St Lawrence Seaway. On his marriage licence, William describes himself as a merchant, and at the time he was living a few doors away from the Allan family in Prince William Terrace. The couple had four children, Isabella Seraphina, Andrew A, Bessie and John Gordon. In the Census of 1871, Jean, William and baby Isabella were staying with her parents.

Early in 1876, an announcement in the *Daily Free Press* under a rather graphic headline proclaimed: "Elopement in High Life, Sir Hugh Allan's niece runs away with son of a railway Magnate." Why Sir Hugh had to be dragged into the announcement is a cause for comment. Everything that happened between his family and his brother's family was inevitably linked to him. Jean had run away with Frederick Henderson Brydges, an English-born Canadian migrant. He was the son of Charles John Brydges, of the Grand Trunk, who like McKenzie was another financial backer when Hugh tried to secure the contract to build the Canadian railway all the way from east to west. In 1871 Hugh had believed passionately that the Americans would bring their money and influence to help expand the railway.

Family pressure was brought upon Jean and she agreed to return to Quebec. However, her return was only for a short period. On 22 October 1877, in Boston Massachusetts, she and Frederick were married, although it has been impossible to confirm the date and place of the marriage. They had two children, Letitia Jean and Charles.

It was said that when she eloped with Brydges, she took two of her four McKenzie children with her, and that can be confirmed in the Census for 1891. She was living in Winnipeg and she did have two of her McKenzie children and her two Brydges children living with her. Isabella and Andrew were not there. It must therefore be a matter of speculation whether her two children Bessie and John Gordon were perhaps not William's, in spite of the fact that John Gordon was named after his McKenzie grandfather. Her elopement and runaway marriage may have caused distress to her parents, but it is obvious that Jean was not estranged from all her family as her brother William Rae was staying with her in Winnipeg.

It was not without reason that occasionally Sir Hugh was in conflict with Government, and not only in Canada: when a Government Department in Great Britain attempted to impose who and what the Allan Line should employ on their ships he could not remain silent. In 1877 the Board of Trade issued an order that all passenger vessels leaving English ports should have a surgeon on board who held a medical degree from a British college. Sir Hugh was justifiably very annoyed. The Board of Trade had tried to argue that they were only trying to safeguard passengers from quacks, but in trying to ensure the safety of the passengers, they certainly caused resentment among Canadian medical men. Sir Hugh argued that to exclude him from employing Canadian doctors was a discrimination too far. He would have agreed with the reporter from the *Daily Free Press,* Manitoba.

Members of the learned profession have yet to be made to understand that any exclusive privileges accorded them are not granted by legislation ... So long as the condition of competency is secured, there should be as much free trade in the practice of professions as in any other mode of livelihood.

The discriminating action of the Board of Trade, is by implication, a slur upon the Canadian medical profession which must be removed. Sir Hugh Allan has already borne testimony in a public manner as to his opinion on the subject, and has stated that the medical gentlemen in his service have given entire satisfaction to the public travelling by his line in professional ability as well as gentlemanly conduct, and that he himself is satisfied with his medical officers.[3]

Sir Hugh was determined to protect his own right to employ who he wished, and as in so many things he did, he chose well. William John Shaw, a young Scotsman, trained at the University of Glasgow, was the sort of doctor neither the British Board of Trade or the Canadian Government could find fault with. Sir Hugh was right when he insisted he only employed the very best of staff for the Allan Line, regardless of nationality, creed or class. Shaw was surgeon on the *Austrian* in 1878. According to a contemporary source a young woman described him as *very agreeable, sweet and nice and handsome, a most charming companion* ...[4] [Appleton, p. 129].

The young woman was Jean Glen-Airston. It has been erroneously suggested that Shaw did not marry Jean, but married Sir Hugh's daughter Jane Crawford. In fact Shaw married twice. In 1884, in Govan, where he was then a physician and surgeon, he wedded Ann Janet Baird, and they had a daughter in April 1885, named Ann Janet Baird Shaw. A month later, Ann Shaw died of typhoid fever. She was just thirty years old. In January 1889, in Sarawak Township, Ontario, Shaw married the young woman who had been so attracted to him on board the *Austrian;* they had a son William Glen-Airston Shaw born in Govan in 1891. A caring and devoted doctor, Shaw died of acute bronchitis on New Year's Day 1893, aged only thirty-seven. Jean and her son returned to Owen Sound, Ontario, where she died in 1935.

This, however, leaves a matter unresolved; whom did Sir Hugh's daughter, Jane Crawford, marry, if she did not marry Dr Shaw? The answer has not been found; she has been linked to so many families searching their ancestors, but they have never come up with conclusive evidence of her involvement. Jane Crawford was born to Sir Hugh and Matilda in 1849, she was with them in the 1861 Census, but that was the last confirmed sighting of her.

The twelve years since the death of his wife Eleanora had been a time of mourning for Capt James, but commercial success and the company of his sons and daughters had helped to heal his suffering. The development of the Allan Line, with the help and guidance of his youngest brother, Alexander of Glasgow, had given him immense satisfaction. His early years at sea had taught him to be a practical man, and he never lost the skills he learned as a "skipper". He was, according to most people who knew him well, a man of sound judgement and good in his dealings with people, whatever their rank or status. He treated the deckhand with the same courtesy as he treated his largest merchant client. He had little interest in civic affairs, and did not strive for high office. The sea was first and foremost of his interests, and he combined management of the Allan Line with being chairman of The Clyde Pilot Board and the Clyde Lighthouse Trust.

He shared with Alexander a commitment and faith to the United Presbyterian Church, and was an Elder of Landsdown Church, under the Ministry of Professor Dr John Elder. A dedicated preacher and a stimulating religious teacher, Elder had moved his congregation from his church in Cowcaddens into a magnificent new building, designed by John Honeyman in 1863. He had officiated at the marriages of Capt James's daughters Jane, Janet and Mary, and his death in 1876 had robbed not just his devoted congregation of a great preacher, but Capt James of a good friend.

In the later years of the 1870s, Capt James's health began to decline, and he withdrew from the day-to-day running of the business. He spent much of his time at his country house in Skelmorlie, Ayrshire. In this spectacularly beautiful part of Scotland he could still see the Allan Line ships as they sailed up the Clyde to Greenock and beyond. He died, suddenly, at Skelmorlie on 25 August 1880, aged seventy-two years. The informant of his death was his daughter Mary's husband, John Graham.

That Mary and John were with Capt James indicates they were aware just how serious his condition was; they had travelled from their usual residence at Princes Park, Liverpool, to be with him.

The death of Capt James left Alexander in sole control of the Glasgow operation, although he did have Nathaniel Dunlop at his side. Dunlop had been with the company since 1845 and had given devoted service to the Allan Line; he had been rewarded with a partnership shortly before his marriage to Ellen Smith in 1866.

If Alexander's business life was well ordered, then it is without doubt that his personal and private life was equally well arranged by Jane, his wife, his strength and his companion in all things. They shared many of the things that made his life worthwhile. Alexander's commitment to the United Presbyterian Church never faltered, yet he was in truth an Evangelical student. He was the first President of the Glasgow United Evangelistic Association.

There are few memories written about Alexander; perhaps one of the best was penned by his friend, from the UP Church, Andrew Aird. Aird knew his friend and fellow parishioner better than most men, for there is little doubt that Alexander, like so many of his contemporaries, was a very private man. He did not flaunt his social and religious activities, as Aird so accurately reflected:

> In matters bearing on Glasgow's welfare Mr Allan was not only approachable but willing to exercise his influence on its behalf. Had he been ambitious for pre-eminence as a citizen he could have obtained civic honours, both on account of his mental and commercial status. It was more his delight to be unobtrusively engaged in those duties which would elevate socially and spiritually his fellow-men.[5]

The welfare of orphaned and destitute children was a concern for all Capt Sandy's five sons; they were always among the first to offer financial support and use their considerable commercial and civic influence to help other like minded men.

William Quarrier was one such man. He was the son of a ship's carpenter, but unlike Capt Sandy, his father did not prosper. William on the other hand had the same determination to succeed as had the sons of Capt Sandy. Quarrier's father had died in Quebec of cholera in 1832, when his son was only three years old. Again like Capt Sandy, the young Quarrier served an apprenticeship as a shoemaker and made a success of his business. In the winter of 1864 he was confronted by the sight of a young boy crying while trying to sell matchsticks, and he remembered when he had been a cold, hungry child:

> I stood in the High Street of Glasgow, barefooted, bareheaded, cold and hungry having tasted no food for a day and a half and as I gazed at the passers by wondering why they did not help such as I, a thought passed through my mind that I would not do as they when I got the means to help others.[6]

In 1871 William Quarrier purchased a forty-acre site at Bridge of Weir for the purpose of building a home for orphans. The unique construction of separate houses with their own staff for the children was, at that time, was very different from that of the Victorian workhouses. Quarrier had a passionate belief that a child who had lost its parents should be treated no less well than the child of a merchant. Quarrier sent many of the children that he rescued to Canada. Although it cannot be confirmed there is a good deal of contemporary evidence to suggest that many of the children went out on Allan ships.

There were others who shared Quarrier's desire to help orphaned children. Alexander, Jane and Richard Hubbard Hunter, and George Smith, son of Smith junior of the City Line, were trustees and benefactors of the Scottish Sailors' Orphan Society which they had jointly founded.

The Allans and the Smiths were all aware that life at sea was dangerous, and after shipping accidents many of the wives and children were left destitute. One of the aims of the new society was that if:

> the mother be alive and a suitable person to bring up her family well, the home was not broken up, but a yearly grant is made for one or more of the children.[7]

It was a philosophy that Alexander and his family could and did wholeheartedly share, and they devoted both their wealth and, more importantly, their time to the many charities they had set up. It is a measure of the true Christian principles that these far-sighted Victorian philanthropists believed in so passionately that many of the institutions they founded still thrive today. They may have changed their way of working, but the abused, neglected and impoverished child still cries out, the world over, for love and comfort.

Chapter 8

Change of Management

The death of Sir Hugh Allan in December 1882, coming just two years after the death of Capt James and eight years after Capt Bryce, robbed the family of three of the founding brothers. Sir Hugh's death, would also have shocked many of his friends and his adversaries. He had seemed invincible and it was thought likely he would continue to dominate Canadian shipping, railways and banking for the foreseeable future. The death of his wife Matilda in June 1881, of blood poisoning, had robbed him not just of the mother of his five sons and eight daughters but of his companion and confidant of thirty-seven years. Many Victorians had very large families, but unlike so many poorer families, Matilda and Hugh saw twelve of their large brood reach the age of maturity. The marriage of his daughters had delighted him and had given him grandchildren to continue his dynasty.

In the autumn of 1882 Sir Hugh made a longish visit to the land of his birth. In December he was at the Edinburgh home of his daughter Phoebe and his son-in-law George Houstoun-Boswall when he had a heart attack and died suddenly. He had been warned by his Canadian doctor to retire and spend more time on leisure pursuits.

It was not surprising that the writers of his obituaries could not find common cause with which to sum up his remarkable career. In the seventy-two years since his birth in a small cottage in Ardrossan, Ayrshire, he had fought to build a shipping empire. The Montreal Steam Ship Company and its associated companies that formed the Allan Line was no mean achievement for a man with only a limited education – he had began work at the age of thirteen. In a fascinating profile of him in the *Dictionary of Canadian Biography Online,* the writers admit that they knew little of Hugh's private life. They do, however, give much attention to his wealth.

Allan's accumulation of wealth, climaxing in an estate estimated at between six and ten million dollars, enabled him, his family, and his heirs to live in privileged circumstances. [*He bought the estate on the slopes of Mount Royal in 1860*] and over the next three years built Ravenscrag, the mansion which in the opinion of one editorialist surpassed "in size and cost any dwelling-house in Canada, and looks more like one of those castles of the British nobility than anything seen here". Designed in Italian Renaissance style by the architectural firm of Hopkins and Wiley, the mansion had 34 rooms included a billiard room, a conservatory, a library, and a ballroom that could accommodate several hundred guests. From the 75-foot tower there was a fine view of the city, the port and the distant Green Mountains of Vermont.[1]

It would also have been out of character for Hugh not to have had a graceful, elegant steam yacht, *The Lady of the Lake* which he kept moored on Lake Memphremagog, where he entertained his friends and business associates.

As with his Scottish brothers he retained his Presbyterian religious beliefs; he served on the board of various church committees. There is, however, no evidence that like Capt Bryce he was ever a member of the Temperance League.

He was a generous benefactor to the Montreal Sailors' Institute, of which Old Andrew was President for many years. Hugh was a lifetime governor of the Montreal Protestant House of Industry and Refuge. He was for many years a member of the Protestant Hospital for the Insane which was, as things turned out, was appropriate for Ravenscrag, for seven decades after Hugh's death it became a Psychiatric Hospital. Matilda, with Hugh's financial help, supported her own two charities, the Montreal Ladies' Benevolent Society and the Protestant Orphan Asylum.

Sir Hugh must have expressed a desire that if he should die away from his beloved Ravenscrag he still wanted to be buried beside Matilda at Mount Royal, in the family's mausoleum. His wish was granted and the committal service was conducted in the Church of St Andrews, where he had worshipped faithfully for so many years. His funeral was held on 27 December 1882 with the due reverence afforded to one of his eminent place in the Montreal society

> causing the closing of the stock-exchange for the afternoon. The hearse, preceded by a squad of city police and a detachment of firemen, was followed by his family; political, commercial and industrial luminaries;

"employees from the manager down to the workers on the wharves"; and some 2000 citizens.[2]

How then does one sum up this quite extraordinary man? It would seem that history has not always been kind to Sir Hugh. It is true that he did not suffer fools gladly, and that in his business relationships he was aggressive and uncompromising. He was a politician, he exploited French and English/ Canadian nationalism, although he remained a staunch anti-annexationist. He was ever willing to invest in all new forms of transportation:

> [he] increased his company's power by carefully attending to the protection of markets, soliciting favourable legislation, and obtaining subsidies, and limiting competition ... His ships carried immigrants, his factories hired them and made material for their clothes, his land companies sold them the land, and his financial agencies insured them and lent them money.[3]

His family and close friends knew the true worth of the man, his detractors would never be silenced. He was a great man, not a good man. His Scottish roots and his religious beliefs were very strong. He had earned, by dint of his own energies and strengths, a place in the history not only of Canada, his adopted home, but also of his native Scotland.

The Allan Line continued to prosper during the early years of the 1880s. The death of Sir Hugh and Capt James meant that there were changes of personnel in both Glasgow and Montreal. In Glasgow, Nathaniel Dunlop's role was greatly increased; Hugh's brother Old Andrew took overall charge of the Montreal operation, assisted by Hugh's son, Montagu. Hugh's son James Bryce in Boston took charge of that side of the business; Alexander Rae, Hugh's eldest son, had already declined to take any part in the shipping company.

Many of the passengers leaving the Clyde were emigrants, and during a short summer period more than 3,000 people left on ships owned and run by the Allan Line and the Anchor Line. The Allans also frequently transported a very different cargo. In January 1882 they shipped eighty Clydesdale horses to Boston, believed at the time to be the largest consignment of horses to go to the United States. A separate item of the manifest was 800 tons of potatoes: apparently Boston was unable to meet the demands of its hungry population.

It is to be hoped that the crossing to the New World for the emigrants, the horses and the potatoes did not encounter too much rough weather. The newspapers at the time reported frequent collisions, near collisions and wrecks caused by icebergs. Death was a constant menace on all ocean crossings.

Births, marriages and deaths of family members must have put a considerable strain on the families's social occasions, especially among the grandchildren of Capt Sandy and Jean Crawford. In 1883, it was their granddaughter, Jean Crawford, the daughter of Janet Allan and Thomas Service, who married. She became the second wife of Albert Yelverton Bingham, the sixth son of Baron Clanmorris, of County Mayo, Ireland and the widower of Caroline Begbe, by whom he had had a son and two daughters. Jean and Albert had one son who died shortly after birth. Jean's father, Thomas, had died in 1880, at Cranley House, Cleghorn, Lanarkshire, the informant being his brother Robert. Thomas's death left his daughter an extremely wealthy young woman, and must have made her an attractive prospect for an impoverished widower. Jean's mother, Janet, had died at the age of fifty-one in 1867. Jean had been known to visit her aunt Margaret MacFie and uncle Claud. It would appear from all the evidence available that the MacFie home at Gogar Burn, Edinburgh was a refuge for all the extended family, when they needed a calm and comfortable place to rest. In 1880 when typhoid fever swept across the Isle of Mull, Alexander sent his wife, Juliana, his two children Bryce and Sheila, and his mother Janet, to stay with Claud and Margaret at Gogar Burn. Alexander also left Tobermory and sought safety at Robert MacFie's Airds House. Isabella Bishop's sister Henrietta did not leave the island, and died of typhoid fever in June 1880.

Jean Crawford Service was not the only family member to marry in 1883; RichardG, the third of Capt James's four sons, married Agnes Aitken Murdoch, the daughter of Robert Murdoch and Hannah Laidlaw, in October of that year. The early years of their marriage did not produce a child; Richard (Dick) arrived in October 1898.

RichardG's two elder brothers, RobertG and JamesH, had been in Liverpool for many years and there was not an obvious place for him with them. His younger brother Bryce of Wemyss Bay took an active part in the Glasgow operation. His Glasgow cousins, sons of Alexander, were being groomed to take their father's place when he retired. It is therefore not surprising that RichardG looked to find a more rewarding role in life. He did this with some considerable success by becoming a very successful yachtsman and an intrepid horseman and mountaineer.

It would have been interesting to have been a spectator at the home of Alexander and Jane when their eldest son RobertS announced he was to be married. His bride to be was Lizzie Kincaid Greenhorne, the daughter of Alexander Greenhorne, a shipowner, and Jane Allan the daughter of Capt Sandy and Janet Crawford. In marrying Lizzie his cousin, RobertS was again carrying on a tradition of inter-relationships within this large and complex family.

Lizzie's father, Alexander, had been born in Port Glasgow in 1824 to Alexander Greenhorne, a sailor, and Elizabeth Waters. As Capt Sandy was a shipowner in Greenock/Port Glasgow in 1824 it is more than possible that is where the families became so well acquainted. Alexander died in San Remo, Italy, in February 1877, although his usual domicile was given as England. As a matter of interest, his London home was at Aberdeen Park, Highbury, Middlesex, where his widow continued to live until her own death. The closeness between the Allan and Greenhorne families can be further judged, in that one of his executors was his brother-in-law Alexander of Glasgow.

RobertS and Lizzie were married in London on 12 March 1885. They had three daughters, Dorothy Kincaid born 1886, Elspeth May born 1888 and the youngest Jane Crawford born 1893. At the time of Dorothy's birth, they were living at 15 Woodside Terrace, a very short walking distance from his parents. It would be true to say that all the family lived in the Park Circus area of Glasgow; it was very much the domicile of the merchant families, and as with the Allans they had summer houses at Dunoon and along the Clyde coast between Wemyss Bay and Skelmorlie. They owned their Park Circus homes, but along with many of the other wealthy industrial families they preferred to take long tenancies on their summer homes. It was only after the Great War, in the 1920s, that they purchased large estates. Capt Bryce had been the exception to that rule in buying Aros in 1874.

Family celebrations had been as usual played out against a background of shipping problems. Conditions for both passengers and crew had by 1886 improved from those first encountered by Capt Sandy and his sons James and Bryce. However, even with better ships, there were still hazards to be faced: the North Atlantic sea crossing between Glasgow/Liverpool was particularly dangerous. In winter the hardy seamen encountered icebergs, fog and tempestuous seas. In summer, conditions could be equally treacherous, with winds, sometimes of gale force, and even hurricanes; the breaking up of the Greenland ice floes constantly added to the dangers of seafaring. Reading the daily reports of the shipping intelligence shows starkly that each journey was potentially risky. On one trip in January 1886, the Allan steamer *Norwegian* coming home from Philadelphia encountered a particularly rough crossing and was in consequence fifteen days late in arriving on the Clyde. As Capt Steven admitted later, the ship had sustained no damage, but his cargo, of 160 head of cattle perished, in the violent rolling of the ship.

It was not only the animal cargoes who suffered. Later that year the captain of the Allan steamer, *Siberian,* which had been in service for a year, arrived at her home port with the sad news that a seaman, Neil McLean, had fallen overboard while they were steaming down the St Lawrence Seaway and was drowned. McLean, according to a contemporary source, came from Tobermory. Again, there is no confirmed proof that his death was passed on to Alexander of Aros. However, it would have been totally out of character for Alexander not to have been informed, and totally out of character for him not to offer assistance to McLean's family.

As in all situations it was by no means all doom and gloom. On one occasion the Allan Line performed an unexpected public service by helping to apprehend criminals.

> Yesterday morning a colliery manager named Thomas Lee, aged 62 years, was arrested in Glasgow on a warrant charging him with unlawfully appropriating various sums of money, the property of his employers, to his own use ... Accompanied by his son, Lee arrived in Glasgow on Monday last, and two passages had been taken by them in the name of Carnaby at the Allan Line office for Boston, America. He was about to embark on the *Prussian* ... when he was taken into custody.[4]

Lee was returned to Northumberland to await his punishment, while the *Prussian* continued on her way.

1886 was not a good year for the *Prussian*. Three months after the incident with Lee, on his arrival back at Greenock the Captain had to report that he had encountered more problems. He gave a vivid description of what he, his one passenger and the ship had suffered on the return journey as a result of

> the severe weather that had prevailed in the Atlantic during the past few days ... Her funnels were whitened by the action of the weather ... for four days of this week the *Prussian* encountered a succession of great gales from the east, and unusually high and dangerous seas. The vessel had occasionally to "lay to", but she was well navigated, and arrived in the Clyde all safe, the only casualty which occurred during the voyage being the death of two cattle out of 290 which the steamer brought into this country.[5]

There is a postscript in the newspaper, which stated that cross-channel steamers had reported that they had never before encountered such a fearful easterly hurricane. Complaints by passengers carried by the Allan Line were rare, but when there were any they were usually about the weather or the standard of service received by steerage passengers, who believed they should have been treated to the same level of service as that afforded to first class passengers.

Chapter 9

Love & Loss

It is a sad fact that once an inaccurate statement gets into the public domain it is rarely possible to amend it, even though at the time it was first printed it would have been so easy to correct. There should never have been any doubt about the issue. In a profile of Capt James in *Memories and Portraits of 100 Glasgow Men*, published in 1886, the writer asserts:

> The originator of the Allan Line of ships, the father of the subject of this notice, Alexander Allan, was born in Saltcoats, Ayrshire, in 1780.[1]

The publication of the book relied on subscribers, and among those were Capt James's two sons, Bryce of Wemyss Bay and RichardG, and also William Stead his son-in-law. A fourth subscriber was Nathaniel Dunlop, a senior director member of the Allan Company. All these men would have known exactly where Alexander was born.

An article appeared in *The Ardrossan and Saltcoats Herald* that October and repeated exactly what the profile had asserted. It was left to Andrew Jack to put the matter beyond argument. In a very full article to *The Ardrossan and Saltcoats Herald* signed once again "One Who Knows" he put the true facts of Capt Sandy's birth in no uncertain terms. He followed up the article with a very long letter to his son Hugh, a mercantile clerk in the Glasgow office of the Allan Line: another example of the families closeness.

> I am sorry to dispel the illusion of Saltcoats people as to their good town having the honour of being the birthplace of the great shipowner, but the truth hurts no just interest, and to the Dundonald Parish in whose church yard the bones of his father and mother lie buried belong the honour that may accrue from the fact of his birth place there, and undoubtedly it was a little Old Rome fatherless boy who became the owner of JEAN the FAVOURITE AND ARABIAN, and the pioneer of the present magnificent fleet.[2]

It is a matter of regret that no memorial stone or indication of the exact location of the grave of James and Jean now exists in the Dundonald Church Yard. Time has destroyed what trace there may have been. That their descendants strode the world and still upheld the virtues of self-reliance and honest pride should be the true legacy of those two good hardworking and honest people, James and Jean, who created a dynasty.

Andrew Jack had a pride in his ancestors and their achievements. He named his home in Kilmarnock "Mavisbank Cottage" after the Quay in Govan where the Allan ships docked.

The difference between the men who worked at Mavisbank Quay and the sons and grandsons of Capt Sandy can be measured, in some respects, by comparing their incomes. A classified recruitment advertisement on behalf of the Company at the time of Jack's letter was a strong and powerful indication of the gulf between the classes. The Company wanted strong able-bodied men, who for working fifty-one hours a week would be paid 7d. an hour. The night rate was slightly more generous, at 8d. an hour. This was roughly equivalent in purchasing-power to the current UK minimum wage. By contrast Capt James, Capt Bryce and Alexander of Glasgow each left an estate of over half a million pounds, equivalent today to about forty million pounds each.

Poverty and great wealth went side by side in Victorian Britain, and never was this division more apparent than in April 1886 when Bryce of Wemyss Bay married Annie Smiley Clark. A lavish wedding was held at Annie's Paisley home, Kilnside House, a majestic mansion bought by her father, Stewart Clark, in 1873. Stewart Clark, a leading member of the Clark family of thread manufacturers, and his wife, Annie Smiley, were well-known for their lavish social gatherings. The marriage of their daughter to Bryce was one such occasion:

> a most distinguished assemblage, and the bridal gifts are numerous, and superb to a degree ... The magnificent collection is a rare sight to those who have been privileged to see them ... signs of rejoicing are to be observed outside as well as inside Kilnside House ... at the ... porter's lodge entrance, a handsome arch of evergreens has been constructed.

The outhouses at Kilnside are decorated with flags, while from atop of the colossal mills of the Anchor Works, British and American flags float proudly in the breeze ...[3]

Annie's grandfather, James Clark, and his brother Patrick had established their first mill at Seedhill in 1813. They were innovators in the method of producing cotton thread on to spools, and before long were the country's leading manufacturer of cotton thread. James Clark had two sons, John and Stewart. John was undoubtedly the major inspiration behind the success of the Anchor Mills. He did not marry. His home for many years was Curling Hall in Largs, a splendid mansion overlooking Castle Bay. His private passion, like that of his niece's husband, and all the Allan family, was yachting. He was Commodore of the Royal Clyde Yacht Club and the Royal Largs Yacht Club. When he died in 1894, his obituary remarked revealingly that John's one aim in life was to surpass the achievements of Paisley's other great cotton manufacturers, J & P Coats.

Bryce and Annie had two children, Annie Clark born 1890 and James Bryce born 1893. As their parents had done they enjoyed life in the Park Circus area of Glasgow and at Wemyss Bay and Skelmorlie, on the beautiful banks of the River Clyde. Bryce would now be known as Bryce of Wemyss Bay.

There is a delightful postscript to the press coverage of Bryce and Annie's marriage which shows that Bryce was very much respected by members of the Allan Line.

From our Glasgow and Greenock correspondents we learn that the Allan and other steamers and ships at the Broomielaw, and the yachts in Gourock Bay, are gaily bedecked with flags.[4]

Conflict between fathers and sons is part of the process of children growing up to become independent adults.

That conflict also involved close friends of the Allans when they lived as close neighbours to the families of James and John Stewart Templeton, Alexander Stephen and George Smith in the Park Circus area of Glasgow. They daily shared the same social, scholastic and leisure activities, and their Presbyterian beliefs were an integral part of their lives. It was not surprising that when the young adults started to widen their horizons their conflicts deepened.

Alexander of Glasgow and Jane had always fostered in their sons and daughters a questioning and an open mind to the world in which they lived. They would not, however, have expected the disapproval of their Park Circus neighbours when their children expressed different views and chose different friends. JamesA and CharlesE were particular friends of James Murray Templeton, the only son of the carpet manufacturer, J S Templeton. The problems became acute when Templeton senior took exception to the engagement of his son to an American girl Jessie Ellen Tuttle née Brown.

It was around 1885–1886, when James Murray was in Paris studying art, that he met Jessie Ellen Tuttle, a young American student with a colourful past. Her elder sister, Annie Maxwell Brown, had studied music in Paris, under the celebrated teacher, Madame Marchesi. Annie became a notable singer and formed a close working relationship with Sir William Gilbert and Sir Arthur Sullivan. She toured Europe with the company and sang in many of their now world famous comic operettas.

The Brown girls, Jessie and Annie, were the daughters of Henry Rolf Brown, an American born in Rhode Island around 1828; he was a Master Mariner. But his connection to the sea and ships went back further than that. His father John was a shipbuilder in Rhode Island and his mother Jane Rolf came from Nova Scotia. Henry was married to a Scottish girl, Jessie Ellen Andrews. As well as the two girls, the couple had a son, Henry Rolf junior. He was to become a well respected Doctor of Medicine.

According to the American Census for 1880, Jessie, Annie and Henry junior were living in San Francisco with their mother, who was erroneously described as a widow. She was not, although Henry senior at the time of the Census, as a Master Mariner, could have been at sea. There is a further complication in the Census as Jessie is described, at the age of twenty, as being divorced. It has been impossible to confirm a marriage of a Brown to a Tuttle, nor has evidence been found of a divorce. It is therefore possible that the marriage may have been "irregular" followed by an equally "irregular" divorce.

In October 1888 James Murray and Jessie were at Knockderry Castle, Cove, Dunbartonshire, for the marriage of his sister Alice to Daniel Henderson Lusk Young. It was then that James Murray told his father that he was engaged to be married to Jessie, a young widow. Unconvinced by his son's assertion that Jessie was a thoroughly good person from a good family, Templeton senior sought the services of an investigator. When the investigation proved that his prospective daughter-in-law was a divorcee, Templeton was deeply troubled by the deception. Fully aware of the Allan boys' connection with his son and Jessie, he took his anxieties to Alexander of Glasgow. Templeton and Alexander sought legal advice and Jessie was made to sign an affidavit confirming that she was a divorcee not a widow.

Jessie's engagement to James Murray was promptly ended; but CharlesE was not to be put off so easily, and he became her supporter and confidant. It is not known what his parents made of their son offering to support the rejected fiancée of James Murray, but it is obvious that they did not altogether share Templeton's cruel rejection of the girl. It is very possible that having heard from CharlesE that Jessie came from a respectable shipping family, they were prepared to forgive what may have been a youthful indiscretion or a tragic error.

A few months later, CharlesE's support turned to romance, and his marriage to Jessie Ellen Brown took place in Manhattan, New York, on 20 January 1890. The day before the wedding, CharlesE arrived aboard the *Britannic* which docked at New York. He must have been grateful that the wild Atlantic winter weather had not delayed his arrival. It is unlikely that members of his Scottish family attended their wedding, which would have been in total contrast to that of his cousin Bryce in 1886. For CharlesE and Jessie there were no flags, no celebrations and if their union alienated them from parts of the Scottish community, it reinforced their relationship with her father Henry Rolf and her sister Annie. In the years that followed Henry and his daughter made a number of visit to CharlesE and Jessie.

The marriage of CharlesE was not the only major change in his life. In 1891 he joined Workman, Clark & Co, shipbuilders in Belfast, as their Technical Director. As a graduate Marine Engineer who had family connections to Workman and Clark, it was only natural for him to join them in Ireland, since he did not want to be part of the management of the Allan Line: too many of his brothers and cousins were already working for the Allan

Company and it is doubtful if he could have found a satisfactory position. He wanted to design and build better and faster vessels that were needed to compete in a rapidly expanding market.

Frank Workman and George Smith Clark had founded the company in 1880; they had previously worked at Harland & Wolff. The Workman connection goes back to George Smith, of the City Line. Frank and George were related to CharlesE through Workman and Clark marriages into the Smith family. It was Smith who supplied them with the initial capital to set up their business. The Clark connection had begun in 1858 when George Smith Clark's mother, Jane Smith, married James Clark of the Paisley thread manufacturers.

George and Robert Smith of the City Line added to the problem of identifying their offspring by both naming their daughters Jane. A family trait which also involved the Montreal Allans.

It was, however, family loyalty that kept the shipyard viable: George and Robert Smith gave the fledgling yard orders for new ships. If orders from the family were the mainstay of the business, the appointment of CharlesE as Technical Director allowed them to widen their horizons. During the next two decades he and Workman & Clark built many superior ships for the Blue Funnel Line, the Canadian Royal Mail Line, and also some very fine ships for the Allan Line.

By 1889 the Allan Line had held the Canadian mail contract for more than three decades, but when it came up for renewal they were reluctant to meet the new terms set by the Canadian Government. There was much discussion as to why they had withdrawn from the negotiations; questions were even asked from the floor of the House of Commons. Two MPs in particular, had an interest in seeing that the status quo continued. Sir George Smyth Baden-Powell, MP for Kirkdale, Manchester, and Justin McCarthy, MP for North Longford, feared that if the Allan Line did not retain the mail contract, the Allan fleet would have to reduce sailings from Liverpool and would not visit Queenstown on either the outward or inward leg of the voyage.

In a letter written from their London Office in Lombard Street, J & A Allan set out their reasons why they had retired from the negotiations.

The Canadian Government naturally desired in these days of swift Transatlantic navigation to possess a service similar in point of speed to that on the New York route and invited, under the offer of an enlarged subsidy, tenders for such a service.

The Allan Line, which for over 30 years have carried the Canadian Mails, were prepared to offer an improved service, but the route and degree of speed which the Government prescribed were such as, in the view of the Allan firms, to afford not only no hope of profit, but to give a certainty of loss. They therefore retired from the negotiations into which they had entered with the Government.[5]

It was unusual for the Allans to walk away from a negotiation, but the terms of the new mail contract, as put by the Canadian Government and the Canadian Pacific Railway, were not in the opinion of the Allan negotiating team achievable. The Canadians were insisting that the new mail contract should be carried in ships that could maintain a steaming speed of 20 knots across the North Atlantic, as against the 17 knots the Allans proposed. In the view of the Allan Line, 20 knots would be impossible to guarantee, and would, in adverse weather conditions such as a winter storm in the North Atlantic, be dangerous to the vessels, their crews and their passengers.

In the final paragraph of their letter, J A Allan could not offer either Baden-Powell or Justin McCarthy that there would be a continuance of the service they had desired.

Freed from the obligation of the mail service, they do propose, as Sir George Baden-Powell seems to have learnt, to improve the Canadian service of steamers, but it does not follow that they will continue as heretofore to call at Londonderry [Queenstown] ... Nor is it the case, as he represents, that the new service to be established under the management of the Orient Line agency will not be in competition with the existing lines to Canada, but only with the subsidised French and German lines. The new service from England will naturally compete for passengers and cargo with all existing British lines.[6]

In the end, the Canadians awarded the contract to a London-based ship management company, a decision they soon came to regret. The Allans took the loss of their very profitable mail contract with a degree of stoicism, perhaps they knew it would return to them within a few months. It was just as well Sir Hugh was dead, he would have fought the Canadian decision with aggression, arrogance and his usual unflagging determination. He would have in no uncertain terms told the Canadian Government that they were making a big mistake.

Capt Sandy and his five sons had been an adventurous, robust and hardy group of individuals. They had been masters of the seas for more than fifty years. They had experienced the horrors and disasters that all pioneer sailors and explorers have encountered in opening up new lands and new sea routes. But they had survived, and they had prospered even more than they would have believed possible. Capt Sandy's grandsons had grown up in a totally different environment. They were better educated and they were used to a life of gracious living with an army of servants to cater for their every need. They had time for leisure: they hunted, they fished and above all they sailed on beautiful, graceful yachts. They gave lavish balls, garden parties and formal dinners for royalty, politicians and for the great and good citizens of Canada, Glasgow and Liverpool.

Yet, having said all that, they did not neglect the shipping business and when the opportunity arose for expansion they took a commercial decision to proceed. In May 1891 they bought the State Line of ships when the company had run into financial difficulties and lost their authorization to sail and conduct business. By Allan standards the number of ships run by the State Line was small, but although they immediately sold two, the remaining four were well worth the price they had paid for them. They had to work hard to restore the reputation of the State Line ships, which had been under a cloud for some time, but with common sense and professionalism they continued to give and offer a good service to all their new clients.

Alexander of Aros, having taken on the task of running the estate after the death of his father, was finding ever more reasons to enjoy his life on Tobermory. As the fifteenth anniversary of his role as Provost occurred in 1890, it is perhaps worth giving a brief account of all he had achieved in such a short period of time:

due to his untiring efforts, Tobermory has been vastly improved. During
his term in office a water and drainage system has been introduced and
everything has been done to give satisfaction to the medical and sanitary
authorities of the county.[7]

He had overseen improvements to the hospital accommodation, and,
with the Hon Miss Greenhill Gardyne of Glenforsa, had established the
Nursing Association of North Argyll. He did not, however, always see eye
to eye with all those officials who thought they were helping to improve
the facilities on Mull. In this context Alexander showed himself a poet,
though unfortunately not in the same vein as his collateral ancestor, Robert
Burns, the Scottish Bard. In a take-off of the children's nursery rhyme,
Nurse Truelove's New-Year's Gift, Alexander wrote his own modern version
of *The House that Jack Built, and* he rather hoped it would be used by the
school children on Mull.

> This is the road the Board built ... / This is the pier put up by mistake/ On
> the shore of an inaccessible lake ... / To carry traffic, which we're bound to
> confess,/ Though it well might be more, it could hardly be less.[8]

The road and pier might well have been built in the wrong place, but
Alexander made absolutely sure that his gift of a splendid public hall and
reading-room, paid for solely by him, was exactly where and what the good
people of Tobermory wanted.

Visitors to Tobermory were greeted by Alexander and Juliana, and
while some only enjoyed the beautiful gardens of Aros House there were
others who could experience the delights and generosity of their hosts'
hospitality.

One such visitor was Isabella Bird (Bishop) the young woman who had
first come into the Allan circle a quarter of a century earlier when she asked
them for help in sending Scottish migrants to Canada. She had kept on
her sister Henrietta's cottage at Tobermory for many years after her death,
and when she returned from her many adventures exploring unfrequented
parts of the world she would trudge round the bay and pay a welcome visit
to Alexander and Juliana.

On one such visit around 1889/1890 she formed the Tobermory Young
Women's Christian Association, and whenever she could she attended
their meetings. Frequently, Alexander and Juliana entertained Isabella and
members of the YMCA to social evenings at Aros House.

The welfare of the people of Tobermory was Alexander's priority. Like his father and uncles he was a staunch member of the Temperance League, and, as with so many island communities, his commitment to the Church was strong and unfailing.

Isabella Bird died in 1904, and she left Alexander a sum of money to commission Charles Whymper to design and have built a clock tower in memory of her sister Henrietta, who had died of typhoid on the island in 1880. Whymper was better known as a painter of wild life, but he had designed a clock tower in memory of his father-in-law George Brown in 1901 and Isabella was known to have been a life-long friend of George Brown and his wife. The Tobermory clock tower is an impressive stone column set on a plinth, with the four-sided clock housed above with a slated roof. In August 1905, a crowd of Tobermory people gathered to hear Alexander of Aros give a short speech and it was Juliana, who on the stroke of six o'clock, set the clock in motion. It is still a feature of Tobermory and in 2005, a hundred years after it first chimed, it celebrated its centenary and in all probability will still be chiming in 2105.

Chapter 10

Sadness

The marriage of Margaret Allan, Capt Sandy's youngest daughter, to Claud MacFie had given her a life of wealth and comfort. She and Claud spent many years at their Edinburgh Home of Gogar Burn House, and it was there that she entertained her nieces and nephews and their respective spouses. That she and Claud never had children must have caused her much unhappiness.

For a week in February 1891, Margaret was ill with an internal haemorrhage; she died on the morning of the twelfth. Her death, rather unusually, was not registered by her husband Claud, but by her medical attendant Dr Alexander Matthews. Her estate naturally went to Claud, but in the event of him predeceasing her she had left her estate to her nieces, Jane and Lizzie Greenhorne.

In the event, not only did Claud outlive Margaret, but eight months after her death he married again. His bride was Mary Young, thirty-five years his junior; he was sixty-nine and she thirty-four. The next two years must have been an anxious but hopeful time for Claud, having remained childless during his years of his marriage to Margaret. His new wife produced a son, Claud William, in 1893, and then a daughter, Catherine Mary, in 1897. As with many sons of wealthy merchants, even retired merchants, Claud William was sent to Ardverick Preparatory School in Crieff at a very young age. Claud's delight in his unexpected heir was however very sincere, and in a letter to the press, he wrote:

My son, aged seven years, found a chrysalis in a room in this house [*Gogar Burn*]. It was put under glass, and produced a moth like Graphiphora C nigrum (Hebrew character). The peculiarity of it is a very strongly marked letter "y" in silver on both wings. I have carefully examined Westwood (1851), and find no trace of any moth with a "y" on it. It may probably interest some of our entomological readers.[1]

The enjoyment of that letter lies in our feeling that Claud must have been sufficiently thrilled by his little son's interest in insect finds to spend time looking up reference books – which he surely had in his own library – and cared enough to encourage his son's interest to write to the editor of *The Scotsman*, telling him of the young boy's find.

The early years of the new decade saw major changes to the lives of many family members. The appearance of the "Grim Reaper" was a constant reminder of the fragility of life, but rarely did his coming effect so many members at the same time.

Alexander of Glasgow was now at an age when he began to think about retirement. He had been involved with the shipping line for the best part of fifty years; he had witnessed the growth of the business and the increase prosperity of the family members. He and Jane were delighted to be grandparents, but perhaps they felt there was something missing in their lives. They had travelled very infrequently during their marriage, but they had financially supported many overseas missions and they decided that they would like to see for themselves the way their money had helped to advance the lives of those in distant lands. In 1890, shortly before they left Glasgow on an extended overseas trip, Alexander and Jane saw the opening of the Almshouses at 19 Westland Drive, Whiteinch, named the "James Allan Trust". The Almshouses were to provide accommodation and comfort for elderly Allan employees. Adjoining the new building was the Glasgow Institution for Orphans and Destitute Girls, a charity that was very much at the forefront of Jane's generous mind.

Alexander, Jane and their daughters, Eliza and Janie, travelled first to Canada, with the express purpose of seeing their Canadian relatives. Apart from Alexander the only other surviving son of Capt Sandy's was Old Andrew, and visiting him would be the first leg of what would be a very long voyage. Alexander had been in poor health for sometime; when he and Jane and their daughters reached Ceylon, it was decided on medical grounds, that they should return to Scotland as soon as travel arrangements could be made.

They returned to Scotland towards the end of 1891, but did not go to their summer residence of Hafton, probably fearing that the winter weather might delay them if they had to return to the mainland for further medical attention. They took up residence at Blackwood House, Lesmahagow, but the return to their home country was not to be for long.

They were, however, in Scotland for the marriage of their son JamesA to Mabel Nora Young on 10 February 1892. Mabel was eight years younger than JamesA. She was the daughter of John Young, a Professor of Natural History at Glasgow University; her mother was Eliza Leonora Schenitz. Henry, following his custom at such times, was a witness at the marriage. It is possible that Jane did not attend the wedding, having been ill with a chill and pneumonia; if she did, then it was more than likely that it was there she caught the chill. JamesA and Mabel were to have three sons, Alexander, Hamish and John (Jack), and a daughter Margaret Mabel Gladys.

In the afternoon of the 18 February 1892, Jane died. She and Alexander had been married for almost forty years, and she had given birth to seven sons, of whom two had died in infancy, and two daughters. If the success of her marriage can be judged in the success of her children, then Jane could only have been immensely proud of their achievements.

It was not the custom in 1892, nor was it usual until the latter end of the 1960s, for Scottish women to attend funerals. At Jane's burial at the Necropolis, in Glasgow, however, there was present a group of women she had befriended.

> A few mourners were deeply touched by seeing, standing near and witnessing the burial, so many of those poor women, who afterwards laid upon the closed grave their memorial wreath of everlasting flowers, which had cost them some pounds, as the last token of their affection, gratitude, and sorrow for their benefactress and friend.[2]

It was not a time for introspection or perhaps even for grieving; less than seven weeks after Jane's death, Alexander died. For Henry, as informant of the death of both his parents, it must have been an ordeal. Although he was not the eldest son, he was the person they all turned to when they needed a cool head and the ability to get things done.

While Alexander chose his sons as the executors of his very substantial estate, Jane, equally wealthy, only chose RobertS, her eldest son, but added two of her cousins, John Service and George Smith. To list all the bequests Jane made would take many paragraphs; her generosity was second to none. One of the largest bequests was to the Sailors' Orphan Society,

Glasgow, which Alexander had been instrumental in setting up in 1889. Children, the welfare of seamen, and the destitute women of Glasgow were among her other bequests, along with a number of Glasgow hospitals. As a life-long member of the Presbyterian faith, it was not at all surprising that she left money to the UP Church's Foreign Mission Fund. She also left a small, but no doubt welcome, bequest to the Fund for the Aged and Infirm Ministers.

Alexander, always a very private man, would not have been surprised that his obituaries tended to concentrate on his role within the success of the Allan Line. It was said of him that:

> Mr Allan was a shrewd business man and thorough in everything he performed. While in active health he also took a share in the management of public bodies. In politics he was a Liberal Unionist. He was an elder in the Glasgow Wellington United Presbyterian Church, having been frequently a representative elder at the Synod of the Church. As a man he was of kindly disposition and widely esteemed.[3]

Alexander did not seek civic or political honours, he believed passionately that he should not be rewarded for doing his best to help and encourage others less able than himself. He did, however, leave a legacy that would live long in the hearts and memories of all who knew him long after any written word had been forgotten. At a City of Glasgow Chamber of Commerce meeting, on which he had been an active member for many years, the chairman merely referred to the loss to the community of Alexander's sudden passing.

The death of both Capt James and Alexander meant that there would need to be considerable changes in the management of J & A Allan. Nathaniel Dunlop was to take a far greater role as he was the only director with the required experience. RichardG and JamesA were nominally on the board of directors, but RichardG's interests lay much more in the world of yachts, mountaineering, horses (both hunting and steeple-chasing), and all things that tested his sporting enthusiasm and courage. JamesA's interests were much more in politics, the arts and music, he gave his profession as shipowner but it is doubtful if his heart was really in the day-to-day mechanics of ship management.

RobertS and his brother Claud, perhaps fearing the break-up of J & A Allan, formed their own company, R & C Allan, shipowners, with offices at 121 St Vincent Street, Glasgow.

In 1892, JamesA was not the only one of Alexander and Jane's children to marry. On 15 November, Eliza (sometimes known as Elsie) married TEL (Thomas Eaton Lander) at Carstairs House, in Lanark. TEL, four years Eliza's junior, had been born in Sydney, New South Wales, in 1865, the son of Dr Thomas Eaton Lander and Isabella Spedding, née Mansfield. A simple statement of fact, but the story of what a young doctor and his wife were doing in Australia in the 1860s needs to be told.

Dr Thomas, the son of yet another Thomas Eaton Lander and Ann Ridley, had been baptized on 8 March 1820 at the small rural village of Shifnal, Shropshire. A successful seedsman, Lander senior was very well known in Shifnal, and especially among the farmers of the surrounding districts. The exact details of Dr Thomas's education are not known, but in the autumn of 1844 he was back in Shifnal practicing his profession when he married a farmer's daughter, Elizabeth Sarah Harriet Eyke, of Stanton, Woodside, Shifnal. In 1851, they were living at Inmage Cottage, Shifnal, but rather unusually for that time, there were to be no children of the marriage.

The local curate at Shifnal in 1851 was Francis Spedding, from Gilling, Yorkshire, and his wife Isabella Mansfield, of Papcastle, near Cockermouth, Cumberland. Isabella was the daughter of the late James Horn Elphistone Dalrymple Mansfield who had died just three years after his daughter's birth in 1823. Isabella's mother was Henrietta Knight, who, though a widow with two small daughters, had been left by her late husband as 'a fund holder', thus implying she had sufficient monies to ensure her daughters had a secure future.

In 1846, at Cockermouth, Isabella married Francis Spedding; James Mansfield, their first son, was born in Flinby, Cumberland, but a year later in 1849, Francis and his family moved to Shifnal. In such a small rural community, there can be no doubt that the Lander and the Spedding families became both professional and personal friends. Indeed, in the first few years that Spedding and his wife were in Shifnal, four more children were born, two daughters and two sons. It would have been very likely that Dr Thomas, with the assistance of the local midwife, was present at all the births.

In 1861 trouble erupted between the Lander and Spedding families. Elizabeth Lander and Doctor Thomas petitioned for divorce. A year later the marriage of Spedding and Isabella similarly ended in divorce.

The shock waves caused by scandal must have had the village gossips entertained for hours; after all such things simply did not happen in their tranquil village. A doctor and a clergyman's wife involved in such an affair would rarely have been discussed in polite society. Francis Spedding was transferred to Donisthorpe, Leicestershire. Doctor Thomas and Isabella fled to Sydney, Australia, but if they thought their happiness would be complete so far from their native land, they were to be sadly disappointed.

Australia, in the mid-1860s, was a hard, cruel environment, disease and conflict were rife, and two of the children Isabella had bought with her from England died of infectious diseases. The first daughter she had with Doctor Thomas also died in infancy. They did, however, have two surviving children, TEL and Mary.

It has not been possible to find evidence of a marriage between Doctor Thomas and Isabella, or to find an exact date and location of Isabella's death, but what can be established beyond doubt is that Doctor Thomas and his two children were back in Shifnal in 1869. His homecoming could not have been easy for him: he must have known that he was dying from a disease of the lungs and throat, and he was utterly exhausted. He died on 20 November aged forty-nine, but not before making absolutely sure that TEL and Mary would have a caring guardian.

Doctor Thomas turned to his brother, Richard Ridley Lander, a farmer in Shifnal, with a stable family life: a wife and four children. Richard, whatever his thoughts about the actions of his elder brother, was more than willing to give Mary a home – he had a daughter Mary himself, so Doctor Thomas's daughter became known as Mamie. Even today it would be seen as cruel to separate two orphan siblings but TEL went to live with his great-aunt Mary Ann, at Rusholme, Warwickshire.

Richard Lander was a kind guardian, but in 1871 he suffered a personal tragedy when his wife Matilda died, shortly after giving birth to her daughter Edith. A year later he married Margaret Osbourne. Richard and Margaret had six more children, four daughters and two sons, Arthur Edward and Ernest Osbourne. One of their daughters, Mabel, deserves a special mention: she became a very well-respected music teacher, and was piano teacher to the two young Royal Princesses, Elizabeth and Margaret Rose.

Richard ensured both his wards, like his own very large family, had a good education. Mamie and her two cousins, Kate and Edith, went to Broomfield Hall in Kidderminster. TEL was sent to St John's College,

Hurstpierpoint, Sussex, which he entered in 1873 and left in 1881. It would appear from school records that TEL enjoyed his years at St John's College where he became a *fleur-de-lis* Prefect, and was a member of various societies, including the Natural History Society. It was reported that:

> Thomas [*TEL*] was the first to collect a thrush's egg and a redbreast's egg in March 1880. [*He also*] it was noted took part in an Assault of Arms, a fencing demonstration organized by an Old Boy.[4]

Life at a public school in the 1880s would have been harsh and uncomfortable, but TEL was not one to complain. On leaving St John's he joined the Bank of Scotland, and in 1890 he went out to one of their branches in India. It was when Eliza and Janie were on their long tour from Scotland to Canada and the East that they paid a business call on the branch in India where TEL was working, and such was his first impression of the young ladies that he decided there and then that the elder girl would become his wife. Shortly after their marriage in Scotland, in November 1892, TEL and Eliza returned to India where their son Thomas Eaton (Tom) was born. Their daughter, Winifred Mansfield, was born in Scotland. The name of Mansfield gives us a poignant reminder of her great-grandmother Isabella.

In 1901, TEL and his young family were living in some splendour at Colguim House, Kilsyth, Stirlingshire, a mansion of some thirty-two rooms, with a domestic staff of nine and an outdoor staff of two resident gardeners. TEL, having decided that thirty-seven was too young to retire, became a director of an electric engineering company. Marriage gave him time to pursue his hobbies: he was an excellent shot and was regularly a competitor at Bisley, winning many of the top prizes.

Marriage, fatherhood, and the death of his parents did not daunt JamesA's love of classical music and choral singing. In the early 1890s – as is still the case – the funds needed to allow the choral society and the orchestra to stage their season of performances had to be found from wealthy sponsors. In his delightful book, *Playing for Scotland,* Conrad Wilson gives us a glimpse into JamesA's commitment to the cause.

In 1893 and earlier, sponsorship took different forms but was equally essential to the orchestra's survival. Annual guarantees from private individuals helped to keep music flowing. Shortage of cash meant fewer concerts; a surplus extended the season. It was a capital sum of £20,000 from James A Allan, a rich West of Scotland shipowner, which made a proper Scottish Orchestra feasible. With the money a limited company was formed for the purpose of organising and maintaining an efficient orchestra which would be suitable for concerts throughout Scotland over a much longer period than has hitherto been possible.[5]

As with all changes, there was opposition from certain members of the Choral Union who objected to merging with a Scottish Orchestra, even though the merger would broaden their appeal and widen their membership.

Meetings and negotiations, lasting over a twelvemonth, followed, which only showed that a compromise was out of the question. In the upshot a trial of strength was resolved upon. Each body decided to carry out its programme, regardless of the consequences.[6]

The first concert of the new season in Glasgow, held in St Andrew's Hall late in October 1893, was not well attended, and, according to a report a few days later, was not without its critics. But as the report was written from an Edinburgh perspective, it should be read with a degree of scepticism.

In one respect at least the opening concert of the Scottish Orchestra in Edinburgh was more successful than that in Glasgow. The *Music Hall* was last night crowded, which was by no means the experience of Mr Henschel and his orchestra in Glasgow last week.[7]

However by 1898, according to reports, the concert held in December was a sell-out. It would seem however that, even with successful concerts, the squabbles between the Choral Union and the Orchestra were not fully resolved for sometime. The older members of the Union wanted to remain as they had always been, a choir, whereas the younger members wanted to widen their the scope and bring classical music to a much larger audience.

JamesA can rightly claim a place in the history of classical music in Scotland for his generous support. He was not, however, silly when he believed further financial support was not in his best interests or that of the orchestra. In October 1909, the Scottish Orchestra Company went into liquidation, and JamesA revoked and cancelled a Codicil to his Will. He said he had already been very benevolent to the orchestra and he believed further funding would not be in their best interest or his. He would not end all connections with the orchestra but would retain his share-holdings in the company.

It is with a sense of sadness and regret that we remember that St Andrew's Hall was destroyed by fire on 26 October 1962. The beautiful old Hall was considered by many concert-goers to have had the best acoustics of any concert hall in the country. For the next three decades Glasgow was without an international concert hall. It was not until October 1990 that the Glasgow Royal Concert Hall finally opened.

The year 1893 was notable for the tragic death of a young man, Arthur Edward, the youngest son of Sir Hugh. Arthur had experienced many tragedies in his young life; his mother died when he was eleven, his father died a year later. To be robbed of both parents at the age of twelve, however wealthy they had been, deprived him of two powerful influences in his formative years. In the Canadian Census of 1891, he was living with brother Montagu, who was not yet married. Arthur's sisters, Margaret and Edith, were still unmarried. A measure of the household's strength was that there were another twenty-three people listed, all of them in the capacity of servant.

An interesting condition of Sir Hugh's Will had been that not one of his children should inherit until Arthur had reached the age of majority, which was on 18 April 1892.

Arthur, now of age and a wealthy young man decided that the time had come to move into his own apartment. There is some circumstantial evidence that as a child and young man, he had suffered bouts of debilitating illness, the exact nature of which are not known. However, in late 1892 he took possession of a flat at Dorchester Street, Montreal, run by Mrs Bessie Bird. It was very much the place for young bachelors; Arthur's rooms were

> the most expensive ... consisting of two large rooms en suite, and a third one which was being used as a sort of study. They were handsomely decorated and the pictures and bric-a-brac ... showed excellent taste.[8]

In spite of his illnesses, Arthur was a great lover of sport; he belonged to the Hunt and Tandem Club, and the Racket Court Club. He was a member of the St James's Club, where he went most days for his meals. He was by all accounts a gregarious young man, but he does not appear to have had any active involvement with the shipping line or with his late father's other financial and commercial concerns, though like his three brothers he was a shareholder in the Allan Line. In the evening of the 15 January, after taking tea and watching a hockey match at the Victoria Rink with friends, he dined at the St James's Club, and his companion commented that Arthur appeared to have a severe cold. His voice was husky and he seemed to have a problem communicating. He left the Club shortly after dinner but returned again at about 11.30pm. He left the Club again at 1.30am. He telephoned a friend to join him at his apartment, but it was revealed later that his friend did not receive the message.

A little over half an hour later, an alarm was sounded at the local fire station and an appliance was immediately despatched to Bessie Bird's address. The fire, according to the fire chief who attended, was an insignificant one, and was quickly brought under control. A number of residents and servant girls escaped from the second floor to the porch over the front door, but once the firemen arrived they were quickly brought to safety. This short distraction allowed the smoke to clear from Arthur's rooms, and when the fire chief went to inspect the damage, he found Arthur sitting in an armchair in his bedroom, as if peacefully asleep.

Dr Herbert Birkett, who had an apartment in the same building, with another resident Dr Frederick Finley, worked for many minutes without being able to revive Arthur.

> A thorough search of the premises was made, but the only conclusion arrived at as to the cause of the accident is to the effect that he [Arthur] must have come home smoking, threw away his burning cigar in some corner, or in the waste paper basket, where it was apt to cause a fire, and then after taking off his overcoat and cap, sat down to await the coming of the friend he had telephoned for, perhaps to read, and had fallen asleep.[9]

According to the report of the incident, there was no evidence of a struggle, although a comment was made that Arthur had a handkerchief and the electric cord from a reading lamp wrapped round his wrist. Dr Charles McEachran, the husband of Arthur's sister Margaret, was informed of the accident. Montagu was in Winnipeg, and it took some time to tell him of his brother's death. Arthur's body was taken to Dr Finley's rooms, where it remained until the arrival of the Coroner for the District of Montreal. Ed McMahon, after taking evidence from witnesses, allowed Arthur's body to be taken home to Ravenscrag.

As in all cases of sudden death, then as now, an inquest was held, McMahon regretted the necessity of such an action, but stated

> that of justice he was compelled to. The Inquest was held not to throw discredit or blame on any family, but to find out whether a crime or negligence was to blame.[10]

The unusual circumstances of the fire and Arthur's death raised doubts in the minds of some people that he had taken his own life.

The first witness was Dr Finley, who gave a blunt statement that he thought Arthur had died as a result of fainting and then being suffocated by smoke inhalation. Fireman Pierre Gagnon testified that he had gone into the back room to break the window and had found Arthur in a chair. He illustrated, to the jury, exactly how he found Arthur sitting in a chair. He admitted that at that moment he had expected he would be able to waken the young man. Gagnon believed only minutes had elapsed from the moment he first entered the apartment until he found Arthur. McMahon explained to the jury that although Arthur's rooms were connected by folding doors, access from these doors had been hampered by the placing of a large wardrobe behind them. Arthur would have had to go along a short passageway to get to his bedroom. A juror wanted to know how the maids had escaped so easily, and Bessie Bird explained that Dr Birkett had broken a window for them and they had climbed out in their nightwear, as indeed so had he.

Mrs Bird was asked if she had been aware that her young tenant was in a habit of throwing his clothes down in the front room. To which she replied yes, indicating that Arthur was so used to having things done for him he was lazy about being tidy.

Many of the jurors seemed to want to continue with the idea that Arthur had committed suicide. Dr Finley was recalled and adamantly denied that such an action was out of the question. He was firmly of the opinion that Arthur had tried to get to the window to break the glass and raise the alarm. He said there was evidence that Arthur had got to the back window as some of his hair been found on the window-ledge. Fireman Gagnon had already put forward the view that in attempting to get to the window to break it with the table lamp the cord had become entangled around Arthur's arm when he fell back into his arm-chair.

Witnesses frequently give conflicting evidence, and in this case, that was most definitely true. McMahon had subpoenaed two further witnesses, friends of the deceased, J B Abbot and Edward McVicar, but Abbot had returned to New York and McVicar was also away from Montreal. The jury, however, was not concerned by their absence: they believed they had heard enough evidence to conclude, after some deliberations, that Arthur's death had been a tragic accident.

Arthur was buried at Mount Royal, overlooking Ravenscrag; his very large and extended family were there to mourn the passing of a much loved young man. The mourners represented a distinguished array of Montreal's elite, and included many dignitaries from other Provinces of Canada, as befitted the unexpected death of the youngest son of one of their most respected old families.

If there is to be a postscript to such a personal tragedy, it must surely be that on the day of the funeral, Wednesday, 18 January, there was a reminder in *Montreal Daily Star* of an earlier business affair that had all but ruined Sir Hugh's last few years of life. There had been bitter criticism of him in a New York paper, by Professor Godwin Smith. He had accused Sir Hugh of corruption and bribery by manipulating Canadian public men and politicians in awarding the contracts to build the Canadian Pacific Railway line. Smith had declared their actions had been nothing short of another Panama Canal scandal. Van Horne, rebutting the allegations, wrote:

> The article is a sort of scrapbook of the utterances of certain opposition newspapers and members of Parliament at the time of the loan acts of 1864 and 1888 which are in most cases copied word for word and strung together in a kind of sequence. Everybody in Canada who has a memory extending back seven or eight years will easily recognize them. The facts are distorted in a shameless way. The statements were fully answered at the time ...[11]

The facts may have been known, but they would never be allowed to go unchallenged. Once a conspiracy theory takes root it is never allowed to wither and die.

The death of Arthur had left a feeling of great sadness in the Montreal family, but the year was to end on a far happier note. The marriage of Montagu to Marguerite Ethel the daughter of Hector McKenzie was held on 18 October 1893. Montagu had been his father's heir apparent for more than a decade, but in marrying into the McKenzie family he must have been aware that he would be courting comment from certain members of the Montreal's chattering classes. The dowager ladies of the Golden Square Mile, while attending their soirées, would have whispered and reminded each other that another McKenzie was marrying into the Allan family. They would have reminded each other that Hector's brother William had had a short and unhappy marriage with Montagu's cousin, Jean Crawford. The dowager ladies were not to know that Montagu's and Marguerite's marriage would last for almost six decades and that they would have four children: three daughters, Marguerite Martha, Anna Marjory and Gwendolyn Evelyn, and a son and heir: Hugh.

PART THREE

1894 – 1914

I'll act with prudence as far 's I'm able,
But if success I must never find,
Then come Misfortune, I bid thee welcome,
I'll meet thee with an undaunted mind.–

ROBERT BURNS
Fickle Fortune (1782)

Chapter 11

Pleasures

As Alexander and Jane's sons grew into middle age it became evident that they shared their parents' concern for those less well-off than themselves. Not just satisfied in following what his parents had done, RobertS widened his horizons. In 1894, he was elected to the Glasgow School Board of Education, and this was to be important for the rest of his working life. He was a total abstainer from the demon drink, again like his maternal grandfather Robert Smith and his parents. One of his missions was to educate the pupils of Glasgow to the dangers they would face if they should partake of the devil's liquid. To prevent this happening, he urged the Glasgow Board to start weekly lessons of the benefits of temperance, and even went so far as to supply the teachers with text books on the subject.

On Aros in the spring of 1895 there was both joy and sadness. Capt Bryce's wife Janet Blair, his widow for more than twenty years died at Dunblane Hydropathic Institution. She had resided at Ards House, Aros, since returning to Scotland after Capt Bryce's death in 1874. Her death was perhaps a relief, she was suffering from senile decay, but one sadness was that her grandson Bryce, who was the informant of her death, did not know the names of her maternal grandparents. They were George Blair and Elizabeth MacFarlan. Admittedly both were deceased by 1895, but it is still a little surprising: Janet had kept in touch with her brother Robert Blair, and when he died in 1886 in Dublin Alexander of Aros had been one of his executors. A sugar refiner by trade, Robert was also an associate of Claud MacFie. Janet and her children Bryce and Sheila had been a welcomed visitor at the Gogar Burn home of MacFie.

Janet's death cast a shadow not only on Aros but on the coming of age of Bryce, since the family were officially in mourning. The celebrations were accordingly a little muted. Bryce was still in Oxford (he did not graduate from St John's College until the end of June), but celebratory bonfires were lit and the employees on the Estate presented him with a "massive gold watch chain".

A week later, Alexander and Juliana entertained over seventy people to a lavish outing.

> At 1.30 the party left the precincts of Aros, where three waggonettes and five carts were loaded with as happy a group of holiday seekers as could be, and set out for Ardnacross ... where a lovely park overlooking a long stretch of the Sound of Mull was put at their disposal ... When the company got assembled, sports were set on foot – races and jumping for married men and boys; married women; single women and girls; in which all joined most heartily. A tea-dinner of the most substantial description rewarded those who had exerted themselves ... the Laird of Aros himself came down in his yacht [*probably Mermaid, built in 1888, by MacLean & Sons, Roseneath, and designed by R D Ferguson, which Alexander kept until 1896 when it was replaced by Gled*] and joined the party ... Presiding over the sports, he threw such enthusiasm into various events that those who thought they could not run at all joined in the games to the astonishment of none more than themselves.[1]

There is a postscript to the celebrations of Bryce's coming of age. On his return from St John's College, Oxford, where he had read Jurisprudence, he was greeted by the people of Mull as a returning hero.

> The streets were gaily adorned with flags, and at two points were arched over with banners in a most tasteful manner. ... Such an event had not occurred for upwards of seventy years, and the occasion was taken advantage of to give a warm welcome to the young heir. Yachts in the harbour were gaily decorated with bunting. A rocket fired from the RMS *Carabinier* when she came in sight announced his arrival, and was the signal for a salute of twenty guns from the rocky bluff overlooking the town.[2]

On disembarking, a great crowd of well-wishers greeted Bryce. Tenants and local boys carried him shoulder-high to a carriage where the horses had been unharnessed, and then pulled it themselves along the main street. In the evening bonfires and fireworks were a fitting end to a remarkable culmination to Bryce's years at Oxford. It is doubtful if the good people of Mull really appreciated that their "young laird's" years in the "city of dreaming spires" had been years of long, hard days of study, and nights spent in revision, though it has to be said that Oxford in the last years of the nineteenth century offered many distractions for rich young students. Bryce spent a good deal of his time as President of the Archery Club; regrettably there is no evidence that he was a member of the Bullingdon Club, but as a former pupil of Harrow School, he could have been offered the chance to become a member of that most exclusive of Oxford clubs.

In the late 1880s, the Allan Line in Glasgow began what would become a yearly event, much appreciated by their employees: a "soirée and lecture", usually in late January, in Glasgow City Hall, attended by as many members of the family as were available on the chosen evening and a distinguished list of official guests. Alexander of Aros acted as chairman on a number of these occasions. In that role, which he played to perfection, his opening speech of welcome to the guests was delivered with humour, and frequently it was laced with a degree of nostalgia. He had a habit of referring to the *"good old times"*

> when he was in the Liverpool office. Those times were, in some respects at any rate, superior to the present. Passengers in those days did not expect to travel at such a tremendous speed. If in those days they took a man across the Atlantic in 14 days he did not grumble particularly; if they took him in 12 days he was pretty well satisfied; and if occasionally they brought him across in 10 days he gave a presentation to the captain and officers.[3]

Alexander of Aros would have been surprised to learn that a little over a century later, passengers would demand and receive compensation from their ship, aeroplane or railways companies if they were delayed by even a few hours. Such is the changed pace of life nowadays. Alexander made another remark that has as much resonance today as it did in 1892.

> Things have sadly changed nowadays, but he did not think the people were any better or happier on account of the express speed they demanded in travelling ...[4]

In concluding his lengthy opening speech he paid tribute to the early pioneers of Canada and the men, his uncles in particular, who led the way in opening up Canada and making the Allan Line the success it was. He was scathing of those people in Canada and the United States who saw progress for both countries as leading towards a merger into one nation of North America. He ended his speech with a comment that would be unthinkable today, although is still probably whispered in certain parts of the world.

> There were prominent politicians who talked about our colonies as if they were things to be handed about and bought and sold. They seemed to forget that the colonies of Great Britain were bought with the best blood of Great Britain, and to talk of them as a mercantile point of view – as to whether we could make money out of them – was a base thing to do. He should like to see the day when there should be a strong federation, offensive and defensive, between Great Britain and all her colonies.[5]

The 1890s dream of Imperial Federation was never made real, but in one sense Alexander of Aros's wishes came true a little over two decades later, when the armies of the Colonies were to come together to fight on the side of the British throne, supporting their allies in Europe and elsewhere against continental aggression.

The soirée evenings usually ended with a concert, and the audience went home with a renewed faith that the Allan Line would continue to play a lasting role in their lives and the well-being of their country.

It is doubtful if all of Capt Sandy's grandsons were gainfully employed as shipowners by the end of the 1890s. Alexander of Aros's primary occupation was the management of the Estate, its tenants and workers. RichardG, unlike his brothers and his Glasgow cousins who were also still employed as shipowners, was looking for additional interests.

In 1896/7 RichardG, Robert Murdoch his father-in-law, and John his brother-in-law together with two other fellow merchants, Robert Smith and George Moir, bought a liquidated coal-mine, Carmuirs near Larbert, Stirlingshire. It was the first time the Allan family had been involved with coalmining in Scotland; the five directors formed a new company, registered in Edinburgh and released a Prospectus offering shares to the public.

A report in the *Glasgow Herald,* dated 13 December 1897, assured prospective shareholders that in the opinion of the directors the Carmuirs mine, taken on a lease of twenty-one years, could again be a profitable mine. It occupied a site of five hundred acres and with its connections to the North British and the Caledonian Railways it had every opportunity of being profitable.

The directors being shrewd businessmen did, however, seek the advice of a Mine Engineer, Robert Frew of Landsdale, Frew and Gemmell. Frew's report was most encouraging.

> On the whole I consider the coal-field, with the existing two seams of coal and the fittings and plant completed in the manner of the rest has been done, will, with the favourable railway dues to the best markets have a good chance of turning out a more than usually remunerative mining venture.[6]

Carmuirs may have been a profitable mine but more importantly it was a comparatively safe mine. Checking the *Scottish Mining* website it has been possible to locate only two accidents at the mine between 1899 and 1902. On 3 March 1899, Benjamin Gibson a fourteen-year-old [he was according to his death certificate only thirteen], was against [A] Special Rule, taking a hutch laden with clay down an incline road by going in front of it, he was overpowered and run-over. His death certificate says his skull was crushed.

The second accident in 1902 was an example where tragedy can strike at just the wrong moment. James Ferguson Thomson a fifteen-year-old miner was

> following his father, who was taking his last tub for the day down a cut chain cuddy brae, dipping 1 in 4 – a partially filled tub was ranced up the braehead. The chain appeared to have knocked out the rance and set the tub in motion. It overtook deceased, crushed him against a prop and broke his neck.[7]

Two accidents that claimed the lives of teenagers, proving, if proof were needed, that whatever rules and regulations the directors of a company introduced, accidents could but should not happen.

RichardG was very much more personally concerned by a terrible yachting accident. In August 1896, *The Times* reported that a Baron von Zedtwitz had been killed at Spithead in a collision between his yacht the *Isolde* and the German Emperor's cutter *Meteor*. RichardG was the Kaiser's racing manager, and may well have been on board the *Meteor* at the time.

> A deplorable accident occurred yesterday at Spithead ... The large cutters and the 52ft class were each completing the first round of their respective courses at the Committee-boat HMS *Ant*, about noon when the German Emperor's cutter *Meteor*, which was following the *Britannia*, after running over the stern of the 52ft rater *Isolde* dismantled her mast with the main boom, and the mast and mainsail fell on the owner Baron von Zedtwitz, who was so badly crushed in the head and body that he died on a steam yacht to which he had been removed about 20 minutes afterwards.[8]

The accident was most unfortunate, added to which von Zedtwitz was a German diplomat who had, since coming to Britain, enjoyed a successful season racing his yacht *Isolde*. For RichardG, that the *Meteor* was the cause of the death of a diplomat, and a countryman of the Kaiser, was extremely regrettable. If RichardG was not himself on board the *Meteor*, he would certainly been at Spithead for the Royal Albert Yacht Club Regatta. The summer of 1896 had seen a series of mishaps for *Meteor*; in July, RichardG had had to telegraph Hunter's Quay to say that the Kaiser's yacht was still in Germany at Cuxhaven and although she was under full tow there was no way she would arrive at Dunoon until Monday at the earliest.

Ten days after the death of von Zedtwitz, the Kaiser announced that he was

> giving a valuable silver cup for a race from Dover to Helgoland after the ceremony to commemorate the sixtieth year of Queen Victoria's reign. The cup had been designed by his Imperial Majesty, and is 3ft high and said to be very valuable ...[9]

A committee was formed, comprising the Earl of Lonsdale, Sir John Burns, Sir Edward Burbeck, Sir Edward Sullivan, Mr Richard Grant, Mr Dixon Kemp and last though by no means least, Mr Richard Allan. The committee met many times during 1896/7 trying to decide and agree the terms and conditions of the race, and occasionally they had to refuse a yacht permission to take part. At a meeting in June 1897 at the home of Earl

Lonsdale the committee agreed the handicap allowances for each yacht, but these were placed in sealed envelopes and were not to be opened until the yachts had reached Texel in the Netherlands.

It is doubtful if the race ever took place. In the summer of 1896 there had been the first indication of a anti-English feeling in Germany. The German press were quick to exploit the growing gap between the rich and the poor. They were scathing of the Kaiser and his love of English yacht racing, and so he withdrew from attending the Cowes meeting that year. It was not a choice he took lightly, but political pressure was put on him and he had no other option, as he said at the time, but to withdraw from a sport he loved.

> Unfortunately upon this occasion the Emperor cannot act in accordance with what we may hope are his own feelings and desires. He is obliged to pay attention to the feelings of others who look upon England and Englishmen with eyes very different from his. There exist, unhappily, men and circles in Germany who regard our Constitution, our habits of thought, our commercial greatness, and our success as a colonizing Empire with a bitter detestation incomprehensible to us.[10]

To RichardG, it must have been a terrible blow to lose not just the Kaiser's wonderful yachts but the pleasure it had given him to work for such a dedicated seaman.

RobertS was interested in the civic and educational affairs of his native Glasgow, and in January 1897 he was elected a director of The Merchants' House of Glasgow. It was a position of great honour in one of the most important civic organizations in the City: membership of the Merchants' House had always been much prized by the merchants of Glasgow. Already in existence in 1605 when it received a written constitution, the Letters of Guildry, the Merchants' House incorporated all the trades of Glasgow, and had been based since 1877 in a majestic specially designed building in West George Street. The extended Allan families would be members of the Merchants House for many decades.

Later in November of that year, RobertS expanded his involvement in Glasgow civic life when he became a Patron of the Hutchesons' Hospital.

Occasionally, even in the largest and most successful companies, a decision is taken by the management which on the face of it seems inappropriate or a little foolhardy. In January 1898, J & A Allan embarked on such a decision. In the City of London Court, they sued the Corporation of Trinity House and the Thames Conservancy authorities for an overpayment of river dues in respect of a cargo of animals. The sum in dispute was put by the Allan Line barrister as being £3.9s.1d.; according to Mr Lauriston Batten, counsel for the Allan Line, it was not the amount that mattered but the principle: if the matter of overpayment was left as it was, then hundreds of other shipping companies would suffer. Batten told the Court that there had been a long running disagreement between the harbour board and the shipowners that dues should be paid upon the basis of the registered tonnage of the vessel and the space needed by the cargo when unloaded. Such an agreement had the backing of the Merchant Shipping Act. In the present case:

> The defendants measured the pens in which the animals were confined: but the shipowners objected because the space occupied by different animals varied, pigs for instance taking up less space than bullocks.[11]

J & A Allan did not object to the change; they did, however, object that when the cattle had been unloaded from their ship the *Austrian* it was before the new rules had been put in place. Therefore, they argued they had been over-charged.

The defendant's Counsel, Mr Butler Aspinall, responded by saying that the 1895 system had been in vogue and the plaintiff had been correctly charged. Mr Commissioner Kerr was of a different opinion, and found for the plaintiffs: J & A Allan were awarded their £3.9s.1d and their costs. It would be interesting to know who in the Allan family had been inclined to bring the action against Trinity House. It could have been a risky adventure for such a small sum, but one thing all the Allan family members agreed on was that where a matter of principle was concerned they were prepared to defend it whatever the cost.

Chapter 12

Problems

The new century was only six weeks old when yet again a member of the extended Allan family married a cousin. On 14 February 1900, at Sefton Park Presbyterian Church, Liverpool, Bryce of Aros married Hilda Mary, his cousin, the eldest daughter of JamesH and Clara. The wedding was a very splendid occasion, as befitted the "young laird of Aros" and the eldest daughter of a wealthy and well-known Liverpool shipping merchant. Bryce's sister Sheila and Hilda's sister Doris were two of the four bridesmaids. A fashion note says they wore "large black hats of velvet and chiffon and waving ostrich plumes". Bryce gave each bridesmaid a gift of a heart-shaped gold and pearl brooch, and a tiny gold heart pendant. The guests included the parents of both bride and groom, RobertG and Margaret, his wife, both resident in Liverpool, and many Stead relatives of Clara from Yorkshire. Bride and groom travelled to London en route to their honeymoon in Algiers.

There was a close relationship between Bryce and JamesH stemming back to the time when JamesH went to work at the Liverpool office of the Allan Line. It is known that he visited Aros and enjoyed a day's grouse shooting on the estate; he was there with Alexander and Bryce in August 1890. Hilda Mary was at Aros for thirty-one days in September and October 1899; her father joined her for the last week, and as it was just a few months before her marriage to Bryce it is fair to assume that plans for the wedding were made during that visit.

Alexander and his son were known for the generosity of their hospitality, and the shooting, hunting and fishing on Mull rarely left them without a day's enjoyment. But in the recreational stakes Aros had more to offer than field sports. Sailing was a passion for male members of the extended Allan family, and (not to be outdone by the male members of the family) Sheila could match any of them when it came to yachting:

> [*She*] inherits her father's taste for aquatic sports, manages a boat with
> intrepidity and skill, and succeeded in carrying off two cups against Clyde
> racers ... A half-gale and a pitching sea convey no terror to her nor ever
> impel her to relinquish the helm.[1]

The Allan women were not typical of their Victorian contemporaries, and
in no way could they be called shrinking violets. They had inherited the
determination of Jean Brown, who showed them that a woman could be
strong, forthright and as good as any man.

Ever since Capt Sandy first sailed his small brigantine *Jean* to Canada, over
eighty years ago, the family had witnessed the building and launching of
many fine ships for their ever-expanding fleet. Frequently when a new
ship entered service on the Canadian run it was an occasion for a special
celebration. One such occurred on 31 March 1900 when the *Tunisian* was
given a trial run. She had a number of reasons for being special: she was
the largest ship ever built by Alexander Stephen & Sons, and she was the
finest and fastest ship to belong to the Allan Line. An innovation, apart
from her engineering and technical improvements, was that she was lit by
electricity – according to a report at the time she had between five and six
hundred electric lights throughout the ship. Her first class passengers may
possibly have been unimpressed by this luxury, but her steerage passengers
must have been enthralled by the magnificent show.

The Allan family, together with members of the Stephen family, and
an impressive array of shipping and political dignities were aboard for the
ship's trial run. The guests travelled from Glasgow by special train, then a
river steamer took them to the anchored liner for a cruise along the Firth of
Clyde and the beautiful coastline of Argyll.

> Till noon a haze overspread the Firth, but thereafter the weather was
> charming with a spring-like mildness. The course taken was round Holy
> Island and back. During the cruise the measured mile was run several
> times, when the highest speed registered was fully 17 knots ...[2]

The assembled company, who numbered between two and three hundred,
were able during the cruise to enjoy a lavish luncheon The Allan family
members were Bryce and Annie, RobertS and Lizzie, CharlesE, but not his

wife JessieE, JamesA and Mabel, Henry, RichardG and Agnes. Nathaniel Dunlop acted as chairman and host-master; the Stephen family were represented by Alex and Daisy, Fred and Agnes, and John, who was known to all the assembled company as "Uncle John" – a designation that was a measure of the old man's position in the Stephen family and beyond.

Dunlop gave a short speech of welcome and proposed the Toast to the Queen. Uncle John followed with a Toast to the *Tunisian* and in doing so emphasized that the Stephens

> had now had over half a century's experience … since his firm had first done business with Messrs Allan. They were then trading to Canada and the East with vessels of some 500 tons. Now they had ships like the *Tunisian*, nearly 11,000 tons … that was a great advance in such a short time … Neither Mr Dunlop nor himself could claim the credit of the *Tunisian*. It belonged to the younger generation, both of shipowners and shipbuilders.[3]

Henry, replying for the Allan Line, showed in a witty speech that his heart was always ruled by his banker's head. He admitted that he had spent a good deal of time grumbling about the cost and probable delays of the vessel they were celebrating that day:

> About five weeks ago they [*The Allan Company*] had to tell Messrs Stephen that it was of the greatest importance that the steamer should be ready to sail on 5 April. Their own expert advisers told them the thing was impossible, but Messrs Stephen had done it … and on that day the *Tunisian* would sail for Canada with 1400 passengers, and so would be able to keep all its dates through the summer.[4] [*The Scotsman*, 2 April 1900 p. 10]

Claud had not been at the launch, because in April 1899 he had returned to Liverpool aboard the Allan ship *California* after visiting his Canadian relatives. Claud's role in the affairs of the shipping line at this time was less defined than that of his elder brothers and his cousins. He was, nevertheless, a man seeking adventure, and when the disagreement between the British and the Afrikaners (the Dutch-speaking Boers) erupted into a full blown conflict, Claud enlisted as a private in 47 Company (Duke of Cambridge's Own) 13 Battalion Imperial Yeomanry.

The history of the Imperial Yeomanry [IY] puts into sharp focus the continuing problem (being) faced by British Governments in funding and fighting wars. The original idea for the formation of the IY was the brainchild of George Wyndham, Conservative MP and, at the time of the Boer War, under-secretary at the War Office, in Lord Salisbury's Government. As Wyndham explained, he could provide the IY with arms, ammunition and tents, but nothing more. Everything else would have to be paid for by the recruits.

It was therefore not surprising that the original recruits to the Duke of Cambridge's Own were, like Claud himself, wealthy, eager young men, experienced horsemen, and good marksmen who had learned the art of shooting on the country estates and moors they frequented each summer and autumn. After an initial training period of three months, Claud and his compatriots set sail for South Africa, full no-doubt with optimism that after a few minor encounters with the Boers they would soon be sailing home.

Claud could not have arrived in South Africa much before the end of August and the beginning of September. His first introduction to the fighting must have been at when they fought the Boers at Mafeking: it was a disaster. Two hundred and seventeen days later, on 16 May 1900, the bloody siege of Mafeking was finally over. Claud, a prisoner of war, was released at Lindley on 12 May 1900. He had been injured during his short time as a soldier in the IY.

His months of war service were rewarded with the Queen's South Africa Medal with three clasps: Cape Colony, Orange Free State and Transvaal. The history of the Boer war has been written about many times, but it is worth mentioning that the treatment of prisoners by both sides was brutal and led to the condemnation of the British for their use of "concentration camps", a phrase that was to haunt the nations of the world forever.

The last of Capt Sandy's five sons, Andrew, died at his home in Montreal on 27 June 1901. He was in his seventy-ninth year. His obituary in the *Montreal Daily Star,* though full of detail about Andrew's childhood in Ayrshire and his arrival in Montreal and the development of the Allan Line with his brothers, was regrettably short on detail about the character of the man. It must be said that he was a less forceful person than Sir Hugh;

indeed, he was much closer in character to James and Alexander. He always carried out his duties quietly and with dignity, never actively seeking the limelight. Yet as his obituary remarked

> he carved for himself an honoured place in Canadian business history, and one which will be remembered for all time. The determined Scotch boy who came out as a passenger in the sailing ship *Canada* [*the first of the Allan full-rigged ships*] in 1838 had before him a career filled with responsibilities and vicissitudes which only such a sturdy nature as his could combat successfully.[5]

As if to prove just how far the determined young Scottish boy had travelled in his years in Canada, the obituary ended with a reminder of that long journey:

> The members of the Royal Family have on more than one occasion shown their confidence in the Allan steamships by crossing the ocean in them. The present Duke of Argyll, the Marquis of Lorne with the Princess Louise came out to Canada on the *Sarmatian* at the beginning of his term as Governor-General and also returned to England on the same vessel. The Duke of Connaught crossed in the *Sarmatian*, as did Lord Dufferin, Lord Landsdowne, and the Earl of Derby and the Earl of Aberdeen.[6]

The obituary could have also said that the Duke of Connaught had stayed with Sir Hugh as early as 1869.

The death of Andrew brought about a change in the management of the Allan Line. Since Sir Hugh's death he had been chairman of the shipping line, so his death left the Allan Line of Companies with a dilemma: who should be the overall chairman? For a couple of years, Montagu continued to run the Canadian side of the business, but his other interests included banking, financial services and industrial directorships, and of course his private interests: yachting, horse-racing and ice hockey.

Sir Hugh's two remaining sons, Alexander Rae and Bryce James of Boston, who were now well into middle age, had taken the decision to retire when they inherited under the terms of their father's Will in 1893, after the death of Arthur. Alexander had married Eva Belford Travers in 1874 and by 1901 they were living in Brockville, Ontario, where he gave his occupation as retired. They had one son, Hugh Travers born in 1875. Alexander Rae died just two days after his Uncle Andrew, just fifty-six years old.

Andrew's five sons seemed to have fared a little better; Andrew Alexander, the third of his sons, had worked for his father and uncle since he was 17, and was by 1901 a vice-president; his elder brother, Hugh Andrew, also worked for the company.

William Rae, Andrew's youngest son, was different: he had carved a career for himself that did not include ship management. Like his brothers, he had been educated in England at the legendary public school, Rugby, where Rev Dr Thomas Arnold had been a towering force in the education of boys between 1828–1842. William Rae returned to Canada and worked briefly with his Uncle Bryce James in the Boston Office until 1882. In 1883, he left Boston for Winnipeg, working for a time in mercantile matters until 1893. In 1904 he took over an insurance company, and formed a joint stock company under the name of Allan, Lang & Killam. Later the company changed its name to Allan, Killam & McKay. The name of Killam is interesting in that in 1909 William Rae married Minnie Whyte, widow of Albert Clements Killam, lawyer, High Court Judge, Member of Parliament, and also (perhaps particularly interesting from an Allan point of view, with their interest in the Canadian Pacific Railway) Chief Commissioner of the Board of Railways Commission.

William Rae also held a number of other directorships, including President of the Board of Fire Underwriters. Rather like his cousin Montagu, he was a great sportsman with a particular love of horses, and was President of the Winnipeg Jockey Club. In a country as vast as Canada the relationships and friendships between the country's elite were a constant source of strength for them.

James Bryce, Andrew's fourth son, had also been educated at Rugby School, and then at Oriel College Oxford and Laval University Montreal, before being admitted to the Bar of Quebec in 1889. He ran his own practice for five years, then joined Campbell, Meredith, Allan and Hague – again indicating family connections, for a Campbell and a Meredith married into the Allan family. The chambers of James Bryce KC were regarded as one of the most influential of all legal firms by the residents of the Golden Square Mile – and at the beginning of the 1900s, according to some sources, these residents held over 70% of all Canadian wealth.

However, wealth, privilege and social status are no respecters of tragedy. Even when that tragedy is not directly related to a family member but to one of their friends it affects all concerned. Just two weeks before his father's death at the end of June, James Bryce must have been horrified to hear of what had happened to one of his own articled pupils, Jocelyn Clifford Redpath, a son of the wealthy Redpath sugar-refining family which was also resident within the Golden Square Mile. He had had a privileged childhood, and was working for his bar exams. However, late in the afternoon of Thursday 13 June 1901, Jocelyn Redpath and his mother, Ada Maria, both died of gunshot wounds in his mother's bedroom. Three shots had been fired from two revolvers, but there was no indication of any intruder. There appears to have been no police inquiry: two inquests were hastily convened the following day, Friday 14 June, one after the other, and brought in verdicts that Jocelyn had killed his mother, then himself, during a period of temporary insanity brought on by an attack of epilepsy. The two victims were buried the day after the inquests and, according to reports, never mentioned again by the Redpaths. The double tragedy was forever to remain a mystery, but out of earshot of the Redpath family it must have been a matter of gossip in the drawing-rooms and salons of the Golden Square Mile, as their neighbours speculated about the events of that terrible afternoon.

Andrew's eldest son, John Smith Allan, was perhaps the miscreant of the family. He was born in 1856, and like his brothers educated for a period at Rugby School. It is also more than probable that after returning to Canada he began to work for the family firm. In June 1879, he married a Canadian girl of Irish descent, Adelaide Stuart Gault, the daughter of Mathew Hamilton Gault, an Insurance Agent, another resident of the Golden Square Mile. As his brother William Rae left Boston for Winnipeg about that time, it is possible that JohnS took his place at the Boston office. Six of his and Adelaide's children, five girls and one son, Andrew Hamilton, were born in Boston.

By the spring of 1891 the family were back in Montreal, but there is evidence that the marriage was in some disarray. In March of that year JohnS and his cousin Montagu travelled from New York to Liverpool, both giving their occupation as shipowners. Adelaide was in England in 1893 when she gave birth to a daughter, Thelma. She was, however, back in Canada later that year.

Some time around now JohnS's marriage to Adelaide finally ended. An intriguing report in the *Manitoba Morning Free Press* of September 1895 announced that JohnS had deserted his wife for a Mrs Hebden in May 1892. The article listed JohnS business interests as banking (including a Loan and Mortgage Company), the Canadian Rubber Company, and the Canada Paper Company – nowhere in the report is shipping mentioned.

The report, however, does emphasize that Adelaide was filing papers with the Canadian Courts, suing her errant husband for alimony of sixty thousand Canadian Dollars a month.

In the 1901 census, Adelaide and her children are together in Montreal – no JohnS – and she describes herself as head of the house. Ten years later she is a widow.

There has often been confusion between Andrew's son, John Smith, and Sir Hugh's son of the same name. Sir Hugh's son was born in 1853 but died the following year.

It is difficult, when the two founding fathers had so many sons, to know exactly who should have inherited the management of the great Allan Line. The matter of succession was made even harder, because since 1897 it had ceased to be a wholly owned family company and had become a limited company, registered in England. It would be a number of years before the reorganization of the company was finally resolved. In the meantime, Nathaniel Dunlop was appointed chairman.

In Scotland Alexander's sons, RobertS, JamesA, Henry and Claud would all continue to describe themselves as shipowners, and apart from their inherited wealth that would be their main source of income. CharlesE however was in Belfast by 1901, working for Workman, Clark & Company as a Marine Engineer; since 1891 he had been their Technical Director, and had worked on many of their finest ships, including the *Victorian,* the first turbine liner to cross the Atlantic.

It is not difficult to contrast the lives of Alexander and Jane's five sons with those of the five sons of Capt Sandy and Jean two generations earlier. Jean is highly unlikely to have had more than one servant in Saltcoats, and certainly not a nursemaid, governess or coachman; by contrast, in 1901 RobertS had seven servants, and CharlesE had eleven female servants of whom the youngest was fifteen and the oldest forty-nine. Not one of Charles's servants was Roman Catholic. JamesA had ten servants living in at Westerton House, Strathblane, including a butler and a coachman, though these had their own lodgings in the grounds.

A feature of the 1901 Census for Ireland was that CharlesE was resident in the townland of Ballymiscaw in County Down on Census night. In 1895 he had taken out a tenancy on Stormont Castle, a baronial mansion in Ballymiscaw on the outskirts of East Belfast. The Castle had been owned by the Cleland family since 1858, when they had employed Thomas Turner to convert the original plain Georgian house into a baronial mansion. The Cleland family had left the Castle in 1893, and CharlesE then obtained a long tenancy agreement.

The 1901 Census is important for another reason: Henry R Brown, CharlesE's father-in-law, was on a visit from America as he and CharlesE had become friends since his marriage to Jessie, in spite of the problems she had encountered in Scotland. In the Census both CharlesE and Jessie give their religion as Presbyterian, although it has always been believed that Jessie was a member of the Church of Christ Scientist, from the beginning of her marriage, and that it was she who converted CharlesE. The membership list, held by the Church Archives in Boston, does not contain the names of either CharlesE or his wife. It is also possible that at the time of the 1901 Census, the Enumerator in Belfast was unwilling or unable to register membership of the Church of Christ Scientist as a recognized religion.

An accurate measure of the place the Allan family occupied in the world can be seen when the observer looks at the Census for Hafton. Henry was resident at the time but not the owner. The estate comprised the main house ["the Castle"], a factor's, gardener's, gamekeeper's, butler's and forester's houses. The estate was supporting in excess of twenty-five men, women and children. That the Allans were good and caring employers is illustrated in that Charles White and the cook Mary Macrae still remained with the family years after the deaths of Alexander and Jane.

In the Census of 1901, Claud was back in Scotland living at Ballochmyle, Mauchline. He married in June Adeline (Ada) Mitchell, daughter of James Lockhart Mitchell, a timber merchant, and Marion Nesbit Miller. There would be four children of the marriage, Marion Mitchell born in 1902,

Sheena Margaret born in 1906, Charles Claud born in 1908 and Robert Alexander born in 1914.

Claud and his family had witnessed many changes in the two years since the beginning of the new century and not all of them for the good. Early in 1901 Queen Victoria died, after sixty-four years on the throne. Campbell-Bannerman denounced the use of concentration camps, and the Boer War escalated further with the Boer offensive against the Cape Colony. It would be another year before a peace treaty between the Boers and the British would be signed.

In spite of the war, Glasgow in 1901 had cause for celebration: the Glasgow International Exhibition opened in June. Needless to say, one of the major exhibits was devoted to shipping; as any visitor would have said:

> No exhibition in Glasgow with any pretensions to completeness could afford to dispense with an extensive section devoted to ships and shipping interests.[7]

It is inconceivable that the Allan grandchildren and great-grandchildren were not among the many thousands who thronged into Glasgow that summer to see the great exhibition and look with pride at the beautiful models of the ships that had served the Allan Line over so many decades. George L Watson had made models of his elegant and stunning yachts, which the Allan family had raced with such success over the years.

Chapter 13

Janie & Politics

In May 1902 Janie was one of the first members of the Glasgow and West of Scotland Association for Women's Suffrage. By 1902 she had already publicly announced that she was a socialist, and a year later she was one of the vice-presidents of the Association, and very active on their various committees. Janie was ahead of her time – or rather the women's movement in Scotland was under way before it began to be taken seriously in England. Janie was quick to ally her movement with Mrs Emmeline Pankhurst, and throughout the turbulent years of the Suffragette Movement she supported her. Janie used her considerable wealth to good effect.

The poor continued for some time to be the "forgotten people", but not by members of the Allan family: Janie's mother's trust funds had done much to help the deprived women and girls of Glasgow. The Scottish Labour Colony Association Ltd was set up in the late 1890s by a group of prominent businessmen with Sir John Stirling Maxwell at its head. The main objects of the Association were

> to organize and administer a labour colony, where food and shelter will be given to able-bodied men out of employment in exchange for work, and to agitate for reformatory legislation with respect to vagrancy.[1]

It was inevitable that Janie would be among the first to donate money; during the first few years of the Association, she gave them regular sums of money, each sum considerably more than a labourer's wage for the year. The aim of the Colony was to lease a farm, where the out-of-work men could be housed in return for working on the farm. The farm chosen was Mid-Lochardwoods, about eight miles from Dumfries and four from Ruthwell. Robert Burns stayed near Ruthwell when he was gravely ill, he believed the waters from the Red Well would cure him, rich as they were in iron salts. The farm at Mid-Lochardwoods:

consists of about 150 acres of arable land of good quality, about 40 acres of reclaimed moss and about 300 acres of unreclaimed moss. In the opinion of ... well-known agricultural authorities ... it is exceptionally well suited for the purposes of a farm colony. The buildings are ample, commodious, and substantially built, and have accommodation for a large number of men. They are well situated, protected by trees, and there is an extensive orchard and garden.[2]

It is the next sentence which sums up the attitude of the Association's executive:

The position is a particularly secluded one, there being no villages or public-houses readily accessible; both of which are important considerations in the management of such a colony.[3]

The Temperance and Presbyterian ethos would preclude any suggestion of drunkenness or promiscuity. Only by hard labour, clean air and good food, would the vagrants turn round their lives. In truth, it did have the hoped-for effect on the men. The farm supported them, fed them and gave them a regular income. In the second year of the scheme forty-five men worked at the colony, where their average stay was only two months before they felt able to return to their home towns and seek work. A condition required by the Colony's Trustees was that the men at the least accept that the aim of the stay at Mid-Lochardwoods was rehabilitation.

Janie, Eliza and her husband TEL, CharlesE, JamesA, Nathaniel Dunlop and his daughter Ellen, who all supported the Colony, must have been delighted to read the comments of the Chief Constable, when he wrote:

A month ago I visited the Labour Colony ... along with a committee of the Town Council, and have pleasure in stating that I was very much impressed with all I saw. The situation of the house, so far away from any town or licensed-premises, is really excellent and the field of labour so varied that altogether I consider the farm well adapted for an institution of this kind. Splendid work is best carried on, and in my opinion the institution is well deserving of the support of the public.[4]

If the new charitable labour colony was doing well, Richard H Hunter was able to announce that a charity he and Alexander of Glasgow had founded, the Sailors' Orphan Society of Scotland, was also doing excellent work thanks to the money raised from many generous benefactors. In November 1900 he admitted:

With the advent of the darker and stormier days the claims upon the society are usually heavier than during the summer. This month we have admitted 24 children out of families where there were 38 children. So many of the cases were specially sad, and all of them in urgent need of help. Only those who come into personal touch with these families know what a blessing the assistance we can give is.[5]

The sea is indeed a cruel master and one that should be treated at all times with respect and due diligence. It is somewhat ironic that in 1903 the Naval Act set up the Royal Naval Volunteer Reserve [RNVR]. On the one hand the Government left the old, the dispossessed, the unemployed, and sailor's orphans to seek charitable assistance; on the other hand it wanted to build up a reserve fighting force for free.

The Admiralty hierarchy did not in fact approve of the idea of a Volunteer Reserve force, but Claud was among the first to welcome the whole venture with enthusiasm. The new Service was formed into Divisions, and the first to be set up in Scotland was the Clyde Division. Again the generosity of the local people and civic organizations was immediate; the Glasgow Corporation and, more important, the Clyde Trust were of the greatest help. The Clyde Trust loaned the Division a new building (which had cost them more than £30,000) for training purposes, until they could raise the funds to build their own head-quarters. In a critique aimed at the demise of the old Royal Naval Artillery Reserve, the Marquis of Graham, a leading member of the Scottish Division, stated bluntly that it would be impossible for the RNVR to continue to subsidize the volunteers as they had in the old days. He cited a Commanding Officer of the old Brigade who had paid out of his own funds more than £300 [closer to £30,000 today] to meet the costs of his unit.

The volunteers had to meet exacting criteria of physical fitness, intelligence and a desire for sea service. Less emphasis was placed on sea experience, but they were expected to have experience as engineers, telegraphists, armourers and shipwrights. They were also expected to pay for their own uniforms and all travelling expenses incurred in attending drills. In a typical demarcation between the Volunteers and the Regular

Navy, the uniforms although similar, had subtle differences. Volunteer Officers wore gold braid, but instead of the straight half inch braid of the regular navy, theirs was a quarter of an inch and waved – hence the term "The Wavy Navy". It was an emblem that came to symbolize the respect they earned, and well deserved.

It was said at the time that few yachtsmen joined the RNVR. (It was generally thought, at least by the Press, that yachtsmen were too busy sailing at the weekends to give up their time to the new volunteer force.) However, even if this generalization were true the Allan family stood out against it: Claud and James Bryce of Wemyss Bay would both play a very important part in the Service at the outbreak of the Great War.

Against all expectations, by the end of 1903 the Glasgow and the Clyde Divisions numbered almost seven hundred men.

Fires in Glasgow and the West of Scotland were almost a daily occurrence. In February 1903 three major fires occurred within a twenty-four hour period; a factory fire, the mansion house of a prominent Member of Parliament, Sir Charles Cayzer, and the third concerned the Allan Line. The yard belonging to William Stevens at Old Govan Road caught fire, and this spread to nearby properties of the Allan Line.

> the store, which was stocked with highly inflammable goods, was transformed into a huge fiery furnace. With alarming rapidity the flames spread northward across a narrow thoroughfare to the Allan Line sheds between the store and the river, and in a short space of time an area of about a hundred yards square was burning with great fierceness ... The yard lies on an incline towards the river, and the burning oil coursing down the slope soon carried the flames across the narrow thoroughfare separating the yard from the old State Line goods sheds on Mavisbank Quay, taken over by the Allan Line when the State Line some years ago was merged in the larger company.[6]

Although the sheds were owned by the Allan Line, they were, at the time of the fire, occupied by the Clyde Shipping Company. The estimated cost of the damage ran to more than £50,000.

In early 1903, the Allan Line were interested in buying new and faster steamers. (The Canadian Mail contract would have to be tendered for during the year, so it was necessary to convince the Canadian Government that they had the ships of the necessary quality.) In January they looked at two steamers in Dundee, *Crown Point* and Orient *Point,* but after an inspection they decided not to buy. Instead, in October, they signed a contract for two new ships:

> The first Atlantic turbine liner has been ordered by a Clyde Shipping firm, and is to be built at Belfast. For several years, Messrs Allan of the Allan Line have been considering the possibility of adopting the turbine for ocean-going boats ... Messrs Allan have placed a contract with Messrs Workman & Clark, for the liner, in which turbines of the Parson type will take the place of the customary reciprocating engines. The new vessel is intended for the Liverpool–Canadian mail service ... she will be the largest of the Allan Fleet, and also the fastest.[7]

It was originally decided that both ships would be built by Workman & Clark, but when it became obvious that there would be an unacceptable delay in completing both in the time-scale demanded by the Allan Line, CharlesE interceded and the contract for the second ship was transferred to Alexander Stephen & Sons yard at Linthouse, Glasgow. The decision was made easier since Stephen's had built other ships for the company, and CharlesE and his siblings had grown up as neighbours and friends of the Stephen children.

Before the new contracts were signed, an erroneous report in the Press announced the Allan Line had been awarded the Canadian mail contract. A retraction was hastily made, pointing out that the tender date did not close until June. The Allan Line advertising continued unabated, with usually two or three announcements a week giving details of ships and their sailing dates. Another important change in the adverts was that the company name now included the words: "Royal Mail Steamers and State Line."

A link with the past was broken in 1903 when Andrew Jack died at his home at St Andrew's Terrace, Kilmarnock, he was seventy-nine. As the grandson of James Allan and Jean Brown, he had for many years acted as the keeper of the family history. His letters to the Press frequently corrected the inaccuracies of other writers who did not know or care about the truth of the Allan family. Andrew Jack took enormous pride in the achievements of his ancestors, and if his grandmother, whom he had never known, could have seen the success that he had made of his life she would have been rightly proud.

Andrew had married Elizabeth Wallace and they had a son, Hugh Andrew, and two daughters, Elizabeth and Margaret [Maggie]. He had been a provision merchant in Kilmarnock; in 1873 he had been appointed the first school board officer, a post he held until 1890. But he was not content with retirement and was delighted when he was appointed caretaker and librarian at Bellfield House, a position he held for the next ten years. Bellfield House had been given to the people of Kilmarnock by the daughter of the late Robert Buchanan, a successful Glasgow merchant.

It was in his personal life, though, that Andrew Jack held fast to the beliefs of his Allan ancestors. A lifelong abstainer, he had held a Temperance card since 1840. In this connection he was a most assiduous worker, and he won for himself the admiration and gratitude for all interested in the movement. For a considerable time he was the indefatigable Secretary of the Ayrshire Temperance Movement ... he was one of the Vice-Presidents of the Scottish Permissive Bill Association. The Permissive Bill was a project in the 1860s and 1870s to introduce powerful temperance legislation to control the sale of alcohol.

Andrew Jack's religious beliefs coincided very much with Uncle Alexander; he grew up a member of the United Presbyterian Church, but later saw that his views were more in line with the Evangelical Union, and he became first a member, then an Elder and President, and was for years Superintendent of the Sunday School. He also had time and a love for music; he taught music for many years, and was one of the first certificated teachers in Kilmarnock. He may not have left the great personal wealth of his five uncles, but there is no doubt that he did leave the town of Kilmarnock, which had been his home for nearly eight decades, "A Better Place".

The year 1903 ended with a particularly happy event, a pre-Christmas sale at the Allan Line's Edinburgh warehouse. The details were announced in the Press: they stressed that it would be a bigger and better sale than ever before. The new warehouse at 82–86 South Bridge allowed for more space for the sale of Christmas stationery, flowers, plants, jewellery, and fancy needlework, at their usual low prices. An added incentive for the good people of Edinburgh to make their way to South Bridge was that a "tea room with convenient retiring rooms" were available for all shoppers.

Rules and regulations were and are a constant source of annoyance to employers; the Home Office sought to introduce legislation that would go some way to minimising the number of deaths and injuries at wharves, docks and quays. In 1904, after months of negotiations, the Government launched a Commission of Inquiry to look into strengthening dockyard regulations. Not unnaturally the shipowners and companies were loath to take on more regulation. The inquiry took evidence from interested parties in London, Cardiff, Newcastle and Liverpool, before coming to Glasgow in April. Wilson, the KC appointed by local shipping companies, insisted that very few accidents had been caused by defective equipment as had been alleged.

A robust reply to the allegations was made by James Smith Park, a member of the Allan board. He said:

> The Allan Line vessels and their cargoes paid at Glasgow … about £44,000 dues or fully ten percent of the total annual revenue of the Clyde Trust, while they disbursed in wages alone at the port about £140,000. He regarded with apprehension the creation of a system akin to factory inspection of docks, quays and ships in port, which could not fail to affect adversely the shipping trade of his company in its competition with foreigners not similarly hampered.[8]

Park finished his evidence with a chilling warning that if the new rules were introduced then they should also apply to foreign ships or it would lead to bitter repercussions. He insisted that a voluntary scheme between all port operators would produce a far better response in reducing accidents.

In 1904 Park may have believed that voluntary agreements would work: history would prove that he could not have been more wrong.

James Smith Park was a director and shareholder of the Allan Line, and, rather like Nathaniel Dunlop, he had begun his career with Allan's at a young age. He was a man of exceptional ability, a Colonel, and a Justice of the Peace. He was a bachelor, the son of Robert Ballantyne Park and Julia Orr Smith, and although the Smith name is not unusual, the number of times it crops up in relationship to the Allans suggests that one day all the links will join into a long, long chain.

The summer of 1904 saw the families involved in the usual round of yachting, shooting, fishing and garden parties. RichardG had success with his yacht *Mavis,* and a glance at the Clyde Week results showed that he was not alone in enjoying success on the water. However, while the Season was occupying the younger members, there were problems to be tackled in the shipping offices.

In May there was the start of what became known as the Atlantic Shipping War. The Red Star Line of Philadelphia and Antwerp had begun to offer cheap fares to any immigrant wishing to leave Europe for the Americas. The Allan and Anchor Lines were reluctant to enter into any kind of price war:

> So far, the companies are viewing a possible war between the lines and a reduction of rates for third-class passengers with equanimity.[9]

Meetings were held between the various shipping lines and their agents, and in mid-June they issued the following briefing:

> the managers of the Dominion, Allan and Canadian Steam-ship lines yesterday held a meeting, at which they decided to postpone the operation of their revised rates from Liverpool to Canadian ports.[10]

The companies still believed a settlement could be reached. It was finally resolved in November, when James Bruce Ismay, chairman of the White Star Line and International Mercantile Marine Company, announced

> that an agreement had been ratified, and it only remained for the Atlantic and Canadian shipowners to accept the terms offered. By the agreement

the normal westward steerage fares would be reintroduced and the dispute would be amicably settled. The terms were agreed to unanimously, and the representatives of the other lines expressed themselves satisfied with the whole arrangement.[11]

It is tempting to say, well they would, wouldn't they, when they got exactly what they had asked for eleven months earlier.

If the members of the Allan family had little control over the antics of other shipping lines, it is regrettably also true that they were not responsible for the conduct of their own staff when ashore. Fortunately it was seldom that members of their very large staff caused them any degree of embarrassment. However, even in the best-regulated families things can go wrong. The sudden death of Isabella McKenzie, a stewardess with the Allan Line, in a temperance hotel in Liverpool in late September 1904, gave rise to much press speculation. The Inquest into her death revealed the whole sad saga, and implicated a steward of the Allan Line.

> It will be remembered that a man named Allan Muir was found in an unconscious condition at the time the woman was discovered. The evidence showed that the deceased was a married woman, living apart from her husband, and that she had lately been engaged as a stewardess on one of the Allan Line steamers.[12]

Letters found in the hotel room suggested that Isabella's death was the result of a suicide pact with Allan Muir. She had taken a large dose of opium, as had Allan Muir, but he survived. One of the letters was addressed to McMaster, a chief steward in Glasgow, accusing him of ruining two lives and bringing disgrace on their children. Reading between the lines, it would seem that McMaster knew of the relationship between the two Allan employees and showed his objections in a formal manner. Muir had not expected to survive the suicide pact for he wrote that: *"My dear and I are going to a better place."*

Allan Muir may have thought he was innocent, but the Inquest Jury disagreed, and found that Isabella had been murdered by him. He stood trial and was found guilty of her murder. In December, the Home Secretary, granted him a reprieve.

It has been difficult to positively identify McMaster, but there was a John McMaster, born in Glasgow in 1871, who in 1891, was a steward on the Allan ship *Nestorian* and might well have been promoted to Chief Steward by 1904. Whoever he was, Chief Steward McMaster might well have threatened to expose the two crew members, or dismiss them; and it is also possible, in view of the despairing resolution of the unhappy couple, that McMaster had made it clear that he had designs on Isabella himself.

There was reason to celebrate towards the end of 1904.

On Saturday 3 December there was an Inspection of the six Glasgow Companies of the RNVR. The Inspection was held in the Drill Hall in Govan, with over 680 volunteers present. The Marquis of Graham was accompanied by Commander-Instructor Heugh DSO RN. Lieutenants Claud Allan and Robert Clark, shipowner with Clark & Service, were the main party in command.

Admiral Rice, with two of his staff, arrived a little before 4.00pm. They were given the customary "general salute". After the Inspection, Rice gave a short address in which he said:

> It was simply extraordinary that, in the comparatively short time the corps had been in existence, the men should have attained the state of efficiency he had seen that day. He would have great pleasure in reporting to the Admiralty the state of the corps both as to efficiency and zeal in drill.[13]

How sad that within a decade the RNVR's efficiency and zeal for drills would be put to a real test in the defence of their country. Then, as now, the young volunteers would not be found wanting. They would go to war with pride and courage.

Chapter 14

Goodbye Old Friends

Christmas Eve 1904 saw the sudden death of Phoebe Houstoun-Boswell, at her home in Edrom, Blackadder. She was fifty-three years old; she had been ill for a week. After her marriage to Sir George she had moved from Ravenscrag to Berwickshire, and it had not taken her long to become more than "the lady of the manor". As her obituary acknowledged:

> the bright, amenable, and kindly nature of the deceased lady won her the love and esteem of all with whom she came into contact. She was ever ready to co-operate with her husband ... in works of public usefulness, and in this way made the acquaintance and gained the respect of a wife circle of Border people, who will now sincerely mourn her death.[1]

Phoebe left two sons and a daughter. Her elder son, Sir George's heir, was an officer in the Grenadier Guards.

Phoebe's death was in marked contrast to that of old Claud MacFie who had died in May 1903. There was no obituary, and very little mention of his passing. He was eight-one years old; he had been married to Mary Young for a little under twelve years. His son Claud William was ten and his daughter, Catherine was six, too young to lose the influence of a father. The informant of his death was his great-nephew J Martin Newton. There did not appear to be a living male relative available to undertake that task. His executors included Andrew Laurie MacFie, Claud's nephew, three Writers to the Signet, and the printer and publisher, Walter Biggar Blaikie. It seemed a sad end for a man who had entertained so lavishly at Gogar Burn House when he and Margaret Allan lived there.

Justice has a reputation of being slow to come to a final conclusion, but four years was still a long time for a man to have to wait to see his reputation and career restored. In 1901, the Allan liner *Grecian* had run aground at the entrance to Halifax Harbour, and had been totally lost. A subsequent Canadian Court of Inquiry had found that the ship's master, Captain Harrison, was responsible for the negligence of the pilot, and his Master's certificate was accordingly suspended. The Scottish Shipmasters' and Officers' Association immediately launched an appeal on Harrison's behalf. The Admiralty in London overturned the Canadian verdict, but were unable to proceed in granting a reimbursement of Harrison's costs. Pressure must have been brought to bear in Canada, Glasgow and London, because finally the Canadian Government changed their minds, and awarded Captain Harrison full recompense for his legal costs. It would have been out of character for members of the Allan family, in Glasgow and Montreal, not to have been involved in seeing that justice was finally done for their innocent captain.

On the first of April 1905 the Allan family had a special reason to celebrate: the *Victorian*, the first turbine triple screw liner to cross the Atlantic, arrived at Halifax, Nova Scotia safe and sound. The voyage had not been without incident; she had encountered fog and ice floes, which had necessitated a change of route and a longer journey. The vagaries of the weather did not detract from the pleasure the *Victorian's* Captain MacNicoll took in the way the new ship had performed on her maiden voyage:

> Never in my life ... have I commanded a better sea boat, and one which responded to orders so readily. Of course, we want more experience before we can decide various technical matters, but, so far as we have gone, I am delighted.[2]

When she arrived at Halifax she was greeted by thousands of cheering Canadians, salvos of gun salutes, and the ringing of bells. Sir Montagu, Hugh and Andrew from Montreal, and Bryce James of Boston were among the official welcoming party. Looking at the passenger lists for the next few years, *Victorian* and her sister ship the *Virginian* were to become favourites with many members of the Allan family as they criss-crossed the Atlantic Ocean.

> The *Virginian* has had her first sea trials on the Clyde. She had over 500 hundred guests on board for her first sea trial, and later made her way to Liverpool, which would be her home port. The *Virginian* then made her maiden trip to Halifax, leaving Liverpool on 9 April and arriving on the 15, having taken six days, fourteen hours and thirty-four minutes to make the trip.
>
> This run creates a fresh record for the Allan Line. The turbines worked well. The ship's speed averaged 15.7 knots. Owing, however, to fog and bad weather, the mean speed was reduced to 15.1 knots net. This is nearly two knots faster than the speed attained by the *Victorian*.
>
> The *Virginian* received a wireless telegraph from the *Victorian* on Wednesday night announcing that icebergs had been sighted.[3]

The captain, on docking at Halifax, reported that he had never before seen so many icebergs that far south at that time of year. A couple of days after the original announcement of the voyage, the time taken by the *Virginian* was given as six days one hour – Moville to Rimonski, "*the fastest passage to Canada via Cape Race on record*". The Allan Line had every reason to be proud of their new vessels. It had been less than a century since Capt Sandy had first sailed his little brigantine *Hero* to the Iberian Peninsula in order to supply Wellington's army.

As with all moments of triumph, there were also moments to stop and reflect on the death of another family member. Only a few weeks after the *Victorian's* safe arrival, John Allan, the grandson of James and Jean of Old Rome, died in Newmilns, Ayrshire, on 20 April 1905. He was ninety-years old. His obituary paints a fascinating picture of his early years, which were very different from the children and grandchildren of the Allan Line family members. After just two years' education, in which he learned to read well and became a good arithmetician, Old John had been put to work as a handloom weaver, his father's trade.

> It is scarcely possible for one life to have spanned a more interesting and progressive period. The first great event within his recollection in the

political world was the passing of the Reform Bill in 1832, at which time he, a lad of 18, walked to Kilmarnock and took part in the procession to celebrate the passing of the measure.[4]

The Chartist Movement also gained John's support; he would often be called upon to read the Chartist pamphlets and newspapers to those of his fellow workers who could not read. A member of the United Presbyterian Church since 1835, he was, when he died, their oldest member.

Old John took after his mother in many respects; he held deep political beliefs, but he tempered them with a broad-minded tolerance.

> In the world of books also he was at home, especially amongst the Puritan Fathers; and few could quote with such felicity and fine expression the poetic gems of Burns.
>
> Very sensibly during recent years he did grow in meekness for the Heavenly Kingdom, and now, after a long and mellowing eventide, made quietly happy by the attendance of devoted friends, he has gone to his grave ... like the typical old man of Scripture, "in a full age, like as a shock of corn cometh in his season".[5] [Job 5:26]

Since the death of his wife, Elizabeth Ross, in May 1879 John had been cared for by his daughter Janet. The relationship between father and daughter was obviously close and they were together until 1886, when Janet, at the age of thirty-nine, married Andrew Miller, a woollen manufacturer and draper twelve years her senior. His first wife had died three years earlier, leaving seven children, three sons and four daughters. Janet, with her father, moved to her husband's home, Purroch Cottage, Hurlford. Three years after her marriage Janet became a widow. She continued to look after five of Andrew's children until they reached their maturity and left home. Alone again, Janet and Old John returned to Mansfield, Galston.

The autumn of 1905 brought an almost unprecedented spell of bad weather to the North Atlantic, a reminder of the dangers and constant threats posed by the weather to the ships, their crews and their passengers.

> It is stated that in the history of Lloyd's there has never been such a large number of vessels on the over-due market as at the present time. The storms and cyclones which have prevailed in the remote parts of the world

are (says the Central News) responsible in many cases for the unusual delays in arrival. The list comprises no fewer than nineteen ships, and several are a month or six weeks overdue.[6]

The Allans needed no reminder. They knew only too well that disasters could and did occur. Three and a half years earlier their ship the *Huronian* had left Glasgow on 11 February 1902; she had been chartered by the Agricultural Department to load hay at St John's for the Cape. Before leaving Glasgow, she had taken on a general cargo and 1,293 tons of water ballast in her tanks. She had a crew of fifty-six and one passenger. The *Huronian* was a relatively new ship, having only completed eight previous voyages; before leaving Glasgow on her last voyage she had been in dry-dock for an overhaul. A slight problem with a twist in her rudder had been repaired, and her captain regarded her as a very satisfactory sea boat.

At first the Allan Line were not particularly worried by her late arrival at St John's; they issued a statement to the press saying that she may have been delayed by bad weather or mechanical problems. February and March passed without further news of the vessel, although it is certain that the Company instructed the rest of their fleet to keep a close watch for *Huronian*. Early in April, the Allan Line made an application to the Government to send a cruiser to search the North Atlantic for the missing ship and her crew.

In September, a Board of Trade Inquiry in Glasgow finally announced that there had been no trace of the ship, her crew or her one passenger. The mystery was never solved; the Allan Line asked the Board of Trade to approve the payment of insurance for the lost ship. The *Huronian* was the only ship of the Allan fleet that was lost without trace. The sea kept her dark secret, until 1907 when a *"tragic message in a bottle"* came ashore near Castle Rock, County Derry, in 1907, The bottle contained a scribbled note by a member of the crew, Charles MacFall, a fireman on the ship. The message read, "*Huronian* sinking fast; top heavy; one side under water. Goodbye, mother and sister".[7] Unfortunately, MacFall had no time or no inclination to give latitude and longitude of the sinking ship and her resting place still remains a mystery. In 1999 a great nephew of Charles MacFall's was still seeking answers to how and why the *Huronian* sank without trace.

CharlesE always had a close relationship and indeed friendship with his father-in-law Henry Rolf Brown, his sister-in-law Anne Lincoln and his brother-in-law Dr Henry Rolf Brown. In checking the passengers lists it can be established that they all made more than one visit to Stormont to see CharlesE and Jessie. It would be simple to dismiss this close relationship as just an example of a kind and loving family. However, that may be, in the light of what happened between 1905/1906, such an explanation appears too simplistic, as more obvious reasons became apparent.

There can be little doubt that by November 1905, when Henry Brown and Anne Lincoln arrived at Stormont, Jessie was very unwell. It had also become apparent, that while Jessie may not have been listed as a member of the Church of Christ Scientist, she was a strong believer in the doctrines of Christian Science.

The Church of Christ Scientist was founded by Mary Baker Eddy, whose doctrines combined Christianity with the theories of Phineas Parkhurst Quimby, a medical mesmerist. The church's fundamental teachings were that faith healing could and did work, that sin and disease could be healed by Faith and Prayer, and until recently the church taught that medical and surgical intervention only hindered recovery. For CharlesE and Jessie's family it must have been torment to watch her become ever more frail. The intervention of her brother Henry, a notable cancer specialist, failed to change Jessie's mind.

In June 1906 CharlesE and Jessie, together with Henry senior and Annie, returned to Boston, where she died on 9 July at the Hotel Vendome. Perhaps Jessie had finally agreed to accept conventional medical treatment, or perhaps she wanted spiritual support from the First Church of Christ Scientist, which is situated in Boston's Back Bay neighbourhood, less than a mile from the hotel where she died. Her death certificate simply states that she died of a Carcinoma Uteri [Cancer of the Womb].

CharlesE returned to Scotland, bringing with him Jessie's body. She was buried in Glasgow's "City of the Dead", the Southern Necropolis, in the lair of her in-laws Alexander and Jane. It seemed a fitting tribute to a woman who had suffered so much in her young life, but who found love and contentment in her marriage to CharlesE.

It is a measure of how far the Allan families had travelled, not just across oceans, but across the social divide. James's grandson from his carpenter's cottage to the magnificent Ravenscrag, gives us one measure. Another measure is that in February 1906, Bryce James and his wife Annie Palfrey were invited to a wedding at the White House in Washington. Alice Lee Roosevelt, the President's daughter, was marrying Nicolas Longworth. Bryce James and Anna were among 800 invited guests, and there is a bleak reference in the newspaper on 17 February that must raise a sly smile:

> There was no great crush at any time within the mansion, the 800 guests present being comfortably placed in the East Room.
> Contrary to the published statement of a week ago, the guests were not confined to certain classes of officials in Washington or to Miss Roosevelt's close friends.[8]

It would have been very odd, even in 1906, if the staff at the White House had not been suitably trained to deal with 800 people at the wedding of the President's daughter.

In Paisley, Scotland, a couple of years earlier, there had been a glittering banquet to honour Stewart Clark, when he was given the Freedom of the Burgh. The guest list included the industrial, political and civic dignitaries of the district. Bryce of Wemyss Bay and his wife Annie, the daughter of Stewart Clark, were among the select guests. Sir Thomas and Lady Glen-Coats together with Stewart and his wife Annie greeted the guests as they arrived.

In his speech of welcome, Sir Thomas gave a short resume of Stewart's work, politics and private activities, including his involvement in yachting; but he was more forthcoming on the work that his wife Annie Smiley had done for the Burgh. And in doing so he again showed that the Clark families shared the very same philanthropic care as did the Allan families, mentioning her connections with

> the Infirmary, the British Women's Temperance Society, the Scottish Girls Friendly Society, the Deaf and Dumb Mission, the Free Breakfast Mission and the fund for providing poor children with clothing ... [Annie] was the only lady now living who had taken part in the former Volunteer bazaar, and she was present at the last one, which was such a wonderful success.[9]

The banquet and the Freedom of the Burgh of Paisley are interesting for another reason; by 1902, Stewart and Annie had become owners of the

Dundas Castle Estate, Linlithgowshire, which is still in the family more than a century later, and of Cairndhu, County Antrim.

Stewart died in November 1907. As well as close relatives, the mourners at his funeral included the Marquis of Linlithgow and Lord Rosebery. His Will published a couple of weeks after his death, was a testament to a man who cared passionately for the poor and dispossessed, and for all the servants both in Scotland and Ireland that had served his family so well. He also included in his list of bequests, the servants of his son-in-law Bryce and daughter Annie. Such kindness, from a man who was once described as solid but uninspiring, surely shows his true nature.

As if in tribute to his father, John Clark added the name of Stewart, and from henceforth was known as John Stewart Clark. There have been many words written over the generations expressing the view that Victorian industrialists were only interested in profit at the expense of their workers. While this may have been true of a few, it was certainly not true of the families associated with the Allans.

The first decade of the twentieth century saw three of Alexander's sons move further away from the shipping business. It is true that RobertS, Henry and Claud were still nominally shareholders of the Allan Line, but control of the company rested in Canada. RobertS was spending more and more of his time with the Glasgow School Board with which he had been involved for the best part of thirty years. In 1905, Henry was appointed director of the Clydesdale Bank on the death of Lord Inverclyde (George Burns, of the Burns-Laird and Cunard Shipping Lines). Henry was also a member of the board of the Caledonian Railway Company.

In 1901 Claud had become a member of the Merchants House, a connection that continued until his death. In 1907 he became a director of the British Crown Assurance Corporation Limited, but a more important change in Claud's life occurred about this time. He became tenant of the mansion house of Kilmahew, Cardross, one of the homes of the late George Burns. A large imposing Victorian house built on Jacobean lines, it had three receptions rooms, twenty-one bedrooms with dressing-rooms, a billiard room and library, and fine wooden staircases. But if the house was splendid, then the gardens were truly magnificent, and it was a tradition that Claud continued. In 1911 his two head gardeners were William McHutcheon, who had been a gardener in Burns's day, and Robert McFerguson; later Frank Dunbar took over as head gardener.

RobertS and his family were still tenants at Hafton Castle and at Woodside Terrace in Glasgow. Henry, however, was experiencing some difficulties with houses and landlords. In November 1908 he was at the Court of Jurisdiction trying to seek payment of an outstanding building repair bill on Ballochmyle House from the Trustees of the late Major-General Claud Alexander. It is unlikely that Henry would go to law for the sake of £29.19s.7d.; it may be that his motivation was not monetary redress, but to test the procedures set up by the new Sheriff Court (Scotland) Act which had come into force in 1907. Lord Sherrington, in a rather lengthy judgment, was of the opinion that the Trustees of Major-General Alexander should answer to the charge in the Sheriff Court of Ayrshire. Henry had won a moral victory, but whether he ever recouped his £29.19s.7d. is not known. He later rented a house in Maybole, before moving to Torrence House, East Kilbride, for the rest of his life.

In 1907 also came the death of Henry Rolf Brown, CharlesE's father-in-law. He died in Dennysville in Maine, at the home of his daughter Anna and son-in-law Arthur Lincoln. His death had come just over a year after the death of his daughter Jessie. In June 1908, CharlesE returned to New York aboard the *Lusitania,* and it would not have been out of character for him to make the time to travel to Dennysville to pay his respects to his sister-in-law.

Chapter 15

Change of Direction

In the summer of 1908, two years after Jessie Ellen's death, CharlesE married Jessie Georgina Stewart, known as Georgie, the daughter of Alexander Stewart, Minister of the John Street Evangelical Union Church, Aberdeen.

Stewart was a man of unfailing belief in the teachings of his Church, and in the advancement of medicine. For many decades he was Medical Director of the Deeside Hydropathic Establishment at Maryculter in Kincardine. It was there that he developed, if not a cure for tuberculosis, a disease which took the lives of so many men, women and children in the nineteenth century, then at least a way of managing the condition and giving the sufferers some hope. In 1899 he moved to a larger establishment at Milton of Murtle, near Peterculter in Aberdeenshire.

He was also, like so many Victorians, a firm believer in large families. He was thirty-four when he married seventeen-year old Helen Stewart in 1869; she was the daughter of William Stewart, a timber merchant and Catherine Graham. During the next twenty-odd years, Helen produced eleven living children, six daughters and five sons. She died in 1906, aged fifty-four, of cancer of the uterus; three years later the Rev Stewart died. According to his death certificate it was shortly after mid-day on 6 October 1909. A Register of Corrected Entries confirmed that his death was from natural causes, probably apoplexy. His daughter Margaret Townsend was the informant and she gave her address as Deeside Hydropathic. How sad that a man who had given his life to God and healing the sick should die alone on a country road while members of his family were so close at hand.

CharlesE was definitely sympathetic to at least some aspects of Christian Science, and it is no surprise that his second wife was, like Jessie, a follower of Mrs Eddy. It can only be a matter of conjecture what the

Rev Dr Alexander would have made of Georgie's conversion to Christian Science. He would at least have heard about the church's teachings and beliefs, but as a doctor of medicine his ethical training would have clashed with their principle that prayer and faith could heal all disease and that medical intervention should be avoided.

In trying to define the teaching of the Church of Christian Science in simple terms, the tenet of the Church is that by a belief in the teachings of Jesus Christ and by faith and prayer, all diseases of the mind and body can be healed.

If marriage to Georgie confirmed CharlesE's religious beliefs, it also brought a new member to his household staff, George E Smith, a thirty-six-year-old Englishman, who became his butler, and stayed with him for the next two decades. It is a measure of the way the Allan family treated their household and outdoor staff that most of them stayed until their employer died. Marriage to Georgie also brought him two sisters-in-law and their husbands, and a close relationship between them developed. Helen had married Charles Frederick Reddie, a Professor of Music at the Royal Academy, in 1898; in 1909 Mary married Alexander Stronach, a Writer [solicitor] in Aberdeen.

Marriage to Georgie also gave CharlesE a precious gift that his marriage to Jessie had never been able to give him. At the age of fifty he became a father with the birth of his daughter Monica Stewart in June 1914. She became known as Mickey, and as a child and young teenager she enjoyed her father's leisure activities of hunting, shooting and fishing. Although the Church of Christ Scientist has no hard or fast rules about taking part in field sports, in later life Mickey did turn away from such activities.

It is rare for the Allan Line to lose a Court of Inquiry judgment, and even rarer for them to appeal the decision of the Court, but there are occasions when an appeal is expedient or even necessary. The collision between the Ulster Steamship Company's ship, *Malin Head*, and the Allan ship *Corinthian* 2, at the entrance to the St Lawrence River in September 1908 had, according to the Quebec Board of Inquiry, been the fault of the Allan ship. The subsequent appeal before the Court of Appeal in London reversed the judgment of the earlier hearing, but in doing so neither side came out of the Appeal as they would have wished. As the judgment of Lords Justices Vaughan Williams, Fletcher Moulton and Buckley made clear:

> both vessels being pronounced to blame for the collision. It was directed that each side should pay their own costs of the litigation. Under this decision of both to blame each side will have to bear a moiety of the other's assessed damages.[1]

Rumour after rumour had dogged the Allan Line for years concerning the contract for the mail services to Canada. As each rumour was denied so another took its place. In 1909, the Canadian mail service was divided between the Allan Line, the Canadian Pacific and the Dominion Line. In a blunt statement that has all the hallmarks of an Allan family member, it was stated that each of the three firms would handle the mail exclusively or they would give up the contract all together. In the same press article, the Grand Trunk Company were said to be in discussion with the Allan Line to form a joint company to build bigger and faster ships. They hoped to become a half-globe encircling chain. The article finished with the comment: [it] will not be at all surprising if the Allan Line becomes an integral part of the Grand Trunk system.[2]

The correspondent may have thought that the Allan Line had other plans. A denial from the Allan Line was printed on the same day. However, it was true that there were major changes taking place in the management of the Allan Line at this time. Nathaniel Dunlop retired as chairman of the Glasgow operation, and as Montagu stated:

> the Allan Line was to be reorganized. In view of the business advantages of Montreal over Glasgow, the business management of the fleet would in future be exercised from Montreal.[3]

Hugh Andrew was appointed chairman and again reiterated that no decision had been taken as to the location of the new headquarters, or to any plans to merge with the Grand Truck. In November, the company issued a press statement giving a list of the shareholders now in place. The four major Allan shareholders were Montagu, Hugh Andrew, James Bryce of Boston, and Andrew Alexander, all part of the Canadian family. The Glasgow shareholders were James Smith Park and two single shareholders,

John A Spens and A D Wylie, both Writers. Not one member of the Glasgow Allan family was listed as a shareholder. Indeed it looked very much as if they were excluded from all involvement, and this was confirmed by Hugh Andrew stating in no uncertain terms:

> I have spent 32 years of my life trying to build up the Canadian end of the business, and it is not likely that we should want to sell it now ... You may rest assured that the Allan Line is not on the market. It is wholly and simply a Canadian Line. That is the only change.[4]

Hugh Andrew gave little credit to what his father Andrew and uncle Sir Hugh had achieved, sounding as if he alone was responsible for everything good that had happened. It seemed a shabby way to treat the sons and grandsons of James and Alexander, considering all they had done to make the Allan Line a successful company. There is a feeling among some current members of the family that the decision would have been different if RichardG had backed his brothers and his Glasgow cousins; but RichardG was not interested in ship owning, and he saw the Montreal takeover as a way of increasing his financial future.

A measure of the dissatisfaction of some of the Glasgow and indeed Liverpool Allan families can be read from the following statement, which very definitely lays the blame for the demise of the British operation at the door of the Canadians:

> The severance of the Liverpool Agencies of the Allan and City Lines, which was arranged by the chairman of the Allan Line Mr Hugh A Allan and Sir John R Ellerman, dissolves the connection that has extended since the opening of the Suez Canal [1869] ... Mr Robert Smith Allan, a member of the Glasgow Branch of the Allan family was a partner of the firm of George Smith & Sons... there have been other family connections with the firm. To a great number of shipping people in Liverpool the transfer of the City Line Agency will seem like a removal of an old landmark. Many a man no longer young will recall how, since boyhood, Allan and the City Line has been to him an institution and inseparable.[5]

Montagu, while still a major shareholder of the Allan Line, also held a large number of other directorships in other companies, including the Merchants' Bank of Canada. In his private life he had an equally wide range of interests: he was vice-president of the Montreal Racket Club, director of the Sailors' Institute, and a passionate supporter of both the Montreal Amateur Athletic Association and the Ice Hockey Association. In 1909 he presented to the Ice Hockey Association a magnificent silver cup, to be competed for by amateur teams in Canada. The original Allan Cup is now in the Hockey Hall of Fame, and each year a replica is given to the winning team. The Cup has been awarded every year since 1909, except for the season 1944–1945. He was devoted to improving the lives of not only people but of animals as well, though within certain limits: for many years he served on the executive committee of the Society for the Prevention of Cruelty to Animals, and yet he was also a keen huntsman, and Master of the Montreal Foxhounds.

If the Allan family in Glasgow were now to play a less important role in shipping, three of the four brothers of Alexander and Jane turned their thoughts to the education of their offspring. It would have been fascinating to be a silent witness to the conversations between RobertS, JamesA and Claud. Henry without any children would not have been involved except as an interested bystander. Their sister Eliza would have been involved with two children to educate; Janie like Henry was childless.

RobertS had for most of his adult life been passionate about the educational needs of the poor of Glasgow and surrounding districts. As a member of the Glasgow Board of Education he pledged to give every child a free education from five years old until they were twelve years old. He wanted them proficient in English, reading and arithmetic, and with religious and moral behaviour playing an important part in the curriculum of the day.

The choice of schools had been easy for their Canadian cousins, they sent their sons to traditional English Public Schools, Eton and Rugby being foremost in the choice. Claud chose a similar institution, Harrow, for his two sons, Robert (Bobby) and CharlesC. The emphasis at Harrow as with the other major Public Schools was on team games and high academic achievement: good preparation for public service with its strong ethical and disciplined codes of behaviour.

Eliza Lander sent her son Tom to Uppingham in Rutland, a school with a strong religious philosophy. Life for Tom must have been less arduous than it would have been if he had been a pupil under Uppingham's previous headmaster Edward Thring. Tom's father had been at Hurstpierpoint

College. In a touching letter written in 1910 he recalled his schooldays under his old headmaster, Bishop William Awdry. Commenting on Awdry's recent death TEL wrote:

> the veneration and affection which I, and, I am sure, several hundred others, have always had for a master and friend who has now left us. ... I had the privilege of more intimate acquaintance with Mr Awdry ... than most boys had ... in my case it was illness. I had a serious case of pneumonia, and, instead of allowing me to be sent to Port Latin, the School infirmary, Mr & Mrs Awdry, took me into their own house and nursed me until I was well again. A professional nurse attended to me during the day, but even then I was not allowed to remain long without a visit from one or other of them ... When I first went to Hurst I was only ten years of age, and my home-sickness was very great. For a long time the only really happy hour was on a ... Sunday evening [when Mrs Awdry] read to us then we would talk.[6]

In the early years of the 1900s it became more acceptable for wealthy families to send their daughters to a boarding school. Eliza sent her daughter Winifred to Malvern Girls' College (now St James's), West Malvern, Herefordshire. As so often happened with the Allans, Eliza's decision made it possible for the family to develop a new friendship, and this one was between Winifred and her fellow student Joan Mews. Joan would later have a closer connection to the Allan family, as well as becoming a life-long friend of Winifred's. There was a strong tradition of music at the school, and the girls were encouraged to become members of the Girl Guides movement, an association to which Winifred devoted a large part of the rest of her life.

As in so many things he did, JamesA did not follow the trend of his siblings and cousins. He chose an avant-garde school for his three sons, Alexander, Hamish and Jack. His daughter, Margaret, would in the fullness of time also become a pupil. His chosen school, Bedales at Petersfield, Hampshire, could not have been more different from Eton, Rugby and Harrow. The pioneer of Bedales, John Haden Badley, had founded the school in 1893, originally as a boys' school. However, he and his wife Amy were both committed to the cause of women's equality and had always intended their new school to be co-educational, treating boys and girls with absolutely equal respect. In those days this was a very bold dream, but they made it come real in 1898. The ethos of the school was on educating the whole child; Badley loathed the public schools' over-emphasis on sport and classical learning, although he himself was a classical scholar. At Bedales each pupil was encouraged to find his/her own path; it will be seen in later chapters that JamesA's children thrived on this and became masters of their own destiny.

Politics had not played as large a role in the affairs of the Glasgow families as they had in Canada. But with the formation of the Independent Labour Party, JamesA became an active member.

JamesA's involvement in the ILP is made clear in Peter Slowe's biography of Manny Shinwell. Slowe writes eloquently about the problems of the Clyde in 1911 when there was a dispute over wages of seamen, particularly around the contrast between the measly pay of the seamen and the income of the shipowners:

> There was cut-throat competition with narrow profit margins and the profits could quickly disappear altogether if a thousand people had to be fed and accommodated on the Clyde. That was not all of Shinwell's good fortune by any means. It also happened that three of the ship-owners were on his side. James All[a]n, chairman of the Allan Line, was a millionaire member of the Independent Labour Party.[7]

The other two shipowners were Algernon Henderson (son of Francis Henderson) of the Anchor Line and Joe Mackay, owner of a large cargo fleet. Allan, Henderson and Mackay were more than willing to pay the seamen the extra ten shillings a week that Shinwell was demanding, but they were almost alone in their willingness to meet the demands of the seamen. That JamesA and Janie had a social conscience alongside their Christian principles makes them stand out amongst other Edwardian industrialists, who argued that profits came before fairness to their workforce.

Comparisons can be misleading, but it might be useful to try to put the wages of seamen into some sort of historical context. In the early part of the twentieth century the annual wages of a butler (always regarded as head of the domestic staff) were £60 a year; a coachman's wages were £18, and a scullery maid's £12. By contrast, the annual wages of a Chief Mate on the *Victorian* and the *Virginian* were £216 a year. An extra third mate's pay was £108; and, rather unusually at that time, the Allan Line paid its officers when their ship was laid up for its annual overhaul or when they were on leave of absence.

It is hard today to visualize what Glasgow and the upper reaches of the River Clyde were like a hundred years ago. The Clyde is now quiet; a few small ships move almost unnoticed down-river; the great shipyards have vanished in the great de-industrialization of the late twentieth century. Only a couple of yards remain, building warships, and the spectator has to wonder how much longer they will survive. How different it was in March 1911, when "over 3,000 passengers left Clyde for Canadian and United States ports ... The Allan liner *Parisian* left for Halifax and Portland".[8]

The aims of the fledgling Trade Union Movement and the Suffragette Movement seem to belong to a distant age, yet their battles are still being fought across the globe. Women wanted equal voting rights with men, equal pay, fairer divorce and property laws and an end to the discrimination that prevented them from entering the professions: a programme which aroused violent condemnation from all too many male politicians.

By 1912 Janie realized that marches and reasoned argument were never going to gain for the movement the female emancipation which she, Emily Pankhurst and the hundreds of thousands of women who supported them were fighting for. Such activities were never going to change the minds of male politicians. If peaceful persuasion were not achieving their aims, them perhaps a campaign of direct action would. The women, unused to violence, began by smashing shop windows and generally behaving in a more aggressive manner. Unfortunately that only brought the wrath of parliamentarians down on them.

James Ramsay MacDonald, Labour MP for Leicester, was among those who voiced his opposition, not so much to the aims of the Suffragette Movement, but to some of the women taking part:

> I have the strongest objection to childishness masquerading as revolution, and all that one can say of these window-breaking expeditions is that they are simply silly and provocative. I wish the working women of this country who really care for the vote ... would come to London and tell these pettifogging middle-class damsels who are going out with little

hammers in their muffs that if they do not go home they will get their heads broken.[9]

Janie would not have been able to stand aside and watch other women take direct action. She did as she had always done: she led from the front. On Wednesday, 6 March 1912, Janie and two fellow Scottish women, Ethel Moorhead, an artist and daughter of a retired army surgeon and Florence Geraldine McFarlane, a nurse and daughter of John McFarlane, a cloth manufacturer of Edinburgh, were arrested for breaking the windows of a shop in High Street, Kensington. Another woman was arrested that afternoon as well for breaking the window of a post office near Earl's Court. The damage was minimal and the cost of replacement put at between £3 and £4. Janie and her companions were charged and sent for trial and each given four months' imprisonment in Holloway, a prison which was notorious at the time for its barbaric treatment of suffragettes.

In May Janie, along with a number of fellow inmates, went on hunger strike. It might be seen as a futile protest, since the prison authorities, with the tacit approval of Herbert Asquith's government, had devised a notoriously brutal method of force-feeding women who took this course, but in fact this aggressive policy was backfiring on the government by developing public sympathy for the suffragettes. Janie, courageous to the last, barricaded herself in her cell; it took three men forty-five minutes using crowbars to break down the door.

In a letter to a friend, written after she left prison, Janie told of her ordeal:

> I did not resist at all, but sat quiet still as if it were a dentist chair, and yet the effect on my health was disastrous – I am a very strong woman and absolutely sound in heart and lungs, but it was not till five months later, that I was able to take any exercise and begin to feel in my usual health again.[10]

The most graphic and horrifying account of force-feeding was given by Emily Wilding Davison; like Janie she barricaded herself in her cell.

> A prison officer climbed a ladder and after forcing the nozzle of a hosepipe through a window, filled the cell with water.[11]

Emily was prepared to drown, but before that happened the warders broke down the door. What followed later that day must have made Emily wish she had drowned.

In the evening the matron, two doctors, and five or six wardresses entered the cell. The doctor said "I am going to feed you by force". The scene, which followed, will haunt me with its horror all my life, and is almost indescribable. While they held me flat, the elder doctor tried round my mouth with a steel gag to find an opening. On the right side of my mouth two teeth are missing; this gap he found, pushed in the horrid instrument, and prised open my mouth to its widest extent. Then a wardress poured liquid down my throat out of a tin enamelled cup. What it was I cannot say, but there was some medicament which was foul to the last degree. As I would not swallow the stuff and jerked it out with my tongue, the doctor pinched my nose and somehow gripped my tongue with the gag. The torture was barbaric.[12]

Emily is still best remembered for the manner of her death, throwing herself in front of the King's horse during the Derby in June 1913.

Janie returned to Scotland to recover, and was gratified that the people of her native Glasgow signed a petition deploring the terrible treatment she had undergone at the hands of the Establishment. Janie's campaigning zeal was not abated: in the spring of 1913 she presided over a public meeting promoted by the Women's Social and Political Union, at which Emily Pankhurst was to speak. It was held in St Andrew's Hall before a very large audience made up mainly of women, but with three hundred male stewards, many of them being dockers and carters. Janie and the organizers had been only too aware that their meeting was very likely to cause a protest. A group of rowdy students interrupted Janie's opening speech by singing or rather shouting the words "take off that hat". A couple of minutes after the students' protest there was another demonstration from the floor. Janie was

making a comparison between the punishment meted to men and to militant suffragists for certain offences when it became apparent that some disturbance had arisen at the back of the hall. ... A determined struggle between a group of male students took place ... The interrupters ... resisted strongly, but the stewards eventually proved too much for them.[13]

Peace finally restored, Janie was able to continue her speech:

Was it statesmanship ... to prosecute women, to pursue them with a policy of repression, as the Government is doing? If members of the Government understood the lessons of history, if they even understood the working of the human mind in any degree, they ought to know that any amount of repression was not going to stop a movement like this.[14]

Janie then introduced Emily Pankhurst; who immediately admitted that a condition of her bail was that she was to refrain from any violent protest and that she had no intention of so provoking her audience that night. The police and civic authorities had other ideas: it soon became apparent to the party on the stage that there were a large number of police in the auditorium. There is some doubt about who throw the first missile but it was enough for the police to move forward in vast numbers. The police tried to storm the platform but to do so that they had to take down the paper decorations surrounding the edge of it, only to discover the paper hiding a length of barbed wire.

> At last one plain clothes constable seized the wire and exerting his strength pulled it down, though he was struck twice on the head and shoulders with flower pots flung from the platform.[15]

Mayhem followed. The police used their truncheons, the women used whatever missiles came to hand; at one point someone fired a revolver, fortunately it only fired blanks. Mrs Pankhurst made her escape from the hall, assisted by some of the stewards, but as she emerged she ran into the arms of the police.

> [*she was practically*] dragged … downstairs to the main door. She was then in a dazed condition, and appeared to faint as she was put into a motor car. Hundreds surrounded the motor, but the police, mounted and on foot, with drawn batons, rushed the crowd to the rear, and Mrs Pankhurst was driven off to the Central Police Station.[16]

Janie had no doubt that the demonstration and the subsequent violence had been pre-planned by the police and the authorities. On behalf of the Women's Social and Political Union she designed a questionnaire to be sent out to as many people as the Union could identify as having been present at the St Andrew's Hall meeting. The women were asked if they were a member of the Suffragette Movement; when did the police first appear; what had they witnessed; and whether Mrs Pankhurst had been given any opportunity to surrender. In reply to one question which asked if the police had been provoked, Grace A Mackinnon, a teacher replied:

> "In no way as far as I could see …" Janie then asked "Did you see any women armed and if so, with what?" To which Grace replied, "Yes with Indian clubs. I did not see them actually used by the women the police were wrenching them out of the hands of the women."[17]

There were thirty-five questions on Janie's list and it is clear that she was preparing a defence in case of her own future arrest, and also to help Mrs Pankhurst with her latest encounter with the police. The authorities' campaign of harassment and persecution of the Suffragettes continued; reasoned argument fell on deaf ears; and inevitably the women took their lead from the politicians and became even more militant. They stooped to arson attacks, and attempted to bomb Downing Street. It took the declaration of war on 4 August 1914 to bring a temporary halt to the women's demands for the right to vote, for equality and an end of discrimination, to the end of domestic violence, to the end of child abuse. A few small demands, which even Janie would have to admit have been partially achieved; but there is still a long way to go before women the world over feel equal and free.

PART FOUR

1915 – 1925

Ye hypocrites! are these your pranks?
To murder men and give God thanks!
Desist, for shame! – proceed no further;
God won't accept your thanks for MURTHER!

Robert Burns
Thanksgiving for National Victory (1793)

Capt James (Courtesy R Glen Allan)

Alexander of Glasgow (Courtesy R Glen Allan)

Albion (Courtesy R Glen Allan)

Sir Hugh (Estate of Sir Hugh Allan)

Ravenscrag (Estate of Sir Hugh Allan)

Matilda Caroline (Lady Allan) (Estate of Sir Hugh Allan)

Charles E Allan (Courtesy Mrs Lorna J Clark)
Jessie (Georgie) Allan (Courtesy Mrs Lorna J Clark)

Aros House (Courtesy Mrs Jane Stedman)

Kilmahew (Crown Copyright RCAHMS)

Lady Margeurite Allan, daughters
Gwendolyn and Anna
(Courtesy Musee McCord, Quebec)

Lady Doris Vernon, portrait by
Hon J Collier, Hambury Hall,
(Courtesy National Trust)

Adeline Allan (Courtesy Michael A Wilson)

Claud Allan (Courtesy Michael A Allan)

Janie (Courtesy Michael A Wilson)

Tom & Joan Lander's Wedding. Elsie, TEL and Winifred on the right.
(Courtesy David & Frances Lander)

Landers at Archtyfardle: left-right: Peter, David, Janie, Elise, Joan, John

Sheena Allan (Courtesy Michael A Allan)

Sir Hugh Allan's Memorial
(Courtesy Mount Royal Cemetery, Heritage Programs, Quebec)

Old Andrew Allan's Memorial
(Courtesy Mount Royal Cemetery, Heritage Programs, Quebec)

Alastair Allan - Aros
(Courtesy Mrs J Stedman)

Susan, Margaret, Jane, (Aros) (Courtesy Mrs J Stedman)

Monica Stewart Allan's wedding (Courtesy Mrs L J Clark)

Margaret Allan & Chris Jenning's wedding (Courtesy Edwin Atkinson)

Margaret Jennings car (Courtesy Edwin Atkinson)

Henry's First car (Courtesy Michael A Wilson)

Commander Robert A Allan, Admiral of the Fleet Sir James Somerville, Washington, 1945 (Courtesy Lady Maureen Allan)

Allan Memorial - Glasgow Southern Necropolis
(Courtesy Michael A Wilson)

Chapter 16

Lusitania

S iegfried Sassoon won the Military Cross for gallantry in the Great War, but that did not mean that he looked upon the awful conflict with anything but loathing. In a very telling poem entitled "Does It Matter?" he poses the question of why sane and sensible men and women would volunteer to go to war, but concludes with the bitterly ironic lines: *People won't say you that you're mad;/For they'll know you've fought for your country/And no one will worry a bit.*

He was right about sane men volunteering to fight for their country, but he said nothing about middle-aged men joining the ranks of the eager young men who flocked to the Recruiting Centres in August 1914.

Three members of the Allan family fell into that category. Bryce of Aros had for more than twelve years commanded a local contingent of Volunteers, and was naturally among the first to seek action. As a Captain in the Royal Garrison Artillery he travelled immediately to their camp at Bedford, followed closely by all the men from his Argyll Mounted Battery. He quickly became a Major in the Ross Mountain Battery and was posted to the Dardanelles with the Mediterranean Expeditionary Force. This was according to contemporary records a "staff appointment", but that did not prevent him from being injured: in August 1915 it was reported he was in hospital in Malta.

Claud was just a few years older than his cousin, and as a founder member of the Royal Naval Volunteer Reserve he knew exactly where his duty lay. He had had previous experience of war, having served with the army in South Africa during the Boer War of 1899–1902. Wartime service in the RNVR did not suit Claud, and in 1915 he transferred to the 9th Glasgow Highland Battalion of the Highland Light Infantry with the rank of Second Lieutenant, and was soon promoted to the rank of Temporary Captain.

Sir Montagu, ten years older than Claud, had every reason to remain aloof from a war in Europe, but he was determined to be part of the struggle. He was an honorary Lieutenant-Colonel in the Fifth Regiment, Royal Highlanders of Canada:

> He volunteered for active service but on account of his age [he was 54] he could not serve in the combatant forces. He was appointed president of the Overseas Canadian Pension Board and served in this capacity in London from September 1915 until March 1918.[1]

The call for action was not answered only by the middle- aged men. Young men fresh from the public schools of Eton, Harrow, Rugby and Uppingham and many others, with little or no experience and barely any training, were appointed Platoon Commanders and sent off to France to face an enemy they knew nothing about. Many of them believed the rhetoric of the politicians and the generals that it would all be over by Christmas. Disillusionment would come quickly.

During the fewer than six decades since Capt Bryce had sailed to Canada in *The Albion*, the fastest little ship of her day, passenger travel across the oceans had been transformed. The early 1900s saw two magnificent passenger liners built for the Cunard line and launched from the John Brown shipyard on the Clyde: the *Mauretania* and the *Lusitania*. This brought sea travel into the realms of luxury; the discomforts suffered by Capt Bryce and his crew half a century earlier were very much a thing of the past. The Cunard ships both took the Blue Riband from the pride of the German fleet, *Kaiser Wilhelm II* – a matter of pride for the Cunard Company and its chairman Lord Inverclyde, though the Germans must have viewed the loss of the Blue Riband with dismay and resentment. Lord Inverclyde retired as chairman in 1905. He was replaced by William Watson, but he only held the position for four years. The man who succeeded him in 1909, and was therefore head of the Cunard Board at the time of the *Lusitania* disaster, was Alfred A. Booth.

The Allan family were not averse to seeing what the new ships had to offer. CharlesE returned from a visit to New York in June 1908 on the *Lusitania*. In March 1911, Lady Marguerite sailed from New York on board the *Mauretania;* she was to spend time in London with Martha and Hugh, staying at the Ritz Hotel. Hugh was to become a pupil at Eton College at the start of the summer term.

In the spring of 1915 Marguerite made a fateful decision to return to England. Her two elder children, Martha and Hugh, were still in Europe; Martha was in France studying art and drama and Hugh was in his last year at Eton College. Marguerite decided that with her daughters, Anna and Gwen, she would reunite her family in England and await the arrival of Sir Montagu later that year.

She would have known that among her saloon class passengers she would find agreeable companionship. If she had been concerned about the stories of U-boat activity, she clearly put her faith in the abilities of the captain and crew to keep her and her daughters safe.

There had been a campaign running in the newspapers on both sides of the Atlantic that passenger liners crossing the Atlantic should be secured from the risk of German U-boat attacks. Cunard repeated that both their liners were not carrying and never would carry armaments and ammunition other than for the protection of their passengers and crew. They also stated that their ships did not carry soldiers on their way to fight in France. A Mr Valder B Paine, in a letter to the Cunard Company, put forward the suggestion that as well as flying the Union Flag their ships should also fly the Stars and Stripes. He believed that as America was a neutral country their flag would be recognized as such. The Americans may have believed that; Alfred Booth definitely did, according to a reply he sent to Paine:

> Your statement that it is right for a British Ship to fly the American flag if the presence of an enemy is suspected as a notice to him that American citizens are on board is one to which I fully subscribe. You may rely upon it that the safety of our passengers is now, as it has always been, the first consideration of the Cunard Company.[2]

But the German High Command did not agree with either Paine or Booth. On the 22 April, they issued a notification that as Great Britain and her allies were at war with Germany, any vessel flying the flag of Great Britain or her allies would be a target for attack if they sailed into the war zone.

The warning did have an effect on some prospective passengers, but most believed that the *Lusitania* would not be harmed. She left New York on 1 May with 1,265 passengers and 694 crew; for the first few days they had a peaceful and trouble-free crossing.

During the voyage from New York, Marguerite made the acquaintance of Sir Hugh Lane who would have made a very charming and interesting companion. Lane was a notable artist, a collector and connoisseur of fine paintings. He was returning to Ireland with a very valuable collection of paintings, which he had bought, on behalf of Lord Duveen, for the National Gallery in London. The paintings included works by Monet, Rembrandt, Rubens and Titian, priceless by today's standards, and insured in 1915 for $4 million. Shortly before he sailed Lane wrote a Codicil to his Will; whether he had a premonition of his own death, or whether he was taking no chances after the warning from the Germany Embassy, we will never know. Unfortunately, Lane forgot to get the Codicil witnessed, and that omission would lead to years of legal wrangling between the galleries of Ireland and England.

The *Lusitania* on that fateful voyage was not under the command of her usual Captain, Daniel Dow; according to some sources he was on leave due to the stress of previous crossings in U-boat infested waters. It is said Dow had also strongly represented to the Cunard management that the ship should not become an armed merchant cruiser, thereby making her a legitimate target for German forces. The evidence that she was carrying military arms and equipment has never been proved beyond reasonable doubt, and it must, therefore, be assumed that she was what she claimed to be: a ship carrying civilian passengers.

The Captain for what would be *Lusitania's* last voyage was William Thomas Turner, known as "Bowler Bill", because of his habit a wearing a bowler hat when on shore. He had previously commanded the *Lusitania* and was regarded by many as an outstanding commodore. Aware of the problems that the ship might encounter as it neared the Irish coast, Bowler Bill ordered the engine room to reduce speed, post extra lookouts and sound the foghorn constantly.

The unprovoked attack occurred shortly after two o'clock on the afternoon of 7 May. Marguerite, Anna and Gwendolyn were in the lounge having just finished lunch. She was in conversation with Frederick Orr Lewis, a fellow Canadian with interests in shipbuilding.

Marguerite's two maids, Emily Davis and Annie Walker, George Slingsby, Orr Lewis's valet, and William Stainton, valet to Charles Frohman, the American theatre impresario, were on a deck below still having lunch. At 14.10 Leslie Morton, an eighteen-year-old look-out at the bow of the vessel, spotted thin lines of foam racing towards the ship. His fear must

156

have been immense but he was able to shout through a megaphone: *Torpedoes coming on starboard side.*

Slingsby, looking out of a starboard porthole, also saw the terrifying wake. He instantly called everyone's attention to it, including Detective Inspector William John Pierpoint. Shortly after their departure from New York, Pierpoint had apprehended three German-speaking men who were hiding in a steward's pantry. He had subjected them to thorough interrogation before locking them in the ship's cells, intending to hand them over to the police in Liverpool when the ship docked.

Concerned about the welfare of their employers, Emily, Anna, Slingsby and Stainton rushed to the first class lounge, but finding chaos raging, they finally came across Marguerite and her daughters and Orr Lewis, on the port deck. Marguerite did not have a life-jacket and Slingsby gallantly handed over his own jacket.

There is a fundamental truth that in all disasters, whether man-made or natural, heroes are to be found. But it is also an inescapable fact that cowards and villains will take the opportunity to enhance their own safety at the expense of others.

In the sinking of the *Lusitania*, there were heroes and there were villains, perhaps even criminal acts. It must be asked, why did the British Admiralty not provide a cruiser escort for the *Lusitania* as it neared Ireland.

There were Naval ships in the vicinity. Why did Captain Turner seemingly ignore the messages of submarine activity in the area? Why were the passengers and crew not better trained in lifeboat drill?

Perhaps the whole truth of what happened that day can never be known; what is not in doubt is that 1,198 passengers and crew died. Marguerite survived, although badly injured, Anna and Gwendolyn did not. Slingsby and the Allan maids survived. The three German-speaking men whom Pierpoint had locked in the cells perished. It did not seem to matter if the passengers were saloon, first class or steerage, the sea took no account of wealth, race, creed or colour.

There were many stories of the courage and presence of mind of the passengers; one memorable story was about David Dalrymple, a young man returning home to Invergowrie after a holiday. He recalled:

> Standing on the deck he overheard a passenger say, "Is that a torpedo?" Looking in the direction indicated, he saw the track. When the boat was going down he dived off the side fully dressed. He was sucked down by

the great ship, but managed to get above the water again, and swam about for half an hour. He eventually made his way to a large upturned boat, and managed to clamber on board. Before long there forty persons hanging on to this boat, one of number being Lady Allan, whom he personally assisted to get on to the keel of the boat.[3]

Injured as she was, Marguerite had to face the loss of her daughters. Gwen's body was found by 17 May, but Anna's was never recovered, in spite of a reward of £100 being offered by her distraught family. Gwen was buried in Mount Royal Cemetery, Montreal, where there is also a memorial to her sister.

There were many opinions, many rumours and all manner of conjectures concerning the last minutes on board the stricken liner. Many cannot be confirmed or denied, others were discredited as long as a century ago.

There is one comment, though, by William Srimgeour, which bears repeating: he remembered that during the voyage most passengers had treated the threat of an attack as a joke. When the joke became all too real, Srimgeour said the joking stopped as the passengers became hypnotized.

Sir Hugh Lane's body was never recovered, and for decades his precious container of paintings lay on the ocean floor. In the summer of 1994 a diver, Tapson, claimed to have found the tubes of paintings; he believed that as the tubes had been sealed the paintings could still be intact. The Irish Arts Minister immediately placed a Protection Order on the cargo; the first such Order for a wrecked ship under a hundred years old.

As with all disasters, either by land, sea or air, an official inquiry was held into the events leading up to the sinking of the doomed liner. The first notice that an inquiry would be held was published on 11 May; anyone wishing to give evidence should contact the Board of Trade solicitors, who would take initial statements.

The full inquiry opened in London on 15 June at Caxton Hall, Westminster. Lord Mersey (John Charles Bigham) was appointed Presiding Officer. He was an excellent choice as chairman since he had wide experience in Maritime Law and had been Commissioner for both the *Titanic* and *Empress of Ireland* sinkings in 1912 and 1914. He had also presided over the drafting of the International Convention for the Safety of Life at Sea in 1913.

Lord Mersey was assisted by four assessors, Admiral Sir Frederick S Inglefield KCB, RN, Lieutenant-Commander Hearn RN, and Captains D Davies and J Spedding of the Mercantile Marine. The lawyers for the Cunard Company were Butler Spinal KC, an Australian-born barrister who had also played a part in the *Titanic* inquiry four years earlier. He was assisted by Lang KC. The Board of Trade was represented by the Attorney General, Sir Edward Carson, assisted by the Solicitor-General, Major Sir Frederick Edwin [FE] Smith, a duo of outstanding advocates of their day. Both had a great reputation for cross-examination and as great orators when addressing a jury; they were passionate, charming and utterly ruthless when trying to get at the truth, or to serve their client.

The opening statement was made by Carson with his usual attention to detail, and it is worth recording exactly what he said:

> Certain statements had been made as between the German Government and the American, and notes had been passed. *Lusitania* was not armed, and was not a transport, and did not carry cargo in the form of munitions. ... There was no such outfitting of the ship as is alleged or fancied, or invented by the German Government.[4]

Carson's statement did not, however, silence all the conspiracy-theorists. Joseph Marischal, a Lecturer in Romance Languages at Queen's University, Ontario, was among the most outspoken, insisting that he had heard a Maxim gun being discharged, saying in his evidence:

> I suggest that the explosion of the torpedo exposed the secret existence of some ammunition. I have experience of explosives. I have served in the French Army as an Officer.[5]

FE questioned exactly where Marischal was at the time the torpedo hit and when he said he was in the second class dining-room, FE again challenged his evidence, whereupon Marischal refused to answer but instead tried to offer his opinion of the evidence given by Alfred Booth, Cunard's Chairman. Lord Mersey silenced him, although he did allow him to complain bitterly that his child had been lost, and that his wife, who was an invalid, his remaining children and himself had been badly treated by the Cunard representative when they arrived in Queenstown. Later in the proceedings, Lord Mersey admitted that he did not believe Marischal, stating that his *demeanour was very unsatisfactory.*

It is strange, Marischal had lost one child but he could only complain that the rest of his family, who had survived, had not received immediate and exceptional care on landing in Ireland.

There was a good deal of discussion between Counsel as to whether the reduction in speed that Cunard had imposed on the liner had in any way caused her to be at greater risk of attack. Alfred Booth stated in his evidence:

> If the question as to increasing the speed by using five boilers had arisen at all it would have arisen in February, when the first submarine attacks were made. His view, and the view of the directors, was that, the *Lusitania* being the fastest ship that was running, the difference between 21 knots and 24 knots was not material so far as avoiding submarines was concerned.[6]

Marischal had already accused Cunard of reducing the speed to save on coal consumption and thus increasing their profits. Notwithstanding that Cunard had reduced the cost of a second class fare from $70 to $50, Marischal said that they *would have been better to attack the pocket of the passengers than their lives.*

On 17 July Lord Mersey delivered the judgment of the Court of Inquiry and his opening statement could not have been more precise, or more clearly stated:

> the loss of the ship and lives was due to damage caused to the ship by the torpedoes fired by a sub-marine of German nationality, whereby the ship sank. In the opinion of the Court, the act was done, not merely with the intention of sinking the ship, but also with the intention of destroying the lives of the people on board.[7]

Lord Mersey singled out two members of the crew for their exceptional bravery and in a warm tribute to the eighteen-year-old lookout who had first raised the alarm, he said:

> Leslie N Morton ... at the time the ship was torpedoed ... was an extra look-out on the starboard side of the forecastle head ... he seemed to have exhibited great courage, self-possession, and resource ... when the torpedoes struck the ship, Morton was knocked off his feet, but recovering himself quickly, he went at once to the boats on the starboard side, and assisted in filling and lowering several of them.[8]

Even then, Morton was not concerned with saving his own life, having done all he could on the sinking ship he jumped into the water. He managed to get hold of a collapsible lifeboat, and with the help of another crew member called Joseph Parry, was able to make the craft ready and helped between fifty and sixty passengers aboard. He and Parry then rowed for some miles until they came to a fishing smack where they were able to transfer their passengers. But that was not the end of things for those two brave young men, they returned to the life boat, rowed back to the struggling survivors and brought another twenty or thirty to safety. As Lord Mersey said:

> This boy, with his mate Parry, was instrumental
> in saving nearly one hundred lives … he has cause
> for being proud of the work he did.[9]

Both Morton and Parry were awarded the Board of Trade Silver Medal for Gallantry in Saving Lives at Sea.

Two days after the inquiry closed Lord Mersey waived his fees and formally resigned. In summing up the whole terrible disaster, perhaps his own words can stand as a memorial to that dreadful day. He said blame must rest solely with those who plotted and with those who committed the crime. He later added an even more poignant comment. The *Lusitania* case was a damned, dirty business.

The controversy surrounding the sinking of the *Lusitania* continues to this very day. There are countless theories involving many conspiracies; a whole library of books has been written about this terrible disaster. The wreck should be treated with respect for what it undoubted is: a War Grave, a memorial of all the people who lost their lives and all the people who survived to mourn their losses.

There is one story for which we have no evidence at all, yet we may reasonably suppose it happened. CharlesE, as a resident of Belfast, would have hurried to the side of his badly injured aunt-in-law, Marguerite and offered her not just condolences but practical help. Did he arrange for her to recover at Stormont Castle, among her own family, until Montagu arrived later that year? The answer must surely be, yes, it was the most natural thing for a member of the Allan family to do.

There had been two other shipping disasters in the years before the *Lusitania,* each caused by a different set of circumstances. The *Titanic,* the ship whose owners the White Star Line declared was unsinkable, was on her maiden voyage when she hit an iceberg and sank with a terrible loss of life. The *Empress of Ireland,* now under the flag of the Canadian Pacific Steamship Company, who since 1909 had taken over financial management of the Allan Line, left her home port of Quebec on 28 May 1914, bound for Liverpool. Shortly after sailing she encountered thick fog in the St Lawrence River, and collided with a smaller vessel: the *Storstad.* Again, the loss of life was appalling.

There is a moving postscript to all this which has been told many times, but still bears repeating: the Legend of Emmy. Emmy was the ship's cat on the *Empress of Ireland,* a loyal orange tabby who had never once missed a voyage in all the previous 200 sailings, but on that fateful morning of 28 May 1914 the crew could not tempt her to board ship; she refused all their cajoling and they sailed without her.

It was said that as the ship steamed away from the harbour, Emmy could be seen sitting on the roof of a shed at Pier 27 which would later become a temporary mortuary for the dead of the *Empress of Ireland.* Perhaps Sir Hugh Lane was not the only one involved in those three disasters who had a premonition of what was about to befall them.

Chapter 17

Quintinshill

If ever a war was misnamed, it was by those who called the First World War "The Great War". It was never a great war; it was the "Slaughter of the Innocents". The death of so many, on both sides of the conflict, was surely a testament to the stupidity of war, confirming those who believe that man has learned nothing about conflict or how to resolve matters other than by the force of arms.

Death by your enemies is at least partially understandable, death at the hands of your own civilian workers is so shocking that when it happens it cannot be comprehended. The Biblical Slaughter of the Innocents may or may not be historical fact, but a event of comparable horror occurred on the morning of 22 May 1915, fifteen days after the loss of the *Lusitania*.

Henry Allan, deputy chairman of the Caledonian Railway Company, awoke on the morning of the 22 May to be told of a train crash close to the Quintinshill signalbox on the main line between Glasgow and London. Henry's involvement with the railway company began in 1903 when he became a director. In 1913 he was appointed deputy-chairman. It is extremely doubtful that the first message Henry received could have told him of the full horror of what had happened that morning. It is worth saying at this point that in 1915 the Caledonian Railway Company was regarded as one of the greatest of the old railways in Great Britain.

> It was a line of immense character, not only in its beautiful blue locomotives, its handsome stations and its many fast trains, but in the splendid solidarity of its management and the way in which vast capital sums were expended on huge schemes for the improvement of traffic and the comfort and convenience of passengers.[1]

As a conservative, thoughtful banker, and indeed as a member of the Allan Line family, Henry had obviously learned that trains like ships should be built to the highest quality, and that their passengers should be given excellent care and comfort during their journey.

In simple terms, if that is possible with such an appalling disaster, a special train, carrying over 500 soldiers of the 7th Battalion of the Royal Scots Territorial Force on their way to Gallipoli, crashed into a stationary local train which had been left on the main line instead of being shunted into a siding. Minutes later, the express train from Euston ploughed into the wreckage, then the train from Glasgow Central did the same thing.

It was a policy of the Caledonian that as the London and Glasgow trains were notorious bad timekeepers, they should always be given priority over the local and goods trains. The shunting of the local trains was, or should have been, another priority for the Quintinshill signalmen, since they had general orders to make sure the main lines were always clear for the expresses. Since the war began, further problems had become apparent with the increase in rail traffic as a consequence of the moving of troops around the country.

Henry was later to say with regret that because of the demand for rail transport they were using out-dated wooden carriages for the troop train. (The modern carriages were steel-framed and a good deal more robust.) The old carriages were lit by gas-lamps, with the oil-gas stored in tanks under the main carriage frame; and unfortunately the tanks had just been filled. The situation was made even worse by the fact that the fire engines had to come from Carlisle – which was some ten miles from Gretna and a further mile and a half from the Quintinshill signal box – then make the last part of journey over rough fields; and when they got there, there was no easily accessible water. The inferno went on burning for two days.

Two hundred and twenty-seven men died that day. Although the number may have been higher, the exact death toll was never established. Human error was given as the cause of the disaster; two signalmen, James Tinsley and George Meakin, were held to be responsible, and were later jailed.

The errors the two men made that morning have been written about many times, and re-reading the graphic details never gets any easier.

> Shunting sometimes took place at Kirkpatrick, but equally … it took place at Quintinshill where the siding accommodation was usually ample … The frequency of a stop at Quintinshill had led the signalmen working

that box into a most reprehensible practice. The box was out in the country, with no dwellings near, the two men [*Meakin and Tinsley*] lived in Gretna. Ordinarily it would have meant a walk, or a bicycle ride of some [*1.5*] miles, from home to duty; but instead, an arrangement grew up by which if the 6.10 was stopping at Quintinshill the relief man rode on it from Gretna and took over his duties on arrival of the train.[2]

Such an unauthorized arrangement frequently made the signalman up to seventeen minutes late for work. In these instances the night man would log the train movements on a scrap of paper for the new man to enter into the log when he arrived. Tinsley was more concerned to get the log up to date than he was to check all signals, and to confirm that all trains were on the right tracks and the signal box locking devices were in place. He failed to do any of those things, and Meakin made no effort to remind his colleague of his duties. Meakin did not immediately leave the signal box, as he should have done, once he had handed over to Tinsley. He remained behind, reading the newspaper Tinsley had brought with him. The two signalmen were even joined in the box by the goods train brakes-men, and the gossip of these three men further distracted Tinsley from his critical duties.

There was a terrible epitaph to the tragedy, which, if true, shows again and again the callousness that war seems to breed. It was reported at the time that the Military High Command ordered the soldiers who had survived the crash (said to number only fifty-two) to be taken to Carlisle, where they spent the night, before being put on another train and taken to Liverpool to board a ship for Gallipoli. As the survivors marched through Liverpool on their way to the docks they were dishevelled and demoralized. It appears that they were not even given new uniforms, let alone shown any kindness or consideration after their terrible ordeal. A group of local people seeing them march past thought they were prisoners of war and verbally abused them.

If they had reached Gallipoli, the likely fate of these 500 would have been as dreadful as that of so many men who served in that bloody and ill-conceived campaign. Col Bryce of Aros could have testified; he had been to the Dardanelles and knew at first hand the savagery of that battle.

Newspaper coverage of the Quintinshill disaster was very muted at the time, perhaps because in times of war it is necessary to keep troop movements secret from the enemy. There was an inquest in Carlisle and later a Board of Trade Inquiry. The BOT report cleared the Caledonian Railway Company of any blame, stating that had the two signalmen obeyed the basic operating procedures and used the safety devices provided the accident would never have happened. They went on to say that in their opinion the Caledonian Railway did not need to make any further changes to their safety rules.

Meakin and Tinsley served just a year of their prison sentences, and were re-engaged by the Company, but not as signalmen. Tinsley became a lamp man and porter at Carlisle, a post he held for more than thirty years. Meakin was re-employed as a goods train guard, but only held the position for a few years. They must have carried a terrible burden of guilt for the rest of their lives. At the time of the accident Tinsley was married with three young sons: was he ever able to tell them of the events of that dreadful morning? Meakin was single.

It appears that Henry, as vice-chairman, and the Caledonian Railway Company as an organization were generous to the four families of the train workers [servants as they were called at the time] who died in the crash.

F Scott [the driver of the troop train] and [his] Fireman J Hannah of Kingmoor, were both killed. Scott's widow received £300 compensation from the company, and £10 annually for her two youngest children until they were sixteen. Fireman Hannah's widow received three years' earnings, equal to £270.5s.9d., plus £10 per annum for five years for her five-year-old boy. Quite recently there was a deeply moving epilogue to this particular side of the Quintinshill tragedy. Many of the Carlisle enginemen, whether they worked out for the English or Scottish railways, were Cumbrians, and Mrs Hannah became a postwoman at Lamplugh ... Eventually she became postmistress and continued in her job until well over eighty years of age. When she retired she was awarded an OBE in recognition of her long and faithful service.[3]

The Company put out a new directive in which it laid down that all its managers and railway employees, whatever their duties, should never again deviate from the Company's "basic operating rules".

The young soldiers were buried in Edinburgh's Rosebank Cemetery, where a large granite cross towers above the names of the dead. Among the dead on the troop train were found the burnt bodies of three young children. They were never identified. It was thought they had stowed away on the train. Somewhere in Scotland there were families who would never know what had happened to their children.

166

It took nearly ninety years for a plaque to be erected at the site of the crash, and the money was raised not by the military or the railway companies but by a group of indomitable ladies of the Leith Women's Group.

Robert Gilkison Allan, the eldest son of Capt James, died at his Liverpool home, Rosemount, Mossley Hill, Liverpool, on Wednesday 14 July 1915. He was seventy-four and had been in failing health for some time. Liverpool had been his home since he had joined the Allan Line offices in 1874 as a young man, after the death of his Uncle Bryce. His funeral, a few days later, was at St Andrew's Church, Aigburth, the service being conducted by the Lord Bishop of Carlisle, Dr Diggle, and the Rev Sidney Nowell Rostron, Vicar of St Andrew's. RobertG's brothers JamesH, RichardG and Bryce of Wemyss Bay attended, with his cousin RobertS from Glasgow. RobertS's brother, Claud, was on active service, CharlesE was in Belfast and Henry was still very much involved with the aftermath of the Quintinshill disaster. As befitted a man who had given outstanding service to the Liverpool maritime community, mourners turned out *en masse* to honour his life. At his graveside there was a contingent of boys from the Seamen's Orphanage, a fitting tribute to the man who had taken a keen interest in the institution set up by his Uncle Bryce.

RobertG's obituary outlined the work he had done in Liverpool to expand and improve the Allan Line Services. He and Margaret never had any children, and it is perhaps this that saw him devote almost all his time to his business.

> He had lofty ideals, and possessed an amiability of disposition which made him *persona grata* in every avenue of his life, whether commercial or social. In this respect he was a pattern to young men. Somewhat retiring in his habits, he never desired to cut any prominent figure in politics, shrinking from the blare of public life, but several institutions benefited from his generous patronage.[4]

In September 1915 Sir Montagu left Montreal for London to take up his duties as Claims Agent for the Fourth Division of the Canadian Pension Board. He would join Marguerite in London, where she was still recovering from the injuries she sustained in the *Lusitania* disaster. His daughter Martha had returned to Canada at the start of the war, and trained as an ambulance driver. According to her obituary, written many years after the war, she bought her own ambulance and took it to France in order to assist in the repatriation of injured soldiers. The mud and stench of the trenches made the evacuation of the injured a hazardous task at the best of times. Martha and all the brave women and men who volunteered as nurses and drivers deserve a very honoured place in the history of the war. Many of the women took their lead from the Suffragette Movement. They served their country with dogged determination and outstanding courage.

In a book of letters written during the war Arthur George Wilson, known as Peter (and later to become a member of the Allan family), wrote graphically of the appalling conditions of life in the trenches.

> Very heavy rains late in August and September – mud and water in the trenches over the tops of our gumboots ... Heavy bombardments often caused trenches and dug outs to collapse and some troops suffocated when overcome with fatigue and when sleeping in lightly built dugouts which fell in upon troops.[5]

In Canada, in Scotland and in England the wealthy owners of large houses opened them up as hospitals and convalescent homes, their daughters often working as VAD (Voluntary Aid Detachment) nurses. Sir Montagu and Marguerite gave Ravenscrag over to the Canadian military as a convalescent home. To the injured servicemen returning from the hell that was the war in Europe, Ravenscrag must have felt like heaven on earth.

Sir Montagu and Marguerite were to suffer another tragedy before they themselves could return to Ravenscrag. Having already lost their two teenage daughters, they lost their only son. Hugh left Eton College and, like so many other eager young men at the time, enlisted. On 23 February 1917 he joined the Royal Naval Air Service at Chingford in Essex. A little over four months later he was killed. He was just twenty years old. Montagu and Marguerite had indeed paid a very, very heavy price to defend their motherland from the enemy. Hugh is buried in the Coxyde Military Cemetery in Flanders.

Hugh was not the only Allan family casualty of war. Phoebe's eldest son, Sir George Reginald Houstoun-Boswall, a Captain in the 4th Battalion of Grenadier Guards, was killed in late September 1915. He left a widow, Naomi Anstey, and two infant daughters. He had succeeded to the baronetcy in 1908 on the death of his father. His brother Thomas was serving with the 13th Royal Scots Guards, and inherited the title.

A third family tragedy occurred in 1915. Claud MacFie's young son, who as an eight year old had been so interested in moths, was killed in France; his grave is at the Le Tournet Memorial. He was twenty-three years old, and had been a Second Lieutenant with the South Staffordshire Regiment, with secondment to the Bedfordshire Regiment.

Eliza Lander's son Tom did not hesitate to offer his services to fight the enemy. He had left Uppingham in 1912, but had had little time to enjoy life after school. In October 1915, he obtained an aviator's certificate from the Royal Aero Club at Hendon, and enlisted in the Highland Light Infantry. An interesting note on his aviation certificate is that he gave his address as Pollok Castle, Newton Mearns. In November 1916 he was awarded a Military Cross for conspicuous gallantry; he was wounded and for a short time returned to Scotland. It was while convalescing that he decided to use his aviator's certificate to join the Royal Flying Corps. Later, on a mission over Mesopotamia, he was shot down; he was both lucky and unlucky: lucky that he survived the crash, but unlucky in that he was captured, first by the Turks, then by the Germans; for him the war was over.

Tom was not the only young man to forsake the army for service with the RFC: Peter Wilson was another intrepid flyer. Again rather like Tom, he had been wounded in France in 1916, but returned to duty in France again joining his regiment, the West Yorks Regiment in 1917. He was terribly unfit for trench warfare, and stayed in a non-combatant role, but he always remained a devoted member of his regiment; he too was accepted for the RFC, and returned to France as a "flyer". Again like Tom he was awarded a MC in 1918 for conspicuous gallantry.

The award of the Military Cross was first introduced in 1914, to be given to ranks between major and warrant officer for gallant and distinguished service in the face of the enemy.

An even more prestigious award is the Victoria Cross for "outstanding valour", first awarded in 1856. For a young man doing his best in the face of an enemy attack, the verbal distinction between "outstanding" and "conspicuous" may not be at the very top of his mind; on the other hand those of us who owe so much to the young men who went so eagerly to war might well feel that they all deserved the highest honours a nation could give.

Chapter 18

Warriors

It was not all doom and gloom in 1916. Sheila, sister to Col Bryce of Aros, was married in Kashmir to Edward Francis Sykes, an engineer born in Essex and some seven years Sheila's senior. She was thirty-six, Edward was forty-three. With the sort of irony that was popular at that time he was known as Bill, obviously named after Charles Dickens's violent criminal character in *Oliver Twist*. A civil engineer working in the harsh inhospitable parts of Kashmir and India, he needed to be tough, hard and even a little ruthless if he was to get things done within the time span of a contract. He was, however, a just man who asked nothing of others that he did not ask of himself. There were two children of the marriage, Bryce Edward born in 1918, and Helen Agnes Elizabeth in 1922, both being born in Rajputana (Rajasthan), India.

Sheila's journey to India was not without incident. She was booked to sail to Madras in October 1915 aboard the *Khiva*, but there is evidence that she cancelled her reservation. It is said that her luggage and her wedding presents went without her, and she never saw them again. Her change of plans may have had something to do with the fact that Col Bryce had been injured and was recovering in Malta. It is believed that she undertook a hazardous journey across Britain to France, then an even more problematic train journey through that war torn country to Marseilles. From there a further sea journey to where her brother was in hospital would again have put her at risk of encountering enemy action. Sheila was a strong-minded resourceful woman, and before her trip to India she must have wanted to reassure herself and send a message back to her parents in Tobermory that Col Bryce, although injured, was not gravely ill and would in the fullness of time return to Aros.

James Alexander Allan died in April 1916, not a casualty of the war, but from the complications of a perforated duodenal ulcer. He was fifty-three, and he left three sons: Alexander was twenty-three, Hamish was twenty, and Jack was sixteen. His daughter, Margaret Mabel Gladys, was a child of seven. His main executors and trustees were his brothers Henry and Claud, and two brothers-in-law, Allen and Charles Young. Alexander had been named as a trustee but he was a young naval officer at the time of his father's death. In August he wrote to his father's solicitors, Moncrieff Warren Paterson & Co, declining to act as trustee at that time, saying that

> [because of] probable frequent absences from the country in the near future without being able to leave an address I wish to defer acceptance of trusteeship under the will of my late father till after the war or such time as I shall be more settled.[1]

The death of her husband would only have added to Mabel's anxieties. Her younger son Hamish had been in Boston since September 1913 reading Chemistry at the prestigious Massachusetts Institute of Technology. He returned to Glasgow for the summer vacation in 1914, but returned to MIT again towards the end of September. He completed his studies in the summer of 1915 with a 1st class honours degree, but his enjoyment of his new status did not last long: he tried to enlist, but was considered unfit for military duties. Not deterred, Hamish joined the British Red Cross as an ambulance driver. By September of 1915 he was in San Giovanni di Manzano, where he was in good company, for another driver was Victor Silvester, later to earn fame and fortune as a dance-band leader. As a sixteen year old, Silvester had joined the army in France for six months, after lying about his age.

Hamish's war came to an end on 1 December 1916, when a high explosive shell caused a compound fracture to his right femur and he was invalided home. The army medical doctors were convinced that the only option was to amputate the injured limb, but Mabel had other ideas. After years of what must have been extremely painful treatment by doctors of his mother's choosing, the leg was saved, though it was to cause him discomfort for the rest of his life.

Alexander was even less lucky than his younger brother. He had been at Bedales from the third term of 1904 until the first term of 1909. For the next four years he had been a naval cadet undergoing training. In 1913 he had joined the sailing ship *Hougomont* as second mate; he gained his first mate certificate in 1914, and his master's certificate in 1916. He then transferred out of the Merchant Fleet to join the RNVR in 1916, with the rank of sub-lieutenant. He was posted to the Royal Naval Reserve (Trawler Section) and by June 1917 he was a lieutenant on the HM *Morococala,* a fishing trawler. In June, after a period of fitting-out at Pembroke, *Morococala* took up escort patrols, anti-submarine patrols and mine-sweeping duties off the south coast of Ireland. Alexander's duties were dramatically different from yachting in the friendly waters off Hunter's Quay and Rhu. His new duties

> entailed escorting ships through the "Danger Zone" of the Western Approaches and the Irish Sea. Anti-submarine patrols entailed running abreast of the coastline keeping watch for submarines, suspicious shipping, floating mines or survivors and wreckage from sunken merchant ships. When reports were received on the newly installed radio apparatus of mines discovered, then a pair of trawlers would set up a sweep and begin the task of making the area safe.[2]

Alexander was an outstanding officer, as was reported by his Commander-in-Chief Admiral Lewis Bayley:

> The *Morococala* was very skilfully handled by Lieutenant Alexander Allan RNR. His reports to me were clear and it was depressing to Lieutenant Allan to see his abilities wasted through the vessel being under-gunned.[3]

The little fishing trawler may have been under-gunned and under-equipped for war at sea, but for a little over one and a half years she performed her tasks with the utmost efficiency. Then, all too inevitably, her luck ran out. On the morning of 19 November 1917, Alexander and seven other trawlers were sweeping an area for mines that had been laid the previous evening by a submarine. A convoy was leaving Cork later that day, and the trawlers had been ordered to make safe a channel for the convoy. The trawlers worked in pairs, and on that fateful morning:

> *Morococala* and *Indian Empire* had set their wire successfully between the two ships and commenced the first sweep at 08.30hrs. Suddenly a massive explosion rocked the *Morococala* just behind the bridge, hiding the stern in a cloud of smoke and flame.
>
> Lieutenant Allan and his signalman were seen to clamber on top of the wheelhouse when a second explosion occurred.[4]

173

Alexander and all his crew were killed. Alexander's body was never recovered but there is a tribute to him at the Plymouth Naval Memorial. To his grieving mother Mabel and to his brothers Hamish and Jack and sister Margaret, words could have offered little real comfort, but perhaps they took solace from those of Admiral Sir Lewis Bayley:

> We have lost some of our brother seamen from the dangers of the sea and some from the violence of the enemy, but the same magnificent spirit continues, and I wish to express to all who serve in the Irish Trawler Fleet my whole-hearted thanks and pride for what they have done in the past and my faith in their actions in the future.[5]

It is not hard to assess the mood of the nation as 1916 gave way to 1917. They looked into the abyss and saw only another year of death, mutilation and destruction. The war that should have been over by the Christmas of 1914 looked as if it would continue well into the future.

At the AGM of the Caledonian Railway Company in February, Henry as deputy chairman must have wondered if life would ever return to the easy, carefree days of the first decade of the twentieth century.

Sir Charles Bine Renshaw, the chairman, gave a deeply moving account of the effects the war had had on the railway employees who had served their country. He said:

> 3,594 men had left the service of the Company and enlisted and of these he regretted to say 266 had been killed in action or died of their wounds or disease; 283 had been wounded, 30 were known to be prisoners of war and 40 were reported missing.[6]

He went on to say that forty-five of the Company's former employees had gained commissions and eighteen had been awarded honours. His remarks were greeted with applause, but he expressed concern that the Government had now introduced the voluntary National Service Scheme to keep critical services manned, such as munitions, shipbuilding, coal-mining, transport and agriculture. He thought that too many of their younger men would rush to join the scheme; he could understand their wish to help the war-effort, but he was concerned that without sufficient men they might be unable to run a proper railway service. He warned it would be helpful if the central Control Authority could have defined to some extent what were essential and non-essential industries. He understood that, as far as the railway companies were concerned, suffering as they did from a great shortness in the supply of labour, no man employed in their service would be taken unless the railway company stated that he could be spared.[7]

Henry seconded the adoption of the report and it was passed. A discordant note, however, was struck by a Mr Macdonald, a member of the Railway Shareholders' Association, who could not understand why the dividend paid that year was no higher than the year before. He said it was a poor return when so many people were rolling in wealth. Was Macdonald looking at Henry and Renshaw when he made his cutting remarks? Renshaw had a scathing reply, which Henry must have enjoyed hearing. He said:

> Mr Macdonald was happily possessed of one of the shortest memories of any man he had ever met … He could remember when they were patted on the back and highly praised because they had been able to maintain their dividend, while another railway in their close proximity had cut their dividend down pretty substantially.[8]

Macdonald had surely forgotten that less than two years before the AGM of 1917 the Caledonian Railway Company and others had been involved in one of the worst railway disasters in history. It was surely a measure of the strength of the Company that even in times as awful as those they could maintain a dividend at all. Henry and the other directors were reappointed and Renshaw, perhaps with a moment's foresight, said he believed that it would be the last time he would seek re-election.

Henry's directorship of the railway was not the only one that was keeping him busy. As a director of the Clydesdale Bank, board meetings were a chance for him to give an accurate assessment of the bank's position and their influence in the financial world:

> The main business at their meetings was the authorization of credits, very few of which were refused, but they also had to deal with appointments, salaries and pensions [*no mention was made of bonus payments in 1917*] and to inspect reports from branches. The last meeting of the financial year was always an extremely busy one for it was then that they authorized the renewal of credits subject to annual revisions. One such credit, to Donaldson Brothers, shipowners, was renewed every year for more than two decades. Less happily … decisions had also to be made on the bad debts incurred during the year, prior to the AGM.[9]

Contemporary evidence is not always a reliable test of a person's genuine character, but it would be a fair assumption to say that Henry enjoyed his life as a director of both the railway company and the bank. It was, however, not his only interest. He was an enthusiastic and dedicated motorist who had his first car in 1903, long before the car was regarded as an essential part of everyday life. His family were a source of comfort and pride to him and he played the role of bachelor uncle with great dedication and enjoyment. When a family member wanted an executor Henry was the first choice. When they needed a witness or an informant Henry was the first to be asked. However when Henry needed advice on hiring a domestic servant he consulted his unmarried sister Janie.

Sir Charles Renshaw had been right when he said in 1917 that he would not stand for re-election as chairman. He died in March 1918. His funeral in Paisley befitted a man of his eminent position. The list of mourners was a *Who's Who* of the political, civic and industrial leaders of Glasgow and the West of Scotland. Among them, of course, was Henry. At the next AGM Henry was appointed chairman in Renshaw's place.

There is a delightful passage in Renshaw's obituary that perhaps characterizes this remarkable man, whom Henry was pleased to call not just a colleague but a friend:

> Sir Charles was one of the few Englishmen who had made his home in Scotland not merely for the purpose of sport but as an active member of the community.[10]

Henry's interests lay along the same lines as Renshaw's; he loved to hunt, shoot and fish, but like his brothers his chief recreation was sailing. It was then with an added sense of sadness that a few weeks after Sir Charles's death he learned of the death of Captain William Hogarth:

> [A] well-known skipper, who died at his residence in Port Bannatyne, Bute, began his career with Mr Henry Allan in the famous small rater *Wenonah* and later equally successful 10 tonner *Dakotah*, designed by Herreshoff for Mr Allan, and so all-conquering that she practically killed the class.[11]

The war continued unabated throughout the winter, spring, summer and autumn of 1917. Names such as Ypres, Passchendaele and the Somme became bywords for death and anguish in every house in the land. Young men continued to fight and to die. Jack left Bedales in the second term of 1918, and like his cousin, RichardG's son Dick, was among those who enlisted in the last few months of the war.

It was hard for the women left at home worrying about their menfolk to know how to fill their days with useful activities. Adeline, Janie, and many other women in similar positions literally rolled up their sleeves and set about raising money for the war effort. They also supported the young women who had taken the place of the fighting men in shipyards, in factories and on the farms. Adeline opened a canteen and shop at the Fairfield shipyard in Govan, as well as keeping her beloved Kilmahew in good order. In February, she was advertising for a "table maid" to take the place of her butler. McInnes was fifty-two, rather too old to be called up for frontline service, but it is possible that he had joined Claud as his personal servant. He was back at Kilmahew after the war, which adds weight to that possibility.

Kilmahew held a wartime fete; a photograph of the day shows an injured service man and members of the Boys' Brigade – too young for service, but still wanting to be a part. Sheena was there to support her mother in her role as a leader of the Girl Guides. At the fete there was a stall selling flowers from the gardens of the house, again very obviously lovingly grown and tended. Parked cars, babies in prams, children playing, a hint of laughter in their movements, and ladies in beautiful dresses all gave an illusion that for a few short hours the horrors of the war could be forgotten.

Then on the eleventh hour of the eleventh day of the eleventh month, the guns fell silent. Across Great Britain, Europe, America and the Dominions, mothers said a grateful prayer that their fifteen- and sixteen-year-old sons would not be called upon to lay down their lives. Too many young men, on both sides of the conflict, lay dead among the mud and destruction that had once been the beautiful forests, fields, villages and towns of continental Europe.

Eleven days later His Majesty George V, Queen Mary and the Prince of Wales arrived in Edinburgh as part of their tour of the country. It was fitting that they should arrive in the Scottish capital aboard the Royal train, which was described in a contemporary report:

> It was drawn by two express engines, and was the longest Royal train ever used by the Caledonian Railway Company. ... The arrangements for welcoming their Majesties at the Caledonian Railway Station were of a simple character.
>
> There was no guard of honour, no band, and no military display. To make it fit for the reception of Royalty, the station had been simply but effectively decorated. Overhead clusters of flags and emblems of the Allies were carried from the gardens along the whole length of the west-most platform ...[12]

The royal party were introduced and shook hands with the assembled party of civic dignitaries and prominent citizens, including Henry and his newly elected deputy chairman William Younger. As if to emphasize that the royal visit was in no way a glorification of victory, there were only a few representatives of the Military High Command in attendance. The route all along Princes Street was lined by boy scouts and girl guides, and in positions where they could get a view there were

> wounded sailors and soldiers ... many firms along the route had given over their windows to the men who had suffered and been broken and bruised in their country's cause. Perched on the top of a taxi-cab were a few Jack Tars [*Royal Naval seamen*], who had obviously been in a "scrap" of some kind, and in passing they and their lady attendants received a special recognition from their Majesties.[13]

Millions of words have been written about the deeds of the men who fought in the Great War, of their bravery under constant attack and of their endurance in the most terrible of conditions. In 1934 General Jack Seely wrote a tale of the courage and tenacity of an often overlooked, but nevertheless vital, contingent of the war effort: the horses and mules who had played their part on the battlefields of France.

Early in the New Year of 1915, General Seely had been summoned to the War Office in London and told that he was to command all the Canadian Cavalry. And so then a link was established back to the late Sir Hugh: among the regiments that General Seely would command was Lord Strathcona's Mounted Horse. Strathcona, before his ennoblement, was Donald Alexander Smith, a Scottish born Canadian, and a contemporary and business partner of Sir Hugh's. Together they had forged a new country in the wilderness that was Canada, always aware of the other's power and influence, and occasionally they were on opposite sides of the argument.

General Seely was to command 3,000 Canadians in what could have become an impossible task if it were not for his legendary horse, Warrior. Cinderella may have gone to the ball as a scullery maid and come back a princess, but Warrior, Cinderella's foal, went to war as a thoroughbred and came home a hero and a mascot to the men of the Canadian Cavalry Brigade. Up until the moment he first met the Canadians, Warrior had been the favoured star among a small group of horses at General Headquarters.

> It was a new life for him. He had experienced for many months the shocks and excitement of modern war and had learnt to control himself at terrifying moments, but he had always been a member of a small and select party ... Now he met some thousands of his own kind and had to be one of them. He rose to the occasion, and made friends with them all, unless, I am bound to add, one of them should prove unduly familiar or quarrelsome. He earned the respect and, indeed, the affection of all of them.[14]

It did not take long for the Canadian Cavalry Brigade to develop respect and admiration for their new commander, and to esteem Warrior as a truly remarkable animal. The war-weary men believed that if Warrior came through the battles unscathed (as he did, although he had many very narrow escapes) they would survive as long as he did. The cry of "Here's old Warrior" would often ring out across the devastated countryside.

In March 1918 the Canadian Cavalry Brigade, led by General Seely and Warrior, were engaged in one of the most deadly battles of the war at Moreuil Wood. Seely, not for the first time nor the last, knew where the courage and determination of both the cavalrymen and the horses came from:

> It is indeed the truth, that so far as I am concerned the credit for this wild adventure, which succeeded in so miraculous a fashion, was due not to

me, but to my horse Warrior. He did not flinch, though well he knew the danger from those swift bullets which he had seen kill so many hundreds of men and horses ... The main attack swept up and the wood soon filled with galloping Canadian horsemen. Both sides, ours and the Germans, seemed to be filled with some extraordinary exaltation.[15]

It seems inconceivable that when the guns finally fell silent the War Office could not, did not even wish to, return all the surviving horses to their homelands. More than a million horses had been sent to the Western Front, but only 100,000 were considered worth saving. In December 1918, the War Office announced that they had provided 50,000 horses to the Belgian Government to help with reconstruction, and only 25,000 of the youngest and strongest horses would be returned to Britain. The French would buy as many as they could afford for their slaughterhouses, but the fate of the rest lay in the hands of the British people. Needless to say, General Seely ensured that Warrior returned to his pre-war home on the Isle of Wight, where he lived the rest of his long life among the lush green meadows overlooking the sea that he loved. He died aged 33 in 1941.

Janie Allan, from the moment she heard of the plight of the war horses, was determined to rescue as many as she could afford. She was helped in her task by another lady, Ada Cole, who had witnessed the terrible treatment of animals in Belgian even before the war had begun. As early as the spring of 1914 she saw the first fruits of her campaign for the better treatment of horses:

> Ada's efforts to raise the awareness of the export of horses for slaughter came to fruition in 1914 with an Act of Parliament (a new Law) which amended an 1898 Government order and prohibited the export of horses unless veterinary inspectors certified the animals "to be capable of being conveyed and disembarked without cruelty". It also stated that every vessel should be equipped to humanely end their lives. [16]

She went on to form the International League for the Protection of Horses (now World Horse Welfare) and to set up the Ada Cole Stables in Norwich, now part of the Redwings Horse Sanctuary. Regrettably, the Act of Parliament that she thought would end their suffering was never enforced. The suffering of these noble animals still continues.

Janie was certain she could find suitable homes among her many relatives and friends. All the horses Janie brought back to Scotland were afforded the very best of accommodation on the ships that she chartered and were well fed. The extent of her intervention can be judged from an article:

> Since the Armistice was signed, up to the present time 62,520 horses have been sold in the United Kingdom for £2,075,858, at an average price of £33.4s … The highest price has been reached in Scotland – £41.11s.7d.[17]

It must be said that there was fervent opposition from the War Emergency Committee of the Royal Agricultural Society of England regarding the repatriation of any horses. Sir John Thorold, as chairman of the Committee, had a resolution passed at one of their meetings, to the effect that

> the War Emergency Committee desires to call the attention of the War Office to the grave danger attending the repatriation of Army horses from France owing to the prevalence of a malignant form of ophthalmia and from other infectious diseases in a more or less epidemic form among those horses. It is hoped that special care will be taken to safeguard the interests of horse owners and live stock breeders in the United Kingdom.[18]

Sir John Thorold did not say what should be done with the sick and traumatized horses, but thankfully there were people like Janie, Ada and General Seely who cared for the welfare of those gallant heroic creatures, never forgetting the debt of gratitude they owed them. Men and women of the Allan family, and many men from all the Dominions, including the Canadian Cavalry Brigade, never forgot Warrior. Both he and they should always be remembered for their heroism and their sacrifices.

During the war Janie and other members of the Suffragette Movement called a halt to their protests. However, the war gave women in all walks of life a taste of freedom. They had left the drudgery of housework for work outside the home and for the first time the working class women had earned their own money. It would be another decade before women were given the vote on a level of equality with men, but Janie never faltered in her beliefs that the demands of the Suffragette Movement would one day be met.

Chapter 19

An Uncertain Future

A mood of enthusiasm and a renewed feeling of confidence swept the nation with the ending of the war. The signing of the Treaty at Versailles with Germany in June 1919, and the first mention of the formation of a League of Nations to prevent any further wars, gave the country a cautious sense of optimism.

Janie Allan would have been among those women who welcomed the news that Nancy Astor had been elected as the first woman to take her seat in the House of Commons. The aims and aspirations of the Suffragette Movement had been suspended since 1914, but now women were hoping that all they had fought for could be achieved without further conflict.

It was not that the horrors of war would be forgotten, but there was a belief that now the country could return to a happier time. Industries would continue to expand, new markets would be found, and the wealthy would soon be able to enjoy their pleasures once again.

Claud came back from his war service and purchased in 1919 the mansion house of Kilmahew and its extensive grounds, having been John William Burns's tenant there since 1908. Around the same time Henry bought Torrance House in East Kilbride, a home he would occupy for the rest of his life. Although not decorated for his service on the battlefield of Europe, Henry was appointed an Officer of the Legion of Honour by the French Government for the services rendered by the Caledonian Railway Company.

RichardG, Agnes and their son Dick were by 1922 living at Dunalton House, Monkton, Ayrshire. RobertS still had a Glasgow home but it appears he had taken over the tenancy of the Hafton Estate.

Col Bryce returned a decorated war hero and immediately took up his role as "the young laird of Aros", trying to relieve his elderly father of much of the day-to-day running of the vast estate.

In April 1919 a special meeting was held on Aros to discuss the re-opening of the Tobermory Golf Club. The club had been in existence since 1896, and from 1907 until the outbreak of war Col Bryce had been their president. The meeting in April agreed that there were funds in the club's accounts to help with the refurbishment, but donations and subscriptions from members would be needed to carry out all the repairs. Although the club was not operating during the war years, Alexander had held the nominal position of President while Col Bryce was away on active service. To further help the club with their project to re-open the club, Alexander offered the services of his head gardener, John Cameron, to get the course ready for play. For the next seventeen years Col Bryce held the position of president, and in 1920 he presented the President's Cup to the club.

It is a stunningly beautiful course, according to those who have played on it, perched as it is on the cliff tops above Tobermory Bay. On clear summer days it has a spectacular backdrop of Ardnamurchan and Loch Sunart, and sometimes the golfer can even get a glimpse of the Isle of Skye. According to a report in *The Scotsman* in January 2008 it is now "the best 9-hole golf course in Scotland". There is a delightful anecdote that in 1924 the course layout was changed to avoid problems with sheep and cattle wandering across the fairways and greens.

Hamish spent the early months of peace recovering from his wounds. He seemed to be disillusioned with the world he had returned to, and had little idea of what the future held for him. He had known Helen Boyce Scott as a fellow pupil at Bedales, and perhaps in her company he felt he could relive the joys of the simpler life he had lived at school. On the 18 September 1919 he and Helen were married at Christchurch, Westminster. She was the daughter of the late John Bell Scott from Philadelphia; her mother Marian Isabel was French but at the time of her daughter's marriage was resident in London. Rather against the convention of the time it was she who gave her daughter away. It would appear from the announcement of the wedding that Hamish was married without the support of his brother or any other member of the Allan family: his best man was a Mr Bourne. Mrs Scott gave a reception at Caxton Hall.

JamesH died on 7 February 1919 at Shrawley Wood House, Worcester-shire; he had purchased the estate when he retired in the early 1900s. It is difficult to sum up JamesH's character. That he was a private man cannot be disputed; that he worked and lived in the shadow of his elder brother RobertG also cannot be disputed. His marriage to Clara had lasted for almost forty-four years, during which time they had had two daughters. The elder, Hilda Mary, was the wife of Bryce of Aros, and they were the parents of his only grandchild, Alastair Hugh. His younger daughter, Doris, did not marry until 1905, shortly after moving with her parents to Shrawley Wood. There is a portrait of Doris still hanging in the dining-room of Hanbury Hall, the home of her suitor. The portrait, by the Hon John Collier, shows a Pre-Raphaelite style painting of an elegant, dark-haired beauty, which indeed she was when she married Bowater George Hamilton Vernon, the only son of Sir Harry Foley Vernon Bt and his wife Georgina Sophia Baillie-Hamilton. He was seventeen years older than Doris, but if JamesH and Clara had any doubts about the disparity in the ages of Doris and Bowater they probably did not voice them to their pretty young daughter.

Doris and Bowater (he frequently used his second name of George) spent much of the first twenty years of their marriage away from Hanbury Hall. They went to South Africa, returning home in 1910. Bowater also had farming interest in Argentina, and they made frequent trips to the Caribbean. JamesH and Clara must have been disappointed that with Hilda now in Edinburgh, and Doris travelling the world, they did not have the pleasure of their daughters' company. Clara must have hoped when Doris returned to Hanbury Hall she would visit Shrawley Wood and her parents more frequently.

As was the custom at the time, JamesH, in his Will, made two bequests, both dependent on Clara outliving him and not remarrying. Clara outlived her husband by some twenty-seven years, during which time she continued to live at Shrawley Wood House. It is doubtful if, when she died in 1945 after the years of depression and another world war, she was able to honour her husband's bequests of £10,000 each to the Worcester Infirmary and the Liverpool Cathedral Fund.

Sir Montagu and Lady Marguerite returned to Canada and Ravenscrag in October 1919. They sailed aboard the *Empress of France.* It is impossible to imagine what Marguerite may have been feeling as she stepped on board the ship; the last ship she had been on was the *Lusitania,* a terrible voyage which had taken the lives of her two young daughters, Anna and Gwen. She may have recovered from her injuries but her mourning for her daughters never fully left her. She was also returning home without her only son Hugh. Only Martha was left of the four children she had before the outbreak of war. She shared her suffering with so many other families in Britain and Canada: across the world mothers had lost not just one son but two or more, and they now rest in foreign graves attended by the Commonwealth War Graves Commission, their white memorials a symbol of the waste and brutality of war.

The death of Nathaniel Dunlop in November 1919 broke a link with the Allan family that had begun sixty-two years earlier when he had entered the service of J & A Allan as a clerk. He became a director on his marriage to Ellen Smith in 1866; she died shortly after the birth of their daughter, Ellen. Nathaniel never remarried. He devoted his life to the Allan Line, to his philanthropic work, and his daughter. She became his hostess and constant companion.

In 1901, on the death of Old Andrew, Nathaniel had become chairman of the company, a position he held until he retired in 1907. It was in that year he was awarded a knighthood and an honorary degree in law from the University of Glasgow.

In 1898 Nathaniel purchased an estate at Shieldhall, near Biggar

> and since [then] he has found his chief recreation in remodelling the old mansion house and improving the condition of the policies and farms on the property. Among other additions he has erected a hall for Sunday services and winter lectures, and a reading room for the tenantry. In

this and other philanthropic work he has the warm assistance of his daughter, Miss Dunlop.[1]

Listing his achievements would take a whole biography, but it is worth mentioning that Nathaniel was very much devoted to the improvement of shipping and ship-management. He served for decades on the Clyde Trust, becoming Chairman; he was also Chairman of the Clyde Pilot Board. He was one of the founder members and the first Chairman of the British Corporation for Survey and Registration of Shipping. Finally, he was the first Scottish Chairman of the Chamber of Shipping of the United Kingdom.

> Outside the arena of shipping he has taken a share in several burning economic problems, notably on the Fiscal Policy, on great currency questions of India, and on the bi-metallic heresy and he has published numerous interesting and instructive pamphlets on these and other subjects.[2]

He died as he was about to enter the ninth decade of his life. Born in rural Campbeltown in 1830, he had witnessed the growth of the shipping from sail to steam. He had seen at first hand the tremendous changes brought about by the industrialization of the world, and in the last few years of his life he had seen the destructive effects of the Great War. A long life and one that should be remembered and honoured.

The military conflict in Europe was over, but the 1920s saw years of political and social unrest throughout the land. The returning servicemen were no longer the silent majority, they wanted a greater say in how their lives were governed. The 1917 Bolshevik Revolution in Russia had sent shock waves through the capitalists and wealthy landowners and they were determined to hold on to what they believed was their birthright. The rise of the Trade Union Movement, and in particular the Triple Alliance of the Seamen's Union, the Mineworkers and the Railway workers was a cause for anxiety among industrialists and employers in every corner of the country. Many on the politically Conservative wing urged the Government to consider sending military troops to help quell the Bolsheviks. A dread and a fear of a Communist take-over was a concern which ran through many sections of society.

The start of 1920 saw Henry receive the Legion of Honour from the French Consul, Monsieur Naya, acting on behalf of the French President Poincare. The presentation was held at the offices of the Caledonian Railway Company, and after accepting the award, Henry made a short speech saying that he *"accepted the Cross as a compliment to the Caledonian Railway Company and a high honour for himself"*.[3]

Less than a week later Henry received yet another honour. He had been a director of the Clydesdale Bank for a number of years, but with the death of Lord Inverclyde, James Burns of the Cunard Line, Henry was elected vice-chairman. It was as if the board of the bank felt it necessary to replace one shipowner with another man steeped in the ways of the sea and shipping. Henry was now chairman of a railway company and vice-chairman of a bank. During the next few years, as industry tried to recover from the hardship caused by the War, Henry was in a prime position to witness the enormous changes in the world. He would see demands for higher pay by the workers, while also seeing the decline in the profitability of manufacturing industries. There was, however, still time for the odd moment of pomp and pageantry: he was again in Edinburgh to welcome HM King George V and Queen Mary for another State Visit. He was also among the congregation at St Giles' Cathedral for an impressive thanksgiving service.

On the domestic front, Janie was advertising for a table maid, and from the wording of her advertisement it would appear that she and Henry were both living at Torrence House, East Kilbride. The war had seen a dramatic reduction in the number of young women who wanted to enter service, yet Janie was able to tell prospective employees that though there were only two people living at Torrance House, the domestic staff numbered eight.

Janie was heavily involved with the Scottish Council for Women's Trade, being joint honorary treasurer with Sir John Mann. At the twenty-sixth annual meeting in 1921, she and the Executive Committee were concerned about unemployment amongst women. They had

> taken various opportunities during the year for pressing on the attention of the authorities the scheme drafted by them some time ago for the establishment of an experimental co-operative small holding colony for

women, as they believed that agricultural and labour colonies offer special possibilities for dealing with the problem of unemployment.[4]

Janie had been a leading proponent of the agricultural labour colonies for men since the late 1890s, and it would have made sense to her to widen the scheme to help unemployed women.

Col Bryce, apart from his duties on Aros, was also involved in the Scout Movement and in 1921 was present at a meeting between the Scottish Scout Executive and the local Forfarshire scouting officials. The Rev Guthrie Law, secretary for Forfarshire, thought the expansion of officials would not lead to greater efficiency. Col Bryce as chairman and R Goudie as vice-chairman of the Scottish Executive had other ideas; they thought the formation of Group Councils (which had been adopted all over Scotland, with the exception of Forfarshire) should be finally accepted by all members. The Executive also thought the time had now come for better training of scoutmasters, and for arranging weekend camps for scoutmasters who could not attend large training sessions during the working week.

In June 1921, Sir Hugh's eldest daughter Elizabeth died in Middlesex; she was the widow of George Carson Gribbon whom she had married in Montreal in 1867. He was a brigade surgeon, some eleven years her senior, of Irish descent and a graduate of Trinity College, Dublin. It would be easy to speculate on how they met, but a dashing young brigade surgeon would have been warmly welcomed into the community of the Golden Square Mile. He and his fellow officers would have been much in demand at balls and parties given for the pretty unmarried daughters of the wealthy merchants.

The couple had seven children, three daughters and four sons. The eldest child, was, according to some records, born in Ireland in 1872 but unnamed; the birth of a second daughter, Rose Maud, was registered in Hampshire. Nora and two of her brothers, George and Henry, were born in the East Indies, indicating that George's army commitments took him abroad a good deal. Two more sons were born in Hampshire between 1883 and 1885, suggesting that George may have left the army some time after his fiftieth birthday. In the 1891 Census the family were resident in Kensington, London, and George says he is retired but still working as an "Examiner of Recruits, Registered Practitioner". Regrettably his retirement did not last for many years: he died in 1894 at Christchurch, Hampshire, just months before his eldest daughter, Rose Maud, married Ernest Kenneth Campbell.

Bryce of Wemyss Bay lived long enough to see the end of the Great War and to know that his son James Bryce and his son-in-law Cyril Falconer Stewart had come home safely. James Bryce had served with the RNVR from 1914 until 1922, and as one would have expected, had served with distinction. Cyril Stewart had married Annie in September 1915 while serving as a Officer in the Territorial Army. In 1920 their son Ronald George Falconer Stewart was born, giving Bryce and Annie their first grandchild.

Bryce died at his home, Cliff House, on 2 August 1922 of pneumonia complicated by a serious heart condition. He was sixty-three. As the youngest of Capt James's sons he played a role in the running of the Allan companies, he was also a staunch supporter of his brother-in-law John Stewart Clark. Bryce and Annie were frequently to be seen at all the grand social occasions which Clark held both in Paisley and at Dundas Castle. Social life and salons did not however occupy first place in Bryce's leisure plans: as with his brothers and his cousins, it was yachting which was his all-consuming passion.

Shortly after Bryce's death, his widow and his son James Bryce, in wishing to honour the memory of a great yachtsman, decided that Bryce's true memorial should be for them to donate a Cup in his name. In July 1923 there was a press announcement under a banner headline "Cup for Royal Western Club":

> In memory of the late Mr Bryce Allan, who for many years took an active interest in Clyde racing, his widow and son have presented to the Royal Western Yacht Club a sum of money, the interest to provide a cup

annually to be competed for at the mid-season cruising matches of the Club. The prize is to be known as the "Bryce Allan Cup". The first will be sailed on Saturday in the Club's cruising matches from Hunter's Quay to Tighnabruaich, the cup going to the winning yacht on a general handicap.[5]

The Cup was first won by D T Cassels, sailing a Pleiad Class yacht named *Merope*. Today the Bryce Allan Cup is still regarded as a prize worth winning.

When Montagu and Marguerite returned to Ravenscrag in late 1919 they must have hoped they could look forward to a period of quiet reflection after the terrible tragedies they had so recently suffered. Their hopes were soon shattered. In March 1922 they were embroiled in yet another banking scandal; Montagu, as President of the Merchants' Bank, and his General Manager D C Macarow, were summoned to appear before the Canadian Department of Finance and Minister of Finance in connection with an allegation that they had jointly been guilty of serious errors in their dealings on behalf of the bank.

> The charge against Sir Montagu Allan is that he signed, approved, and concurred in reports which, it is alleged, contained false and deceptive statements with regard to the Bank's financial position.[6]

The charge against Macarow was the same but with another allegation that he wilfully made false and deceptive statements in returns to the Department of Finance. A summons was issued by Judge Cusson of Montreal, and the report went on to say that other charges would involve other members of the Montreal banking elite.

> The whole of the Merchants' Bank affair is almost certain to come before Parliament, Mr Meighen, backed by the Progressives as well as his own party, demanding an investigation. It is not without interest that Mr Ballantyne, the former Minister of Marine, was one of the directors of the Merchants' Bank, and that Senator Webster, a most influential Conservative politician, was also a member of the board.[7]

The reporter, for reasons best known only to him, had to remind his readers that Sir Montagu was the son of Sir Hugh Allan. Sir Hugh had been dead for more than four decades, but if there was mischief in high places

in Montreal, his name was always recalled. The case against Montagu
dragged on for months. At an earlier hearing both he and Macacrow had
been found not guilty, but his persecutors could not let the matter drop. In
November the matter of guilt or innocence was finally resolved by Chief
Justice Decarie. In his summing up, Decarie declared:

> The president cannot be charged with negligence in not doing what
> it is impossible for him to do. On this occasion the accused used the
> greatest possible diligence with the greatest prudence. He was facing very
> heavy responsibilities towards the bank, its directors, shareholders, and
> depositors. His conduct in these grave days was that of an honest man, of
> an honourable man. As soon as he could, at great sacrifice to himself, he
> saved the bank from what he feared would be a great disaster [8]

Sir Montagu had saved the Merchants' Bank after they incurred enormous
losses resulting from making a number of very bad loans. Eight decades
later, more banks with impeccable reputations would make similar terrible
mistakes, but few of their directors could walk away, as Sir Montagu did,
with their reputations for integrity intact. A day after the end of the trial Sir
Montagu, Marguerite and Martha sailed for England, a chance to recover
from the strain of those dark days of 1922.

The year 1922 ended on a much happier note. On Boxing Day, RichardG
and his son Dick were at Fairlie House, near Kilmarnock, for a meeting of
the Eglington Hunt. Did they, as they set off to chase the fox that day, look
around and muse that in 1750, their great-great-grandfather, James, had
been born in an estate worker's cottage in the grounds of Fairlie House?
Would James have shaken his head in wonder that his descendents were
sharing a day's hunting with the Marchioness of Bute, Lady Mary Stuart,
and the Earl of Dumfries? The Allan family had come a very long way since
1750.

Chapter 20

Sayonara

There is no direct correlation between two incidents that happened between the end of 1922 and the beginning of 1923, except that they both took place in the Valley of the Kings in Egypt. In early November 1922, after years of excavating ancient Egyptian burial sites, the British-born archaeologist Howard Carter finally repaid all the hopes (and money) that the 5th Earl of Carnarvon, George Edward Stanhope Molyneux Herbert, a passionate Egyptologist, had invested in searching for the treasures of the Valley of the Kings. On the 5 November Carter and his team of workmen broke through the last remaining obstacle of the Tomb of Rameses VI and entered the chamber of King Tutankhamun.

Hugh Travers Allan, son of Alexander Rae Allan and the grandson of Sir Hugh, was in Egypt on holiday from his home in Brockville, Ontario. He was, according to all who knew him, rather like his late father: a quiet, gentle man who did not enjoy the cut and thrust of business and commerce. Again like his father, he had spent some time working for the Bank of Montreal, but he retired in his late forties, and spent his time in leisurely exploration of Europe and North Africa.

He visited Luxor in January, very probably because he was aware of the excitement caused by Carter's amazing discoveries, and wanted to see the site for himself. It was a fateful decision. On 1 February, news reached Montreal that Hugh Travers Allan had died at Luxor on 30 January. The reports were initially rather vague, but it became soon very clear that Travers had been brutally robbed and murdered. The police in Cairo and the British consular officials were sent to Luxor to investigate the circumstances of his death. Reports in the British newspapers said that Travers's death was a consequence of the political, religious and tribal unrest that had swept Egypt since it had gained its independence from Britain a year earlier. Added to which there were rumours circulating that in desecrating the

193

Tomb of Tutankhamun, Carter had unleashed a Curse on all who looked on the Face of the Boy King. It was left to a British correspondent in Cairo to try to calm fears, but the report would have done nothing to alleviate the distress of Travers's relatives and friends in Canada.

> Lest intending visitors to Egypt should be caused unnecessary concern … it is desirable that it should be understood that this crime has no appearance of being an outrage such as committed in Cairo last year.
>
> Investigation has yet to establish the full facts, but on the face of the matter there is not the slightest indication of racial hostility or even hostility against foreigners. It is apparently an ordinary sordid crime with repulsive aspects, and noteworthy merely because it happened to be perpetrated in the same locality as Tutankhamun's tomb.[1]

Poor Travers was just in the wrong place at the wrong time, and his murder, however horrific, could not be allowed to deter the tourists wishing to visit Egypt. It is not even possible to ascertain if any one was ever convicted of his murder. A few months later the death of the Earl of Carnarvon from septicaemia at the age of fifty-six eclipsed poor Travers's murder in the newspapers, since it gave the myth-makers an opportunity of building up the legend of the Curse of Tutankhamun's tomb. (Howard Carter, the other discoverer, lived until 1939 and died aged sixty-five.)

Henry and the rest of the Allan family must have viewed Travers's death with sadness and dismay, but as they all knew there was little they could do in Canada to bring to justice unknown and unidentified criminals in Egypt.

Henry was busy with board meetings in the early months of 1923, although it was noted that it was not unusual for him to be absent from monthly board meetings. It was said on more than one occasion that he preferred to be out fishing or shooting rather than sitting in a boardroom. In this, of course, he was not alone. RichardG and Dick rarely missed a meeting of the Eglington Hunt, and had little time or enthusiasm for the rigours of commerce. Col Bryce of Aros, apart from his responsibilities for the estate, could always find time and enthusiasm for scout meetings. In June 1923 he was at a conference at Dunblane Hydropathic Hospital in his role as President of the Boy Scouts' Association of Scotland.

At the AGM of the Clydesdale Bank in February 1923 it was Henry's task as deputy chairman to respond to the decision of Sir James Bell to retire from his position of chairman, a post he had held for twelve years. Henry spoke eloquently of Sir James's contribution to the work of the bank:

> I think we must all recognize that we owe a great debt of gratitude to Sir James for his wise and successful guidance. The announcement of his retirement will be universally felt as a great loss to the Board and to the Company. I do not wish to anticipate subsequent proceedings [*Henry knew that he would be elected to replace Sir James*], but I feel that we should not pass over the public announcement of Sir James's intention to retire without trying to express our very high appreciation of his great services to the Bank. [2]

Henry's appointment as Chairman was duly made and he took up his duties in good time for the Bank's next AGM in January 1924.

The early 1920s were not a good time for banks, bankers or industries. As Henry pointed out in 1925, the over-expansion of heavy industries during the war had led to a significant decline of orders. He warned that in Scotland, with its reliance on heavy industries and exports, they were not in a position to forecast the future with any degree of accuracy. He feared the next few years would be even more troublesome; he gloomily predicted that industrial and trade union disputes, high unemployment and low wages would cause major headaches for much of the next decade.

It was, however, not just banks and banking problems that worried Henry. He was also concerned about the state of the railways. As he admitted at a meeting in February:

> although railway wages in many grades are still too high, there has been a considerable reduction in working costs since 1921 due largely to the reduced costs of fuel, and many other materials, as well as some reductions in wages. [3]

He had been grappling for some months with the proposed merger of the Caledonian with the London, Midland and Scottish Company. He was opposed to the merger, and when it became obvious that it would take place, Henry relinquished his connections with the new company.

Henry was first and foremost a banker, but his early years as part of the Allan Line management team had given him a broad insight into the commercial, political and social problems which faced the nation. He could articulate these problems better than most men and he found himself

> on the side of the employers, although he believed that the root of the problem was a growing class conflict which he attributed to the deflation which had caused unemployment and wage reductions. The solution was to find some way of restoring prosperity to the "depressed industries".[4]

Almost ninety years after he gave that warning, we may feel that there was indeed something very prophetic in Henry's words.

Friendship between Bedales ex-pupils was not unexpected but it must have been unusual for two brothers each to marry their former school friends. Hamish had married Helen Scott in 1919, and a little over four years later, in December 1924, Hamish's younger brother Jack married Gwyneth Howard Jones. Gwyneth was the daughter of Alfred Ernest Jones, an export commission agent, and Hilda Straker, the daughter of Frederick William Straker, a stationer and printer. Jack's and Hilda's marriage was registered in Alton, Hampshire; their only son Hugh Andrew was not born until May 1942.

After leaving Bedales in 1918, Jack went to Denmark and studied for a diploma in physical education, and it was education that would occupy him for the rest of his working life. But, unlike his uncle RobertS, it would not be the restricted curriculum of State board schools but the more social progressive education that had first attracted his father, JamesA, to Bedales. Around 1926 Jack became a member of staff at Dartington Hall, near Totnes, Devon. The school was the creation of two extraordinary people, Leonard Elmhirst and his American heiress wife, Dorothy Whitney Straight. Their desire was to build a school community that would be as opposite as possible to that provided by the traditional public and state education system. They wanted children to be free to learn at their own pace and to follow their own interests and talents. They passionately believed that learning by rote was against the interests of the child. The school was to be a co-educational boarding establishment, again in contrast to the single-sex public and private schools.

Jack's decision to join the staff at Dartington could well have been influenced by the similarly progressive education he had received at Bedales and in Denmark. Like so many of his Allan relatives he was essentially a private man dedicated to social progress and improving national welfare, and (again like so many Allans), he valued physical fitness and healthy outdoor activities above academic learning.

As with all new and experimental ideas, there were exaggerated and outrageous claims made about Dartington. It was said by some to be a hot-bed of free love; or, perhaps even more alarmingly for prospective parents, a nudist colony. The staff (rumour had it) had all been trained in Moscow, and were communists to the core. It is true that the ethos of the school leaned towards socialist principles, and it was there that Jack first encountered the concepts of contributory pension-schemes, sickness benefit, health benefits to provide for medical treatment, a minimum wage for all workers, and an additional amount paid to married staff.

Two men influenced Jack's time at Dartington: the first was William Burnless Curry, who went to Dartington in 1931 as headmaster. He had previously been at Bedales. The second was Dr Roger Henry Bolton, of the Peckham Health Centre; the connection between Jack and Peckham continued for many years. Peckham, like so many London boroughs in the late 1920s, was a deprived district where disease and poor diet were rife and where life expectancy was low. The Peckham Experiment begun by Dr George Scott Williamson and his wife Innes Hope Pearse aimed to encourage families by giving them a small amount of money in return for them taking part in physical activities, and by eating more fresh food. The two pioneers were certain the health of the parents would eventually bring about an improvement in the health of their children.

To encourage the growing of their own vegetables and fruit, in the 1920s there was an expansion of the allotment scheme, whereby for a small yearly cost a family could rent a plot of land from the local council or from the Church of England and grow their own fresh food. The idea of allotments was taken from the kitchen gardens of the country estates, which supplied the "big house" giving the cooks reliable access to fresh produce.

CharlesE had been in Belfast for a little over three decades when he decided to return to the mainland. He had observed the destruction caused by the Easter Rising of 1916 and the savagery of the troops as they fought to put an end to the nationalism which was sweeping the whole of the island; then more recently Belfast people had suffered in the Irish War of Independence, and this was followed by the turmoil of Partition and, south of the new border, the Civil War which had followed the setting up of the new Irish Free State. The desire of the Irish people to be independent of British rule has ancient roots; in 1923 for many republicans it was a still unfulfilled dream, while for many protestants in the north it had become an increasing threat.

CharlesE left Belfast only too aware that the city was vulnerable not only to political turmoil but also to forthcoming industrial conflicts. In September 1921 Workman & Clark had been acquired by a syndicate of powerful shipowners headed by Lord Pirrie and the Northumberland Shipbuilding Company. Workman & Clark had been under a cloud for a number of years, even though George Smith Clark had been knighted in 1917 for his services to industry and politics. He had been the Conservative/Unionist Member of Parliament for Belfast North between 1907 and 1910. It is also worth noting that in 1913 Workman & Clark had allegedly been involved in gun-running for the Ulster Volunteer Force. It is impossible to know CharlesE's views on the political machinations of the Irish protestants, but with Georgie a member of the Church of Christian Science, and his own family's liberal traditions, it is hard to believe he was a supporter of any religious or political extremist faction.

CharlesE must have realized that the takeover of Workman & Clark was a good time to signal his wish to retire; he was fifty-five, with a wife and young daughter, Mickey. As he contemplated retirement he was not to know that his involvement with Workman & Clark would continue for many years after he left Belfast.

However, the decision to leave Ireland and his home at Stormont left him with another dilemma: he did not have a home on the mainland. In February 1924, CharlesE purchased from Sir Herbert Frederick Cook, barrister, art connoisseur and historian, the imposing and magnificent estate of Baynards Park, Cranleigh, Surrey. There is evidence to suggest that CharlesE only bought the lease from Cook.

Baynards once formed part of a royal demesne of Gornshall, and was held
by Harold. After the Battle of Hastings the manor was given by William to
Baynard, from whom it takes its name. Sir George More built the present
mansion, which stands in the centre of a park, the estate extending to
1,519 acres.[5]

The mansion up to that point had had a rather chequered past. In the
fifteenth century a Tudor mansion had been built by Sir George More of
Losely, which later became the home of Sir Thomas More, Lord Chancellor
of England under Henry VIII. More found it hard to square his conscience
when Henry wished to break away from the Church of Rome in order to
divorce his first wife, Catherine and marry Anne Boleyn. More was willing
to swear fidelity to the new Act of Succession, but he steadfastly refused
to take the oath that would have denied the Pope's authority and given a
legal basis to Henry's divorce of Catherine. This could not be tolerated by
Henry. More was charged with treason, and on 6 July 1535 he was executed
by decapitation at Tyburn. As was the custom at the time, his head was
exhibited at London Bridge and Catholic Europe was justifiably angered by
Henry's savagery of the treatment of his once trusted servant.

More's daughter, Margaret Roper, bribed a guard and brought her
father's head back to Baynards, where for the rest of the life of the great house
Sir Thomas's ghost was said to roam the premises, holding his decapitated
head in his hands. Shortly after CharlesE purchased Baynards his nephew
CharlesC stayed at the house, and was one of those who believed he had
seen Sir Thomas's ghostly figure. On future visits to his uncle CharlesC
refused to stay in the room he had originally occupied.

In 1832, the original Tudor house had been rebuilt by the Rev
Thomas Thurlow, and the Thurlow family did not sell the entire estate
until 1952. Baynard Park mansion, as it was when CharlesE lived there,
no longer exists; rather like Sir Thomas it had a less than grand demise.
In 1965 it was purchased by Sir Alan Bristow, of Bristow Helicopters, who
was unimpressed by the dark and dingy house and sought permission
to demolish it and build a modern home fit for the twentieth century.
Unfortunately Sir Alan had not taken into consideration the opposition
such a plan would create in the hearts of the conservationists and amenity
groups. Regrettably, they could not, and never were, able to raise the
money needed to buy the house and restore it to its original condition. For
the next eleven years the house slowly died of neglect, and in 1979 it was

destroyed by fire. Rumours abounded that the fire was the result of arson, but no one was ever convicted. It leaves open the question, has any one seen the ghost of Sir Thomas More wandering the grounds as he looks for refuge in a new home?

The Hon Jean Crawford Bingham died in July 1924 at the Sutherland Arms Hotel, Golspie. She had been at the hotel for some time and had been ill, according to her death certificate, for three weeks or more. Her usual residence was given as Doris Street, London. She had been a widow since 1907 when her husband Albert Yelverton Bingham died in Plymouth. Strangely, for the times in which they lived, and his aristocratic background, they left very little information as to their lives, or the contribution they made to the world around them. They travelled widely, visiting Australia and South Africa according to the shipping passenger lists, but whether these were pleasure or business trips it has been impossible to determine. Albert's obituary was very sparse, noting only that he was Deputy-Lieutenant for County Mayo and the sixth son of Baron Clanmorris.

The informant of Jean's death was RobertS, and it is to be assumed that he was called to Golspie when it was feared she might die alone in the hotel. As a wealthy woman in her own right, Jean chose as her executors her Allan cousins, RobertS, Henry and Claud, and Frederick William Workman. There was no mention of Albert's son by his first wife.

CharlesE was certainly determined to enjoy retirement to the full. He took a long tenancy at Dunbeath Castle from Vice-Admiral Sir Edwyn Alexander-Sinclair. The Sinclair family had owned the stunning castle perched on the rocky coast of Caithness for more than three centuries. Dunbeath would afford CharlesE a base for fishing and shooting, although in 1923 he had also been fishing at Aboyne and had a record catch that year. Later he had a fishing lodge at Drumnagesk, but the sea was in the blood of the Allan family and it was not surprising that he should decide to take a long voyage on a yacht. Characteristically, CharlesE did not choose any ordinary yacht for his cruise to Norway: he rented a superior royal yacht, the 766 ton *S Y Sayonara,* from Grand Admiral the Archduke Charles Stephen of Austria. Launched from the Ramage & Ferguson yard of Leith in 1911, *Sayonara* had provided the Archduke with much enjoyment until the Great War saw the end of his yachting activities in Britain.

CharlesE, Georgie, her maid Kennedy and ten-year-old Mickey together with her governess … Miss Cohen left Guildford by train on 1 July. At Euston Station they met four of their guests, Georgie's sister Mary, her husband Alexander Stronach and their fifteen-year-old daughter, Helen Sybil Graham (known as Sybil). Mickey and Sybil were cousins, indeed there were some who thought the two girls were sisters. The fourth member of the party was "Threlford".

It has been difficult to identify this "Threlford" with any degree of accuracy; assumptions and guesswork are sometimes unavoidable. There is one man who would have made a very plausible companion for CharlesE and his family: William Lacon Threlford, who was born in Essex in 1883 and educated in London, Boulogne and Strasbourg. He qualified as a chartered accountant with his own practice in London. He had joined the RNVR in 1906 and served with distinction in the Royal Navy during the War, with the Grand Fleet. He was also at the time of the cruise unmarried, and it is clear that CharlesE's "Threlford" was the only member of the party who did not have a female companion.

The party from London were joined in Aberdeen by Francis and Alice Henderson. A contemporary of CharlesE, Henderson was a shipowner. George Smith, CharlesE's butler, had arrived in Aberdeen two days before the party, to make sure everything on board was ready for the guests.

Mickey's governess kept a diary of the voyage to Norway, and it would be very tempting to recount all she wrote; however, it would be impractical to do more than mention some of the delightful insights the diary offers into the pleasure CharlesE was affording his quests. Regrettably the printed diary rarely gives the full names of the passengers, which has made it difficult to establish exactly who was of the party. However, "Mr A" is presumably CharlesE.

> Poor Mr A, who was pestered without mercy as to the exact definition of fjord, and when we should see one, informed us at tea time that we were about to enter Sogne fjord.[6]

Like all who see the beautiful coast of Norway for the first time, Miss Cohen was impressed by the magnificence of the mountains and "*waterfalls of great height, casting their exquisite reflections in the calm water*".[7]

The next paragraph is remarkable: while surrounded by the extreme beauty of a Norwegian cruise, Georgie has the ladies sitting on deck the next day

> busily employed sewing cushions in that fascinating cross-stitch. Mrs A surprised us by producing pieces of work for us all, complete with wool, needles, and they were greatly appreciated, as also the kind thought which prompted her to think of us.[8]

Later in the voyage Miss Cohen comments that Mrs Allan is the only one still interested in the needlework, as she sits wrapped up in her coat. Georgie obviously believes that the devil makes mischief for idle hands. Mickey and Sybil had much more fun playing hide-and-seek, but they seemed to get most pleasure from being on the bridge. "*The captain and officers are very good natured and anyone is always welcome up there.*"[9] CharlesE, whenever they went ashore, always found somewhere to fish, while Threlford found a quiet spot in a hotel where he could settle down with his coffee.

On 10 July the *Sayonara* sailed into the Arctic Circle at Hestmannøy; the day was very cold and bleak with rain and a mist. Activities on deck were not recommended, as Cohen explained. In the afternoon they were entertained by the Hendersons, Mickey and Sybil with an impromptu play.

> Mr Smith [*the butler*] as "Slim Jim" made us hold our sides with laughing. I was sorry for the desperate plight Mrs H's fox fur must have finished in, after having been made good use of, tied round a pole to represent a horse. ... In spite of the rain we were nearly all, with perhaps the exception of Mr T, who preferred the warmth of his cabin, either on the deck or on the bridge watching the Svartisen Glacier ... It was not hard thus to realize that we were in the vicinity of ice, because of the green water, and small pieces of ice floating round us.[10]

The cruise continued until the end of July. There were many trips ashore; Mickey and Sybil were also kept amused with deck games. As Miss Cohen records, these games were not always played with great success. CharlesE and Henderson had fixed a fishing net across the upper deck, but the holes in the net meant that quoits were frequently lost overboard. Georgie continued to pass the time with her needlework, and in quiet moments

Miss Cohen would be found reading a recently published best-seller, Lowell Thomas's *With Lawrence in Arabia*. Finally on the 27 July they docked in Scotland. Miss Cohen wrote in her diary:

> With great sorrow we gathered together our things, bade our final adieux to the officers, and left the yacht at 11. Sybil was nearly in tears, and I feel bound myself to say that I should have made a complete ass of myself had I not the vision of Dunbeath in my mind.[11]

After CharlesE's cruise with his family and friends the *Sayonara* had a chequered career; she was sold in 1927 and in 1939 she was acquired by the Admiralty for service as an armed boarding vessel. At the end of the war she was sold on again, until finally in 1948 she was deliberately destroyed by fire. A sad end to a very graceful old lady.

PART FIVE

1926 – 1955

Peace thy olive wand extend,
And bid wild War his ravage end,
Man with brother Man to meet,
And as a brother kindly greet:
Then may Heaven with prosperous gales
Fill my Sailor's welcome sails, . . .

ROBERT BURNS
On the Seas and Far Away (1794)

Chapter 21

Death of a Laird

If 1926 is remembered for anything it is for the industrial unrest that swept the land. The General Strike in May had not lasted long, but ships and shipping were disrupted for a much longer period, and the miner's strike went on even longer. Yet for a section of society their world continued as it had always done; the Derby was run, as usual on 2 June; Royal Ascot had its usual gathering of the aristocracy and wealthy race-goers; and there was the usual "Glorious Twelfth" on 12 August with King George V shooting on Lord Sefton's estate in Aberdeenshire. (The weather was typical of that part of the country, with frequent showers, but it did nothing to dampen the enthusiasm of the shooters.)

Henry remained extremely sceptical that the Government could, or would, tackle the problems of unemployment and industrial unrest, and then begin to introduce measures that would bring about period of substantial economic and industrial growth. He foresaw a long period of depression/recession. For him at least the outlook for the next decade would indeed remain dismal.

Retirement for CharlesE should have been all about cruising in beautiful yachts, enjoying the summers at Dunbeath in Caithness and his Drumnagesk fishing-lodge near Aboyne and perhaps winters at Baynards Park. Unfortunately, he was to be embroiled for years in the affairs of Workman & Clark.

The Northumberland Shipbuilding Company, which had bought up Workman Clark & Co in 1918–1919, had hit bad times a few years later and defaulted on guaranteed interest payments to debenture holders. These debenture holders took action against the Workman Clark directors.

Shortly before he took his family on the *Sayonara* in July 1923 CharlesE heard that the proposed legal action by debenture holders had been dropped after the death of Alfred Tucker, who had been leading the fight for compensation. But it turned out that this was not the end of the affair.

In March 1924 a legal ruling was given that the old directors of Workman Clark & Co had no case to answer in a Court of Law. Six legal counsel had been consulted and they were all of the opinion that the original loan to the Northumberland Shipbuilding Company, on which the legal action was proposed, was *ultra vires* [beyond one's legal power].

Tucker's executors had declined to continue with the action. Matters should have ended there, but there were other debenture holders who refused to accept the ruling, and they decided that the legal proceedings should go ahead as planned, regardless of the cost of such actions.

Philip Wright, who chaired the meeting in London, commented

> that those against whom they were taking action were men of good financial standing and well able to make restitution of a considerable amount should the decision of the Courts be against them.[1]

It was a foolhardy decision. The debenture holders were led by William Urquhart, a Belfast coachbuilder, who had only invested a very small sum of money when he bought his shares. CharlesE, Sir George Smith Clark and Frank and Robert Alfred Workman were all named as "Old Directors"while the new directors were headed by Sir Edward Mackay Edgar and Sir John Esplen. In all, fourteen directors of Workman & Clark and the Northumberland Shipbuilding Company were named as defendants.

The allegations against the defendants were that they were guilty of fraud, misrepresentation, conspiracy and breach of trust, when they originally issued a prospectus to raise three million pounds by the sale of debenture stock. It was further alleged that in raising the money they had not, as the Prospectus had outlined, passed the money on to the Company to develop the Belfast yard but had diverted it for other purposes.

No one could have known in the summer of 1926 that the case against the directors would drag on for years, nor that there would be tragedies along the way. In November 1927 Frank Workman died. He had been very ill for some time, and there can be no doubt the strain of the legal action had made his last days unbearable. The day after his death, Counsel for

Urquhart asked the court if Workman's Estate would be liable if the present action went against the defendants. Shortly after Workman's death Mr Justice Brown made a statement to the effect that while the "Old Directors" knew about the issue of the Debentures and the prospectus there was no evidence of criminal intent and therefore he could not put their actions to the jury.

It is impossible to know if CharlesE travelled to Belfast to take part in the proceedings, but he would not have enjoyed reading his daily papers. Claims and counter-claims continued to be made. At times it must have seemed that the High Court in Belfast was like a pantomime performance. Events were further complicated when the Northumberland Shipbuilding Company was placed in liquidation. In November 1927 Mr Justice Brown announced that in view of the changed circumstances, he had no alternative but to dismiss the jury from their arduous task. He was pleased to tell them they would be paid one guinea each for their service and they would be exempted from jury service for at least twelve years. The jurors "*chorused a cordial, 'thank you, my Lord'.*"

Unfortunately it was not the end of the matter. In June 1928 a case came before the court from another group of disgruntled debenture holders. They hoped to bring a class-action, but this was dismissed by the Lord Chief Justice; the plaintiffs then threatened to take their case to the House of Lords. Indeed, in June 1929, the matter was raised in the House of Lords; finally in December 1929 a agreement was reached by both sides: the debenture holders would be compensated to the sum of £33.6s.8d. for every £100 of stock they had bought back in 1921. In a letter of agreement submitted to the court by the plaintiffs they wrote:

> that having fully considered all the circumstances in the light of the explanation given by their legal advisers, they are prepared to withdraw as against the Belfast directors, Sir George Clark, Messrs G E Clark, Charles Allan, and the late Frank Workman ... all charges of personal fraud and conspiracy.[2]

It had taken six years to reach a solution. Legal costs amounted to £150,000, and the settlement of the plaintiffs' award would cost between £250,000 and £300,000. As the newspapers commented "[*it*] *is believed to have been the most expensive suit ever brought before the Irish Courts*".[3]

CharlesE would surely have said it was a very high price to prove one's innocence; he might equally have repeated what had been said a number of times during the various Court proceeding, that he, Frank Workman and Sir George Clark had not agreed with the sale of Workman Clark & Co to the Northumberland Shipbuilding Company when it had first been suggested back in 1919. It is more than probable that the sale of the company that he had worked for with such enjoyment for more than thirty years was the reason he decided to retire shortly after the sale had gone ahead. After the court actions ended, the company changed its name to Workman & Clark (1928), but it never regained its reputation and in 1935 it went into receivership.

The whole affair was a multiple tragedy: not only did it cost so much in monetary terms, while not giving the debenture holders what they had hoped for, but the long drawn out litigation also put unbearable pressure on the families of the defendants: these years saw not just the death of Frank Workman but also the death of Sir George Clark's wife, Frances.

CharlesE also heard, at that time, of the death of Walter A Denholm, a much respected manager of the Workman & Clark team. A Scotsman, Denholm had a brilliant scholastic career in Glasgow before being employed by two Scottish shipbuilders, D & W Henderson and William Denny & Bros. He joined Workman & Clark in 1911 and during the years of the Great War the added workload had made heavy demands on him and his workforce. He had been awarded an OBE for his wartime services.

How many Winnipeg citizens turning from Thames Avenue or Tweed Avenue into Allan Street stop for a moment and ponder who was the person that gave the street its name? William Rae Allan, the youngest son of Old Andrew, died at his home in Roslyn Road, Winnipeg in March 1926. He had been in Winnipeg since 1883 and had seen the town grow from a frontier trading post into a thriving metropolis. William's partnership with Killam and Robert McKay saw the trio become one of the main financiers and insurance investors in the Province. His marriage to Killam's widow, Minnie, had added to the contentment he found in life. As one would have expected, tributes to William focused on his business affairs. It is noticeable that, as with so many of the Allan male members, the later years of his life were concerned with banking.

William's life, though, was not all about business: he had a consuming interest in, indeed a passion for, thoroughbred horses.

> [*He*] was president of the Manitoba Jockey Club ... one of the founders of the club which is an old association of owners of running and harness horses ... He was president of the Prairie Thoroughbred Breeders' and Racing Association ... He was a true racing man himself and a lover of every kind of clean sport. Mr Allan was a man of outstanding reputation and his influence in the racing business always has been a great inspiration to others, being largely responsible for the high plane racing is on today.[4]

If a man can be judged by his family then William was a lucky man. His wife Minnie had predeceased him, but his brother Hugh came to the funeral from Montreal. His brother James Bryce was not there, but he had come over from his home in Rome the previous June and spent a last holiday with William. Two other brothers had predeceased him, Andrew Alexander and JohnS, the man with a very colourful and chequered past. William's sister, Jane Crawford, and her husband Frederick Brydges, in spite of their earlier marital problems, had remained on very good terms with William. They had settled in Winnipeg, and in 1916 they were living at Roslyn Street, just a short walk from William and Minnie. Jane had died in 1922 in Victoria, British Columbia; Frederick died in 1928.

Kilmahew in its long history had witnessed many glittering social occasions, but few could have been more enjoyable than the marriage of Claud and Adeline's second daughter, Sheena. In September 1927 she married Arthur George (Peter) Wilson, a survivor of the Great War whose account of life in the trenches was quoted in Chapter 17. In the years following the Armistice Wilson had qualified as a doctor of medicine. The world of female fiction is littered with stories of pretty young nurses falling in love with handsome young doctors, and it is true that Sheena was nursing at St Thomas's Hospital in London when they met and fell in love. Peter was twelve years' her senior. The couple had two children, Michael Allan and Fiona Margaret Ann. But this was not romantic fiction, and Sheena and Peter were not destined to share the dream of being happy ever after. They later parted.

The life of a family doctor between the Wars was very different from the role now played by group practice doctors. In Peter's time most family doctors worked alone or at best with one junior assistant. In a rural practice like Radlett in Hertfordshire Peter would have been on call seven days a week, twenty-four hours a day. It would not have been unusual for a formal dinner or a weekend house party, or even a hunt ball, to be interrupted by urgent demands from his patients.

Sheena, as a nurse and a doctor's wife, although she would have had a number of household servants, would still have been expected to play an important role; for example, she would provide comfort and support to distraught mothers with very sick children. The reasons for Sheena deciding to leave are unimportant. Peter stayed at Radlett, and for the next forty-eight years he was a loved and respected family doctor.

Sheena's marriage was followed a few years later by the wedding of her elder sister Marion in March 1931 to Lieut-Commander (retired) Denis Walton Harrison Last. He was the son of Walter Arthur William Last, Deputy-Commissioner in the Indian Civil Service; his mother was Kathleen Fforde, but both parents were deceased by 1931. Denis had been born in Muzuffargarh, Punjab and in 1911 was a cadet at the Royal Naval College at Osborne on the Isle of Wight. He had been just about old enough to see service in the last couple of years of the Great War, a war that left its mark on all who served in that terrible conflict.

The wedding of Marion and Denis had taken place at Burns Church, Cardross. Neither of the two witnesses were family members, although too much should not be read into that simple statement; it is possible that Marion and Denis wanted their wedding to be low key as a mark of respect to Sheena, who was pregnant with her second child. The fact that the wedding took place a few days before the Easter weekend may have made it difficult for Charlie and Bobby, Marion's brothers, to attend. Charlie had left Harrow School in 1926 and had gone up to Pembroke College, Cambridge in October, but by 1931 he was working for the Imperial Tobacco Company in Bristol. Bobby followed Charlie to Harrow School in 1928, and was still a pupil at the time of Marion's wedding.

In Aros, Alexander and Juliana Elizabeth celebrated their sixtieth wedding anniversary on 18 September 1926. During their long marriage she had been a constant and devoted companion, joining him when he left Liverpool to run the Aros Estate after his father's death. The anniversary was overshadowed by Alexander's failing health, but in the event it was Juliana who died first, of influenza, on 6 November. Her memorial reads: *"loved and respected by all who knew her"*.[5] But that tells you very little about her character. In a book by Lady Nora Fairfax-Lucy, the daughter of a well-known family on Mull, the Mackenzies of Calgary Castle, she gives a detailed picture of Juliana and life at Aros House. At the time she was writing about she had still been a child, but observed that when

> on several occasions the Allans gave a dance [her] parents, sisters and brothers got up in full evening dress before starting the long drive in the wagonette. The Allans were very grand but strictly teetotal and when it came to driving home after a long evening most carriages only got as far as the bend in the avenue before the horses were halted and flasks produced.[6]

Lady Nora then writes, with some humour, that Juliana would frequently engage her female guests in conversation on domestic matters. Juliana had a very distinctive voice and her discussions centred on the problems of hiring domestic staff. She was much concerned that those she employed should be not just be pretty but should also be of a high moral character. She was also concerned that if she employed pretty girls to wait at table or in the laundry she would have problems with her young male employees, while if she employed elderly plain women she could not allow them to wait at table.

> Mrs Allan was a stickler for morals as well as being a determined "do-gooder". When sending old copies of such magazines as *Punch* to the village institute she would carefully cut out any picture she considered might corrupt.[7]

Nora's sister Tina (Christina Marion) was one of those guests whom Juliana frequently consulted on domestic matters. Tina was also, of course, a contemporary of Juliana's daughter Sheila, and the two families remained friends through the subsequent generation. There is another connection between the Allans and Calgary Castle; when Isabella Bird sent her Hebridean laddies to Canada in the 1860s, various sources suggest that the Canadian settlement of Calgary was named after the Mull village whose crofters had been turned off their land by the landowners, and replaced with sheep.

Alexander's health continued to decline: he died on 15 December 1927. He had been Provost of Tobermory for forty-seven years, ever since it had gained burgh status. He had served on the Mull District Council, he had been appointed JP for the county, and had acted as Honorary Sheriff-Substitute. He had been instrumental in setting up the Nursing Association of North Argyll, together with the Hon Miss Greenhill Gardyne of Glenforsa. For thirty years he had served as Chairman of the Kilninian and Kilmore School Board.

He was, though, first and foremost, a landlord to the tenant farmers and crofters, and it was this work that won him the respect and trust of his tenants. He was passionate in offering help to the poor of Mull, and rarely was a plea for assistance ever refused.

If he worked hard, his leisure activities also gave him great pleasure. He was a fine yachtsman, and with his only daughter Sheila he had won many trophies. He enjoyed a day's fishing and on the "Glorious Twelfth", he would, for more years than he could remember, entertain a party of family members and guests.

It is indeed no small matter that Alexander was known throughout Mull as an "ideal landlord" and a true friend. His funeral saw all the shops at Tobermory close for three hours. The mourners included town councillors, parish councillors, members of the school management committee and a goodly proportion of the people of Mull. Col Bryce and his son Alastair were chief among the mourners; Sheila, home from India, was also present.

> Numerous wreaths were received, including one from the estate workmen, who carried the body from the church, the remains thereafter carried by the general public in relays of four to the place of internment.[8]

Capt Bryce had bequeathed to his son Alexander while still a relatively young man the future of Aros, and for almost six decades Alexander had worked to endure that he had earned the right to be the "Laird of Aros".

Col Bryce of Aros may have been reluctant to end his marriage to his cousin Hilda while his parents were alive, but on 5 March 1928, in an undefended case, Bryce was granted a divorce on the grounds of her desertion. She had never enjoyed life at Aros; perhaps, after a childhood spent in Liverpool, she found the lack of cultural pursuits not to her taste. She moved to Edinburgh and at the time of her divorce was living in Great Stuart Street, in the heart of the beautiful new town and a short stroll away from the magic of Princes Street, with its shops, art galleries and restaurants, and the forbidding Castle looming over it all.

Four months after his divorce, Col Bryce married Margaret Mary [Madge] Melles, in St Cuthbert's Parish Church in Edinburgh. Madge was the daughter of Joseph William Melles, a warehouseman of Sewardstone, Essex, who had links to Mull: the Melles had a house at Grulin. Madge's brother, also called Joseph William, and Sheila, still home from India, were witnesses at the marriage. Madge had been the widow of William George Kepple Gough for fifteen years during which time she had raised three children, a son George Hugh Bloomfield, and two daughters Daphne Margaret and Ann Theadora, known as Barbie.

It is possible that under the strict teachings of the Free Church on Mull and the rest of the Western Isles, the Church would not countenance the marriage of a divorcee and a widow; this might be why they went to Edinburgh.

Col Bryce and Madge were not the only members of the family to court controversy in 1928. In January, James Bryce of Wemyss Bay announced his intention to marry the Contesse de Cippico. On the 26 April, the marriage duly took place at the Scots Kirk in the rue Bayard, Paris. It was a lavish occasion. The Very Rev Charles L Warr, Dean of the Thistle and Chapel Royal in Scotland, Chaplain-in-Ordinary to HM The King, officiated, assisted by Rev W Cowper Robertson.

The Contesse de Cippico was, in fact, Marguerite Lucile Jolivet, a French film and stage actress known as Rita Jolivet. Not only was she in a profession that would not have appealed to the older members of the Allan family, but she had two previous marriages, both of which had ended in divorce.

There is a fascinating aspect to this marriage: one wonders if James Bryce knew quite who, or what, he was marrying. It was said by one of Rita's nephews that James Bryce was a quiet, retiring man who was far from being worldly wise, while she was a beautiful woman, three years older than him, and even though he was in his mid-thirties, he was unlikely to have become an expert on the whims of aspiring French actresses. She, on the other hand, had a colourful past and an equally colourful family. She had no children from her two previous marriages, but she knew exactly what she wanted from her marriage to the son of a very rich shipping family. But whatever the truth of their relationship, the romance of James Bryce and Rita lasted for the next three decades.

There has been a suggestion that Rita was introduced to James Bryce by Lady Marguerite, but that is impossible to confirm or deny. Two things, however, are confirmed: Rita was, like Marguerite, a survivor from the *Lusitania,* and her film career might have brought her to Marguerite's notice through her daughter Matilda, who was very interested in the theatre and drama.

James Bryce took a tenancy at Ballikinrain Castle just outside Balfron in Stirlingshire. It had fifty bedrooms, twenty-five indoor staff and twenty-five outdoor staff. It is reported that a piper played them and their guests into the dining-room every night. James Bryce must have thought he was living in some kind of fairy story.

On her third marriage Rita had given up the Italian title she had gained from her second husband, but in entering James Bryce's world she was soon an attraction at all the county grand social occasions. In October, she, her mother, Pauline Helene Viallant, the widow of Charles Eugene Jolivet, and James Bryce were guests at a glittering ball in Stirling.

The whirl of social balls, dinners and salons would have delighted Rita, but for James Bryce, who up to the time of his marriage seemed to have found his enjoyment in sailing, hunting and shooting, it must have felt as if he had entered an alien world.

He was employed as company director with his mother's family firm, Clark's, the thread and cotton manufacturers. In that position James Bryce travelled widely, with frequent visits to Canada. On such trips Rita rarely went with him. On a visit to Japan in 1932, via British Columbia, Rita did accompany him, but on that trip they were both described as tourists.

Chapter 22

Fatal Times

There were many times in Janie's life when she must have believed that finally she had achieved her life's ambition. In the General Election of May 1929 women under the age of thirty were able to vote for the first time, and not just alongside men of property but as part of true universal adult suffrage. On the other hand, though Nancy Astor (Viscountess Astor) had been the first woman to take her seat in parliament as far back as 1919, ten years later the representation of women in the House of Commons could still be counted in single figures.

Very little seems to have changed in the succeeding nine decades; there is a parallel between the 1929 election and that of 2010. In 1929, the Conservative Party won the greater share of the public vote but not enough seats to form a government. They refused to do a deal with the Liberal Party under David Lloyd George, even though he had fifty-nine seats. Lloyd George formed a coalition with the Labour Leader Ramsay MacDonald, but this could only govern for two years before the leaders were forced to admit defeat, and another General Election was held.

In 1929 there was a world-wide financial crisis; banks collapsed; countries verged on bankruptcy. Unemployment rose to staggeringly high levels, manufacturing industries could not invest, and there was a mood of despondency across the whole nation. In the vacuum created by the inability of politicians to solve the nation's problems the mood of the people turned inward. Fascist Parties in Italy, Spain, Germany and Great Britain promoted their philosophy as a way of countering the Bolshevik Revolution. Memories of the War slipped from people's consciousness, and both fascists and their enemies were beginning to whisper ominously about the prospect of another world war.

The history of divorce, since civil divorce was first recognized in 1560, has developed very slowly: in particular, it has taken many centuries to remove the social stigma associated with the breakdown of marriage. The Victorians viewed divorce among the aristocracy (virtually the only class to whom it was available) as something that had to be tolerated but concealed; they deplored the sensational reporting of such cases. A change in the law in 1923 in England made it a little easier for women to petition for divorce, but even then the obstacles were daunting, especially to women who did not have the financial resources needed to pursue such an action.

The divorce of Col Bryce from Hilda in 1928 was the first to occur in the Scottish Allan family. In Canada the situation was even more complex; Old Andrew's two children, Jean Crawford and John Smith, would have had to seek the passage of a Private Act of Parliament before their marriages could be dissolved leaving them free to remarry. There is no doubt, however, that in the late 1920s and the early 1930s Col Bryce's divorce set something of a trend in the Allan family.

Doris Vernon, Hilda's sister, was less good-natured about her husband Bowater George's infidelity. He had inherited the baronetcy on the death of his father in 1920, becoming the 2nd Baronet Vernon of Hanbury, at which time he dropped the name of Bowater and became Sir George. Doris accordingly became Lady Vernon. In 1930 Lady Vernon refused to give her husband a divorce; instead, she separated from him, leaving him to live with his mistress at Hanbury Hall, and returned to her mother Clara at Shrawley Wood House. Fortunately, Doris was financially independent and could afford to stand by her principles. Sir George remained a sad and lonely man, over-burdened by the responsibilities of the management of Hanbury and its estate; the recession/depression in the agricultural industry depleted his income and as a consequence Hanbury suffered from a lack of care which Doris would have ensured it received.

It must have been known within the wider family that Hamish and Helen's marriage had not been a great success. Hamish had continued his medical studies at University College, London, and the Middlesex Hospital, and these must have left a young married man little time for social activities. Nevertheless, in the spring of 1923 they went to Fontainebleau together to join a group of like-minded people who wished to live the simple life, away from the day-to-day pressure of city living.

Less than a month after their arrival Hamish decided he preferred to return to London and complete his studies. Helen remained at Fontainebleau for another five months, and on her return to London she confessed to Hamish that while alone in France she had met another man and they had become lovers. Hamish's reaction would not have been pleasant to witness: it appears he was so angry he left the marital home and was away for a fortnight nursing his wounds before he returned. A reconciliation between him and Helen was agreed but it lasted less then two months.

Helen was not keen on being just a doctor's wife. She became a student at RADA and later worked at the Old Vic. She left the marital home and took a flat in Baker Street, and it was known that the man she had met at Fontainebleau visited her. Hamish again begged her to return; she did, and Rosamund Helen, his only daughter, was born in July 1924.

If Hamish hoped that the birth of a child would repair his broken marriage he was to be disappointed. In April 1925 he went to Norway on holiday and when he returned to England he did not return to Helen and his daughter. In November 1925, when Rosamund was just a toddler, Helen took her on a protracted visit to America, and did not come back until May 1926. When Hamish heard that she and Rosamund were back in England, he wrote to Helen saying

> that their marriage had never been anything but a failure, and that he was convinced that it was useless to make another attempt to live together . . .[1]

He did not seek to apportion blame, and being the gentleman he was he enclosed with the letter a hotel bill which showed that he had spent the night at the Wellington Hotel, Tunbridge Wells, with a woman who was not his wife. As the unreformed divorce laws stood at the time this perfunctory evidence was what Hamish and Helen needed to enable Helen to apply to the courts for a divorce. She was granted a *decree nisi* in November 1926. Hamish of course had to pay the costs even though he was in many respects the innocent party. Helen re-married twice, in 1933 and 1939.

Discretion was the watchword of the Allan family and it was rare that they allowed divorce and separation to become a *cause célèbre*, but there is always an exception to every rule. Dick, RichardG's only son, was to experience all the weight of press attention when his infatuation with an earl's daughter became public knowledge.

In the years since his birth in 1898 Dick had led a conventional life as the only son of a rich man. His education had followed that of his Scottish/Canadian cousins, prep school from an early age, followed by teenage years at Rugby. He left Rugby in 1916 and instead of university he went to the Royal Military College Sandhurst, leaving towards the end of 1918 to join the (Royal) Dragoon Guards as a junior officer. He did not see service in the Great War, as his first posting was to Ireland. He may have thought he had been lucky to miss the carnage of that terrible war, but as he was soon to learn Ireland would not be all about enjoying a constant round of social engagements and enjoying the feminine beauties of the Emerald Isle.

Ireland had been in a political turmoil since the Easter Rising of 1916. In January 1919 two constables of the Royal Irish Constabulary had been shot dead by two masked gunmen. A reign of terror began and in the next year fourteen policemen were killed and many more injured. The British Army was sent in to put an end to the bloodshed, and Dick Allan found he was having first-hand experience of the horrors of a civil war. He left the army in 1923 and became a student at the Cirencester Agricultural College.

In November 1926 Dick was cited as co-respondent in the divorce of the Hon Herbrand Charles Alexander, younger brother of the 5th Earl of Caledon. Alexander, like Dick, had been a soldier, but by 1926, on the insistence of his wife Millicent Valla Meredyth, he had left the army and settled in Wiltshire at Tilshead House, where he proposed to breed and train horses. It was while Alexander and Millicent were in Ireland that they met Dick. He quickly became attracted to her and she to him. They enjoyed dancing together whenever they were invited to the same parties.

Not content with leaving things to chance meetings, Dick telegraphed Millicent and invited her to a dance in Cork. Alexander earnestly tried to persuade her not to go, and to end her infatuation with Dick Allan. In the end, Millicent declared that it was not infatuation; she truly loved Dick. Millicent, like Doris Vernon, had the advantage of being a wealthy young woman, having inherited an income of £3,500 a year from her father, Sir Henry Bayley Meredyth of Easthorpe Hall, Warwickshire.

Dick, as was the custom at the time, gave evidence of his adultery with Millicent at the Grosvenor Hotel, London, and a *decree nisi* was granted to Alexander by Mr Justice Hill in November 1926. Two weeks after it was made absolute on 16 May 1927 Dick and Millicent were married, but there was not to be a happy ending. In spite of her declaration before her divorce that she loved Dick Allan, in less than three years she had deserted him, again running off with her partner at another Hunt Ball. Dick returned to his farm near Moreton-in-Marsh, presumably to contemplate the folly of his youthful indiscretions and to try to put a purpose back into his life.

There was a long-drawn-out and rather sad squabble between Alexander and Millicent over money, which eventually had to be settled by the High Court. In his summing-up the President of the Probate, Divorce and Admiralty Division, Lord Merrivale, made an interesting observation:

> As the matter had been the subject of consideration in public, he thought it proper to say that the present applicant [*Millicent*] was a women of large fortune who had married a man of high position [*Alexander*], but of very much smaller fortune.[2]

Divorces, separations and minor scandals did not mean that the rest of the family were not still busily carrying out their day-to-day responsibilities. Henry was, as always, fully occupied with events at the Clydesdale Bank. The depression continued into the 1930s, but at the beginning of every general meeting Henry usually had to tell the assembled shareholders of the death of yet another member of their esteemed staff. In 1929 it had been the death of John Henderson, a long serving man with an impeccable reputation among his staff, shareholders and customers. Later in his chairman's report Henry was keen to refute current rumours – rumours that again pre-echo financial problems of today:

> There are many who attribute the prevailing depression of trade to financial causes, and criticise the alleged deflationary policy of the Government and the Bank of England. It seems to be supposed that there is a deliberate policy of restriction of credit, for which the Bank of England is specially blamed. A recent cartoon in *Punch*, inspired by this idea, represented the Bank as the Old Lady of Theadneedle Street obstructing traffic; but *Punch* was badly informed. It is not the province of the Bank of England to finance trade and industry – that is the business of the joint stock banks.[3]

Eighty years later governments and banks are still at loggerheads as to who is responsible for ensuring that business, commerce and industry have access to credit. Nothing ever changes!

Henry would surely also have noticed the retirement of Robert Burns, a Saltcoats man who had worked for J & A Allan since 1887, transferring as chief accountant to the Canadian Pacific Company when they took over the Allan Line. Burns had served both companies for more than forty-years, working his way up through the accounts department before becoming a chief accountant. Many Allan employees took the same pathway: they entered the business on the lowest rung of the ladder and through their own talent, assisted by their employers' training, rose up towards the top of their trade.

The general meeting of the bank in 1930 was again a very bleak occasion. The economic and political turmoil continued to worry Henry and his fellow directors. The uncompetitive interest-rates charged by international banks and a few private investors who still had money had led the bank and its Scottish competitors to seek an easier solution to their problems.

> Like other Scottish banks, we have found that the experiment, begun last year, of taking in small deposits on pass-books, has been fully justified. The amount so deposited is very substantial, and is increasing month by month.[4]

Like many economists and businessmen, Henry became concerned about the economic damage being done by Britain's continued adherence to the gold bullion standard. He was definite in his views about popular misconceptions concerning the gold standard, and about contemporary government policy.

> The gold standard has become so embedded in the minds of our people that it would require some very strong influence to make any change acceptable. It may be more practical to secure, by international agreement, both economy in the use of gold and a cessation of needless hoarding by the nations which have adopted the gold standard without allowing free export of gold.[5]

A year later in 1931, conditions for banks and industry, and the level of unemployment, were still showing no signs of recovery. Henry, however, was becoming strongly optimistic: he believed that the world-wide depression would pass. His chief concern, as it had been back in 1925,was that banks and governments – in particular the lock between banknotes and gold reserves, and speculators being effectively encouraged to hoard gold – were slowing any chance of a full industrial recovery. In his opinion this was a recipe for disaster. He may have felt the first breezes of the winds of change, for it was in September 1931 that Britain at last abandoned the gold standard. The pound sterling settled at a more realistic international value, and governments could at last start to take effective measures to improve the economy.

A few months later in May, all financial problems were put on hold as Henry was a pall-bearer at the funeral of the bank's general manager David Young.

Tom Lander had come through the War, albeit with a serious injury to his leg, and now that peace was assured and his future secure he was determined to indulge himself in his love of flying. It was of course a risky decision for a young man with a wife and family. Tom had married Joan Mews, his sister Winifred's school friend, in 1923; she was the eldest daughter of Herbert Mews, a brewer from Steyning, Sussex, and Florence Augusta Helfrick. Tom and Joan had three sons: John Eaton (born 1924), Peter Allan (1926) and David Robin (1929). In 1931 the family were living in The Old Rectory, Harpenden, Hertfordshire.

Tom Lander was one of the earliest and most enthusiastic members of the newly formed British Gliding Association. He had obtained a glider pilot's certificate, which should have ensured that he was fully able to fly the fragile craft. As an engineer he was also keen to try and find a more effective way of launching gliders from the flat. He was joined in this adventure by his cousin Hamish Allan; both young men were keen flyers and owned their own gliders. The trouble with being a pioneer is that all too often it leads to trouble, when the heart is allowed to rule the head.

On Sunday 8 March 1931 Hamish and a group of Tom's fellow gliders, including Charles Elliott, met at Tom's Harpenden home to discuss a new way of launching a glider. Shortly after lunch they went to Faulkner's End Farm, taking with them their new experimental launching device, called "The Skud". They hoped to launch the glider using a cable connected to a winding drum that was fixed to a car engine, rather than manually, as they had done previously. They had even bought a car earlier in January especially for the first experiment. No-one watching that afternoon could have been anything other than horrified when the glider rose unexpectedly swiftly into the air and immediately nose-dived into the ground. Tom died of a fractured skull, even though Hamish was there to give him immediate medical attention. An inquest was held on Tuesday 12 March, and all those present learnt the full horror of Tom's accident.

A juror at the inquest asked Elliott if they were aware of any extra danger in the experiment. Elliott's reply may have startled those present in the room.

> No, my only doubt was whether it would work. I quite expected that the glider would fail to leave the ground.[6]

Hamish had a much harder task when he gave his evidence. He admitted that the glider Tom had been using that day was his, but he and Tom had previously used it for half-a-dozen flights. It was reported in the Press that:

> Lander and he worked out the velocity of launching the glider from the car. They had previously found that the calculated figures were not approached in practice and it was thought that with the engine under load the actual velocity attained would be under the calculated 30 miles an hour. Presumably the figures on which they had been going with regard to the maximum revolutions of the car had been faulty, and the load in this instance proved too small to slow up the engine revolutions.[7]

There could only be one conclusion for the Jury to come to, that of "Death By Misadventure". Perhaps the last words of the events of that terrible Sunday should come from Captain Needham, chairman of the Technical Committee of the British Gliding Association. He thought the accident was due to the fact that the question of velocity had not been given as much attention as it should have done, bearing in mind the lightness of the glider Tom was using that day.

TEL attended the inquest on his son and on his return to Auchtyfardle, the estate in Lesmahagow that he and Eliza had moved to in the 1920s. He would have told Eliza and Winifred whatever he could to ease their grief.

A memorial plaque was erected by Joan, Tom's parents Eliza and TEL, and Winifred, at St Andrew's, Shifnal, the church where so many of his ancestors worshipped and whose graves lay in the churchyard. In the early years after Tom's death a peal of bells would ring out across the village on the anniversary of his death. Time and changes in the world have now silenced the bells, and how many of the worshippers and visitors to St Andrew's now stop to read the words on the plaque and wonder about the man they commemorate? The plaque gives a brief history of Tom's short life and the cause of his death, but words in gold cannot and will never be able to convey the sense of loss the family suffered that day in March 1931.

Joan's family and the Allan family would rally to support her and her sons in their day of need, and in particular Hamish, as Tom's executor, would be a dear and compassionate friend, always ready to help when he was asked. Joan and her sons spent their holidays at Auchtyfardle, but grandmother Eliza, while enjoying seeing her grandsons grow, must always have been reminded of the son she had lost. They would also spend some of their holidays with Great Aunt Janie at East Lodge, Invergloy, near Spean Bridge, Inverness-shire, but wherever they were there would always be reminders of the father whom they never really knew.

Tom's untimely death was not the only one to occur in the Allan family in 1931. In October 1931 RichardG died at a nursing home in Prestwick at the age of seventy-three. In trying to assess RichardG's life it is worth remembering that he was the eighth child of Capt James and Eleanor Gilkison. His mother had died when he was only nine; his father had died when he was just starting out on his career. His two elder brothers, RobertG and JamesH had moved to Liverpool when he was at school; his three sisters Jane, Mary and Janet had married, and lived in England. Only his youngest brother Bryce had remained in Scotland, living as he did at Cliff House, Wemyss Bay. RichardG and Agnes had only one son, Dick, but a rough count of nieces and nephews suggests RichardG must have been a very busy uncle. Only one of his siblings, his eldest sister Eleanora, had remained unmarried, but she had died in September 1918. RichardG had been the informant of her death. Until her last illness she had lived in her parents' family home at 2 Park Terrace, Glasgow.

On RichardG's death certificate his son Dick gave his father's occupation as shipowner, retired. As a statement of fact it is true, but although RichardG had worked in the family firm he had very little interest in the day-to-day business of ship management. There is a story, told by family members, that it was RichardG's reluctance to oppose the takeover of the Allan Line that was the reason for the sale to the Canadian Pacific Railway Company back in the 1910s.

RichardG had a love and a passion for hunting, and from November to March every year he was an active participant at most of the major hunts across the West of Scotland. He also enjoyed riding as an amateur in point-to-point races, and he rode in the Grand National steeplechases on more than one occasion, although, regrettably, he never came in first. He was also a notable mountaineer, which rather suggests that he liked the thrill of conquering the unknown. But it was in the world of sailing that he should be most vividly remembered: a perusal of contemporary yachting papers shows that he was first amongst equals in a family of yacht owners and yachting racers.

He and Agnes had been married for forty-eight years, and although his sporting activities must have taken him away from home on many occasions their marriage was happy and had endured. Agnes survived him until 1951, continuing to enjoy the delights of Ashcraig, their home at Skelmorlie.

Chapter 23

More Tragedy

The four years between 1932 and 1935 were for the Allan children, grandchildren and great-grandchildren a period of re-adjustment. The world they lived in was changing by the day. The birth of the British Fascist Party founded by Sir Oswald Mosley, the election of National Socialist Leader Adolf Hitler in Germany, growing disquiet among the Trade Union workers and those without hope of finding a job, all contributed to social unease or even personal despair, and made the days increasingly violent and insecure on the streets of Great Britain and Europe.

Col Bryce of Aros was finding that rents from his farms and cottages were not keeping pace with his expenditure. Wages for farm workers, gardeners, and domestic servants had risen sharply, and the number employed declined accordingly. Claud at Kilmahew would also have been concerned that the estate employed so many people, although a number of his employees had been with him for decades and would remain with him until his death. He did, however, have many other interests to concern him: he was a member of the Dunbartonshire County Council, and did much charitable and education work. In 1932 he was appointed Convener of the Finance and Property Committee, of the Royal Technical College, in Glasgow, a post he held until his death. The Royal Technical College was the leading science and engineering institution of its day, and in 1964 became the University of Strathclyde.

In February 1932 RobertS died at Hafton, Hunter's Quay. He was seventy-four, and had been in failing health for a number of months. RobertS's death left Claud as the only remaining member of R & C Allan, and he had to decide whether he wanted to continue running the shipping company that he and RobertS had set up back in 1892.

RobertS had been more interested in education than he had been in ship management, although he continued to call himself a shipowner. In tracing his career it will be seen as one of achievement and service to his native Glasgow. He continued to support the charities his parents had set up as well as other institutions that were of a particular interest to him.

> [*He was*] a member of the Council of the Royal Scottish Geographical Society ... He was also convener of the Educational Committee of the great 1901 Glasgow Exhibition. In recognition of Mr Allan's services to the cause of education and to the city generally, Glasgow University in 1909 conferred upon him the honorary degree of Doctor of Laws. At his graduation it was stated that Mr Allan, by his patient and devoted labours in the cause of sound education, had proved himself a loyal servant of the city and a good friend of the University.[1]

It has been impossible to establish with any degree of accuracy whether RobertS or his parents at any time actually owned Hafton Castle, as opposed to being the leaseholders. It is definite, however, that RobertS did own Sandbank House (also in Hunter's Quay), and that he also spent much of his time on the Isle of Bute. At the time of his death he was commodore of the Clyde Corinthian Yacht Club; he was a passionate sailor, his last yacht being the six-metre *Lintic*. He and his family would each summer have attended the Cowal Highland Gathering, a festival of Scottish pipe bands, dancing, caber throwers, wrestlers, and all manner of athletes, young and old. The Games still today attract crowds from not just Scotland but all over the world, in particular Scottish descendents from the Americas and Australia.

RobertS left a widow, Lizzie, with whom he had shared forty-seven years of marriage; she outlived him by five years. Again, on her death certificate her address is given as Hafton, Hunter's Quay. Of their three daughters, Dorothy the eldest had married Major David Percival in 1922. He had trained at the Royal Garrison Artillery, Woolwich, where in 1901 he was described as a "gentleman cadet". He was the son of Edward Hope Percival of the Indian Civil Service from Kinsbury House, Upton, Gloucestershire. Dorothy and Percival's main residence from around about 1927 was also in Gloucestershire, at Priors House, Bream.

It has been possible to identify three children born to Dorothy and David. A girl, also called Dorothy, was born in Fyzabad in 1923, then a son, Allan (registered in Woolwich in 1926), and Claud (registered in Chepstow, Monmouthshire in 1929).

Elspeth and Jean, RobertS's younger daughters, never married, and they spent their remaining years at Hafton.

For the first time in many a long year, early in 1933 Henry was unable to attend the AGM of the Clydesdale Bank. The acting chairman, Archibald Walker, told the assembled company

> how much the directors regret the enforced absence of our Chairman, Mr Allan, who has been laid aside by illness.
>
> This is the first annual meeting Mr Allan has missed during the past 24 years. I am pleased, however, to be able to state that he is making good progress, and I am sure that it is your desire that we send to him our earnest wishes for his speedy restoration of his accustomed vigour.[2]

Henry must had read the report of the AGM with a good deal of pride; the bank had come through some incredibly difficult years, but if the headlines were to be believed "*Very Satisfactory Result of Year's Working*", and "*Stability of British Sterling Prices and Forces of Recuperation Growing*" he could hope that the results at the next board meeting in February 1934 would give him cause for even greater satisfaction. However, there was a caveat, as if not to lighten the mood of shareholders overmuch:

> even a greatly improved trade is not likely to absorb the whole amount of unemployment, as any adjustment to shorter hours of labour must be international, and if possible world wide, and that will take a very long time.
>
> Till the arrival of the time visioned in the report of the experts of technocracy – and it is a very distant vision – when men can get all they require by working a very few hours a week, the unemployed allowance must be continued, and those who are working must continue to help to keep those who are unable to get work.[3]

There is a depressing irony in those words: it is almost as if they were written in the second decade of the twenty-first century. Technology did not, as the bankers hoped it would, and has not led to a fall in unemployment, nor has it led to a reduction in working hours. In 1933, a shipyard worker, a coal miner, a teacher, a nurse, even bankers, and office staff, almost without exception, worked within walking distance of their workplace. Now, commuting vast distances has added to the amount of time workers are away from home. The unskilled and the semi-skilled languish on state benefits, despised by those in work, and by the Government who too often label them as work shy or scroungers. Technology would not turn out to have helped the poor and the dispossessed, and it is rare to find a Government Minister or anyone else offering a realistic solution that would satisfy the economists.

Sir Hugh, and men like him, did not look to others to make their fortunes: they saw opportunities and took them. In the early years, when Sir Hugh first ventured across the vast Atlantic Ocean, he endured years of hardship and unremitting work, but the reward for his labour was all the more satisfying because he could say with a degree of pride, "I did it myself".

In January 1933 TEL died at his Lesmahagow home of Auchtyfardle shortly after he and Eliza had celebrated forty years of marriage. It was just a little under two years since Tom's death; for his parents these must have been two difficult years of adjustment. According to his obituary in the Hurstpierpoint College magazine, Major Lander was

> kindly and helpful ... [a] generous contributor in every sense to anyone, or any cause, requiring his counsel or assistance. He was eminently practical, gentlemanly, and courteous on all occasions, and, as many will know, a wise counsellor.[4]

Eliza and Winifred stayed on at Auchtyfardle; Winifred took over the role of running the estate and expanded the role of the farm by breeding a herd of Jersey cows. She became, as one would have expected of an Allan woman, a breeder of prize-winning animals. There is a story told by William Gemmell senior, of Bankend Farm, Coalburn, of Miss Lander coming to visit his father James, a notable breeder of Clydesdale horses. William remembers that Miss Lander's usual mode of transport was pony and trap. She was often accompanied by her trusted servant, Donny McGregor. Winifred also had a long commitment to the Girl Guide Movement which began when she was at St James's School, Malvern. She was Division Commissioner in Lanarkshire from 1922-1947, and Ranger Captain of Lesmahagow for twenty-years.

Questions relating to moral, cultural and religious beliefs are never easy to answer, nor is it easy to find a solution that would satisfy all parties involved in an argument. There is no doubt that CharlesE and Georgie were prepared, as early as 1911, to declare they were Christian Scientists, even though CharlesE's name never appeared on any membership list. Georgie however was definitely a member, and a dedicated follower of the Church's teaching from an early age. The exact date she met Charles William John Tennant of the Church of Christ Scientist is open to question, but he played a significant role in Georgie's life.

He was in many ways a very interesting man, the son of David Tennant, a wealthy Irishman who married Isabella Craig, the daughter of an Edinburgh papermaker. In 1911 Isabella was a member of the Church of Christian Science, and it is possible that it was her son Charles who influenced her decision to become a member. Charles had been educated at Bedford School, but in 1898 he travelled to Vienna, where according to his obituary he received healing for an incurable disease. From that moment on he devoted his life to the Church of Christ Scientist; first by studying in Boston, then returning to Scotland, first as a Reader, then on the Committee of Publications in London.

A handsome, charismatic man it is not surprising that Georgie became enthralled with him and his teachings. In 1928 he tried to argue that the Church of Christian Science and orthodox medical practice would never be able to agree on the treatment of disease. He insisted that:

> Christian Scientists have no quarrel with the members of the medical profession although they differ radically from them. Christian Science is fundamentally a religion. It is the re-discovery of the divine principles which underlay the works of the Prophets, Christ Jesus, his disciples, and the early Christians. Jesus never resorted to material means of healing.[5]

231

Georgie's and Tennant's shared beliefs were put to the test when CharlesE became ill while at his fishing lodge of Drumnagesk in the summer of 1933. He did not receive immediate medical attention from the local doctor; in fact Georgie would not hear of a professional doctor being sent for. Instead she called on the services of Charles Tennant. CharlesE spent his last few days in the care of Tennant and Georgie, and died on 21 August. Mickey was present, and it was she who was the informant of her father's death. The death certificate, as was required by Scottish Law, was signed by Dr Donald Meek, of Huntlyfield, Aboyne.

CharlesE was, rather as his father Alexander had been, a quiet unassuming man who disliked the limelight, and preferred to fulfil his civic duties away from the public gaze. He supported many sporting organizations and when his help was requested he rarely, if ever, refused to help. He had been an outstanding engineer and had revolutionised the manufacture and production of ship's engines. The legal struggles which engulfed Workman Clark & Co after CharlesE's retirement caused him distress and anxiety. He was happiest, as he would have been the first to admit, when on the riverbank, the grouse moors or the golf course. It was at Stormont Castle that he laid down a nine-hole course; unfortunately, the visitors' book at Aros does not show if CharlesE ever played on the beautiful Tobermory course with Col Bryce.

CharlesE had made his Will in late December 1931, updating a trust fund he had established in 1919. The 1931 Will was witnessed by his old trusted butler, George Smith, and the Rev John Fenwick Starforth, who had been Vicar of Axmouth in Devon from 1896 to 1928. It would be interesting to know how CharlesE came to know Starforth, a man of similar age to him, but so different in his views on religion. From all the evidence available CharlesE was a supporter, but perhaps never a full member, of the Church of Christ Scientist, while Starforth was a member of the Orthodox Established Church: they must have enjoyed some interesting discussions. But friends they certainly were, if Starforth was at Baynards Park in 1931 and was to be trusted to witness CharlesE's final Will.

Mickey was only twenty at the time of her father's death, but under the terms of his Will she became a very wealthy young woman, though the money would be held in trust until she reached her majority. CharlesE left the other half of his estate to Georgie, which is not at all surprising, but it was rather against the convention of the time that he made no restrictions on Georgie's inheriting were she to remarry. He could not have known that a little over twelve months after his death, Georgie would marry Charles William John Tennant.

The Scottish Episcopalian marriage took place at Inverness Cathedral in September 1934; Georgie gave her address as Dunbeath Castle, and Tennant's address was Stratton House, London. An interesting link with CharlesE was that John Starforth officiated. The witnesses were Alexander Stronach and his wife Mary; if Mickey was present it was not recorded. Georgie and Tennant left Southampton for a honeymoon in America, arriving in New York aboard the *Berengaria*. Again there is no evidence that Mickey went with them.

Georgie's marriage to Tennant lasted until his death in 1944; Georgie outlived him by twenty-two years.

In the early spring of 1933 the Mudhook Yacht Club held their diamond jubilee; Claud was on the committee and was selected to be a representative at the Clyde Yacht Clubs' Conference later that spring. There were rumours that the oldest of all, the Royal Northern Yacht Club, was thinking of moving their centre from Rothesay to Rhu, but the Conference did not discuss the rumours of impending transfer at any great length. They were rather more interested in finding a way to encourage more young yachtsmen to become members. Cadet Centres were set up at Hunter's Quay, and at the Gareloch, and during the season opportunities were given for cadets to gain experience on board some of the boats used in actual racing.

> Contests for crews drawn from Universities and public schools were held recently. Already entries are coming to hand from school crews which were unable to take part in this year's racing, but wish to sail next year, and one of these is from a girls' school.[6]

The Clyde Conference may have believed they had silenced the rumours about the Royal Northern making a move, but like all rumours they rumbled on. The move eventually took place in 1937.

Yachting was not the only interest of Claud that summer, he was also on the committee of the Glasgow Mission to the Outdoor Blind. A very generous financial supporter, Claud served as President from 1936 until his death in 1944.

In 1934 there were some early signs that the terrible years of the depression might be easing. The opening of the Mersey tunnel between Birkenhead and Liverpool was an indication that transport in the north-west was beginning to improve. On the Clyde, the launch in September 1934 by the Cunard-White Star Line of the Atlantic passenger liner *Queen Mary* brought a new age of luxury to sea travel. The Chairman's announcement at the launch that an order for a second liner was being considered gave the shipyard workers the prospect of future work, and the *Queen Elizabeth* was indeed launched just four years later.

The Allan family were at the same time involved in the launch of a very much smaller vessel, but one nevertheless, much needed in Scotland. James Bryce of Ballikinrain was an active member of the Royal National Lifeboat Institution, and the need to raise funds for lifeboats was (and is) never-ending. The generosity of members of the public in Glasgow was far greater than in London: Glasgow fundraising enabled the RNLI to commission two more lifeboats. A gift of £11,000 from Miss M D Rankin, in memory of her two brothers John and Matthew, both noted marine engineers from Greenock, was greatly appreciated. A similar donation from Elizabeth Sinclair allowed the first motor lifeboat to be built on the Clyde, even though the Trustees had received a lower tender from Cowes. At a meeting of the RNLI Association in May 1934, James Bryce was appointed chairman of the Glasgow branch, as replacement to Leonard Gow. Gow, supporting James Bryce's appointment, said that he was a noted yachtsman and an active social worker, and always ready to offer his services when called upon, even though his busy professional life left him with little free time.

Dick's short marriage to Millicent Meredyth did not stop him from trying to find another bride who would be more compatible. In March 1933, from his mother's home of Ashcraig, Skelmorlie, he married Phyllis Maitland Bibby. She was the daughter of William John Bibby, who in 1911 had given his occupation as manager of oil distillery in Birkenhead; however, on her marriage certificate she said that her deceased father had been a stockbroker. Her mother was Amy Christina Phillips, the daughter of John Phillips, a corn merchant in Ormskirk. Phyllis had a brother, William Gerald, eleven years her junior. One of the witnesses at Dick's marriage was his cousin James Bryce of Ballikinrain. Dick and Phyllis had a son, Richard Glen, in 1933.

William Bibby had died in New York in 1921, and was certainly, at his death, not a wealthy man. His widow Amy sadly died a year later, after having been in a mental hospital for some years. The administrator of both William's and Amy's small Estates was Amy's brother Archibald Phillips, a fine art dealer in business with his partner Rayner MacConnell in Burlington Arcade. Phyllis and William Gerald were left orphans, she as a sixteen year old, William just five. There is, however, no doubt that both children were taken care of, either by the Phillips or the Bibby family. Not unnaturally, Phyllis felt a great affection and responsibility for her brother, and perhaps as a Christmas present that year she, or William's guardian, paid for him to take his pilot's certificate at the Liverpool & District Aero Club. It was a fateful decision. Less than seven years later, William had become a Pilot Officer in the RAF, and while attached to No 8 Service Flying Training School, based at Montrose, he died in a crash. He and John Frederick Palmer, two years his junior, were killed at North Mains of Luthermuir, Marykirk, Aberdeenshire. It is impossible to imagine the feeling of loss that Phyllis must have endured: she had devoted her life to her brother and now he was no more.

The Bibby connection is worth pursuing. Her father William John was born in Birkenhead in 1874, the son of William Bibby, a master mariner, and Elizabeth Powell. His grandfather, John, had also been a master mariner. In the 1891 Census William John and his younger brother Everett George were respectively a junior clerk and an apprentice in a shipping office.

In Liverpool there was, and indeed still is, a long-established ship owning and management company called Bibby Line Group Limited, founded as long ago as 1807. The early history of the company partly covers the period when the Allan Line was running its ships out of Liverpool. Within the Bibby Line there were members who wished to increase their sailing to America, but James Bibby considered the American trade already well-served – perhaps by the Allan Line?

Unfortunately, Dick's marriage to Phyllis ended very much as his marriage to Millicent had. Phyllis left him and their small son, and sought pastures new. Early in 1940, she married Sir John Duncan Orr-Lewis, a man with a colourful past. He had had two previous marriages: his first wife Marjorie Milne died, and his second marriage to Doris Blanche Gibbons, whom he married in Paris in 1929, ended in a messy divorce in 1936. It was stated at the divorce hearing that he had committed adultery for two years with Mrs Bunny Cooper. The Orr-Lewis connection with the Allan family had its roots in Canada: Sir Frederick Orr-Lewis had been a Welsh immigrant to Montreal, who among his other activities set up the Canada Steamship Lines and was a member of the Merchants Bank of Montreal. He had also been a passenger on the *Lusitania* with Lady Marguerite. It is inconceivable that Orr-Lewis and Lady Marguerite were not acquainted. Did she even introduce Phyllis to the son of her old friend Sir Frederick?

Dick, alone again, was left to ponder his incomprehension of women's minds. He had twice thought he had found a soul mate, but ended up taking refuge at his Gloucestershire farm from a world he did not understand. He made no further attempt at matrimony, but continued to enjoy the company of delightful young women.

In April 1934 *The Scotsman* announced the engagement of Alastair of Aros to Anne Wilkie Sutherland, the youngest daughter of the late John Sutherland JP of Kirkcaldy, Sheriff-Substitute and banker, and Mrs Janet Sutherland of Edinburgh. Sutherland had died in 1918 of Bright's Disease, a disease of the kidneys, leaving his widow Janet to bring up three daughters, aged fifteen, thirteen and eleven.

The year had begun well for Alastair. He passed his chartered accountancy final examinations in February, and at the time of his qualification he was employed with Lindsay, Jamieson and Haldane in Edinburgh. He had spent part of his education at the Royal Naval College Osborne.

A second announcement in *The Scotsman,* two months later, stated the marriage of Alastair and Anne would be held on Saturday 7 July in

St Giles' Cathedral. Both in the *Scotsman* and elsewhere it was announced that there would be no invitations sent out, and no reception, but that friends wishing to attend the service would be welcomed. It would seem that neither Alastair nor Anne wanted the more usual glittering social occasion one would have expected for the heir-apparent to the Aros Estate. Their decision may have been influenced by a desire to skirt round a social difficulty. Since Col Bryce's divorce and remarriage there was a family rift to consider, and Alastair knew that his mother Hilda and his stepmother Madge would not wish to be seen together. In the event neither Col Bryce nor Madge attended the wedding ceremony.

They missed the opportunity of seeing a pretty bride dressed in a gown of pearl-tinted satin, with a skirt flowing into a train, over which was draped a family heirloom of beautiful lace. The train was carried by a posse of little boys dressed in kilts with white silk blouses and lace jabots. It has been difficult to identify all the boys, but two, Lowrie and Iain, were the sons of Anne's sister Mona Carmichael Sleigh. Mona was Anne's Maid of Honour; she had married in 1925 William Lowrie Sleigh, the son of the William Lowrie Sleigh who was Lord Provost of Edinburgh. His mother was Jessie Anne Sime. Anne's other sister, Retta, had married two years earlier Robert James Clark, a university lecturer in natural philosophy.

Alastair's best man was his friend Jack Dunlop of Seton Castle near Prestonpans, and Anne was given away by her uncle, John Fraser. As one would expect, although there were no official invitations, the generosity of the family and friends made the wedding a very special occasion. Five gifts are worth mentioning: Alastair gave his bride a diamond and platinum watch, she gave him a field cigarette case. Anne's mother gave them a cheque; the absent Col Bryce gave them a string of pearls and table crystal; Madge is not mentioned. Hilda's gift was lavish (though to modern eyes regrettable): she gave Anne a beaver fur coat and a silver fox fur.

Alastair and Anne spent their honeymoon in Tobermory, and though their wedding in Edinburgh had not been celebrated with a reception, the people of Tobermory turned out to welcome the couple back to Aros. It is highly likely that neither Col Bryce nor Madge were in residence at the time; Col Bryce, not wishing to cause any more dissent, probably took Madge off to see her family.

Alastair and Anna's three daughters were Susan Mary and Margaret Doris (both born in Dumfriesshire), and the youngest, Jane Elizabeth (born in Tobermory). There was a family tragedy shortly before Susan's birth; Anne's mother Janet was knocked down by a motor car as she was crossing Dean Bridge, Edinburgh, on Saturday 29 February 1936. She was taken to the Royal Infirmary, and although the press gave an indication that her condition was not that serious, saying only she had head injuries and concussion, Janet died five days later of a fractured skull. It was a sad end for a lady who had delighted in seeing her three daughters happily married, but did not live long enough to enjoy her grandchildren.

Chapter 24

Prelude

Margaret Mabel Gladys was another of the Allan women who did not conform to stereotypes of the "flapper generation" of women in the late nineteen-twenties and early nineteen-thirties. She had been too young to follow in the footsteps of her elder female Allan cousins in seeing service in the Great War. Her education, like that of her brothers, had been at Bedales, where she had learned independence and her spirit of adventure had been encouraged. In 1930 at the age of twenty-one she took part in her first motor trial, the London to Gloucester run, winning the ladies' prize. The motor car in the 1930s was still regarded by much of the population as a rich man's toy, and not unnaturally there were protests from members of the public and local authorities about these monsters ruining the peace and quiet of the countryside. The Somerset Standing Joint Committee were particularly concerned about the trials being held in narrow lanes at night and asked the Home Office to prevent them or at least restrict the times they were held.

The Royal Automobile Club were mindful of the complaints and admitted it

> is in sympathy with the public feeling that these reliability trials should be confined to the highways that are wide enough to leave room for other users ... this organization had repeatedly urged on local motoring clubs the importance of bearing in mind the rights and convenience of other persons when arranging trials.[1]

Margaret may well have had some sympathy for any alarmed pedestrians who dived into ditches to escape from the wheels of the motor, but she had no intention of giving up a sport she so obviously enjoyed from the moment she first sat at the wheel of a racing car. It was not long before she was no longer content just to take part in local trials. In 1932, with her co-driver Eve Staniland, she entered the Monte Carlo rally in a Lagonda, and finished tenth – an amazing result for an inexperienced rally driver in a long and gruelling race. In the same year she raced at Brooklands, the world-famous racing track in Weybridge which flourished between 1907 and 1939 and even today is considered to have been a very testing course for both car and driver. These were to be the first of many such races. She could well claim to have been an extremely successful and accomplished driver.

Local road trials around southern England, Brooklands and even Monte Carlo were not quite exciting enough for Margaret. Also in 1932, she competed in the Alpine Trial, the most demanding and complex of the racing season. It was a six-day-long trial from Munich to San Remo, held at the beginning of August; Margaret and her co-driver were in a Wolseley Hornet, and they came fourth. Her co-driver was none other than her brother Hamish. It is clear that even after the tragic death of his cousin Tom Lander, Hamish was still seeking excitement. His and Margaret's generation had inherited from Capt Sandy an eagerness for challenges, and the skill and endurance to try new adventures whether on land, by sea or in the air.

There was praise for the British drivers even before the trial had finished. With two days still to be completed, it was said of the cars:

> The excellent performances of the British cars ... have created a great impression on the Continent. The Germans, Swiss and Italian Press are loud in their praise of the British representatives ... the British motor industries will have made one of the most imposing displays ever undertaken in Europe.[2]

In 1933 it was not just the cars that were worthy of praise; there was warm praise for the British drivers from a correspondent, J E Montgomery of Splügen, who wrote to *The Times*:

> The international Alpine motor trials passed through this village on their way to the San Bernardino Pass, and your readers may be glad to know that the British drivers produced a favourable impression locally by their numbers, the careful manner in which they negotiated a sharp turn in the village (in contradistinction to the somewhat over-dashing style of others) and their general coolness and modesty, especially in the case of one car which stopped to change a wheel. It was remarked by some of our Swiss friends, that a number of the British drivers were wearing their ordinary clothes, as if the trials were an everyday event ...[3]

240

Claud and Adeline may have wondered at the enthusiasm with which their young nieces and nephews encountered these challenges – fast cars, gliders, fast ocean-going yachts and point-to-point horse races. At the beginning of the 1930s both of them were nearing the seventh decade of their lives, not that this meant either of them had any intention of retiring from their social and charitable commitments. Claud became Commodore of the Royal Northern Yacht Club in 1933, and during the summer months this occupied a good deal of his time. In the dying days of summer, and as autumn gave way to winter, Claud could be found enjoying a day's shooting. In winter he and Adeline would frequently be found curling on a frozen loch. The spring and summer months would occupy Adeline with a myriad of charities, her two main activities being the Red Cross Society, to whom she had presented her own Cup, and the Scottish National Sweet Pea, Rose and Carnation Society, of which she was the president. She presided over many of the annual shows held in Glasgow. Closer to their home at Kilmahew near Cardross she was an ardent supporter of two organizations, the Helensburgh and Gareloch Horticultural Society and the Women's Guild.

All this was part of their day-to-day lives; they were also watching over the lives of their sons, Charlie and Bobby, their daughters Marion and Sheena, and their grandchildren Michael, Fiona, and then Marion's son Denis born in 1937. Sheena, having left Peter Wilson, moved into a beautiful Manor House in Shamley Green near Guildford; it was a house of great charm. The large formal gardens and rolling lawns were a haven of peace and quiet. Not that Sheena would have time for such luxury; she offered a home-from-home for boarding school pupils who could not join their parents for vacations, and she used her nursing skills to offer convalescent care to many young pupils who needed a safe environment to recover from illnesses and accidents. She never lost her desire to help others, and in this she was surely her father's child, and a granddaughter who had inherited all the care and compassion that her grandparents had shown.

In September 1930 there had been a formal announcement in the *London Gazette* that a Helen Boyce Allan, now known as Helen Boyce Young, renounced the latter name and wished to be known again as Helen Boyce Allan. This was very odd, since her surname had never been "Young" at all, though when she enrolled at RADA while married to Hamish she had adopted her mother-in-law's surname and called herself "Helen Boyce Young", but as far as is known she had never acted or lived under that name.

In the first term of 1936 Hamish and Helen's daughter Rosamund became a pupil at Bedales, where both her parents had been educated. And that spring, after ten years alone, Hamish married again. He had known his bride Lucy Wyatt when he was a young doctor at Middlesex Hospital where she had been a nurse. On this occasion romantic fiction worked: they really did live happily ever after. They were to have four children, two sons (David Alexander and Andrew Wyatt), and two daughters (Claire Margaret and Fiona Lucy).

By 1936 Hamish had bought a medical practice in Southgate, North London; many of his patients would have been from the wealthy middle classes of what in 1936 was a delightful part of the sprawling metropolis, but it is almost certain that just as Jack was involved with the Peckham Experiment, Hamish must have given freely of his time and his expertise to the poor of the district.

Henry Allan had been a banker, a railway-company director, and a ship-owner; he was a Justice of the Peace and a member of the Merchants' House. To his family he was a jovial, kindly man, ever willing to put his vast experience at their disposal. There was, however, another side to his character. His years as director, vice-chairman and chairman of the Clydesdale Bank had been fraught with financial difficulties. His managers and senior staff did not always find him an easy man to deal with. He had strong views and probably, like his uncle Sir Hugh, he did not suffer fools gladly.

Like Janie, Henry never married; how far he shared her suffragette and socialist beliefs is unknown. They were both strong minded people, and their political views could well have been expressed dogmatically. If there were differences these did not prevent them from being close, and she was the informant when he died in February 1937. He had been ill with colon cancer for six months, and for the later part of that illness he had been a patient of Sir David Wilkie at his private clinic in Drumsheugh Gardens, Edinburgh.

In some ways Henry was particularly fortunate to have as his doctors Sir David Wilkie and Henry Wade. In Wilkie he had one of the most eminent abdominal surgeons of his day. He was very unlike the typical surgeon so often depicted: he was not domineering, not ruthless and certainly not aloof. He was charming, kindly and approachable. Wilkie had been born in Kirriemuir, the home of J M Barrie, but was not a contemporary, although in later life he and Barrie became friends.

Henry Wade, on the other hand, was a Robert Burns enthusiast and frequently gave lectures on the subject of Burns and the medical profession. It would be delightful to think that in his last days on earth Henry Allan might have discussed his own family's collateral links to the great poet.

In 1937 there were another two family weddings. The first was when Margaret decided to retire from motor racing and settle down to a more gentle form of life. She did not, however, give up racing altogether: her last race was in 1950, when she won the Ladies Race in the Circuit of Ireland Race. In February 1937 she married Richard Edward Christopher Jennings, a fellow competitor in the motor racing circle. Chris Jennings was born in 1911, the son of a retired army officer, Edward Jennings of Gellideg, Kidwelly, Carmarthenshire. He had been educated at Repton School. In 1931 he had joined the motor car company Riley of Coventry, and it was with Riley that he had driven for many years. In the year he married Margaret he was appointed Midland Editor for *The Motor,* and this started a connection with the magazine that would last until the Second World War interrupted all their lives.

Shortly before her marriage, Margaret was reminded that her father JamesA's attempts to register her birth back in 1909 had been disastrously muddled. His first attempt had been to register her as Mabel Gladys, then he tried Margaret Nora, but finally, in January 1937, her mother Mabel

Nora was able to sign a "A Register of Corrected Entries of Birth" and Margaret officially became Margaret Mabel Gladys Allan.

Shortly after Margaret's marriage her cousin, Monica (Mickey) married Robert MacDonald Sutherland on 19 May 1937 at St Conan's Church, Loch Awe. As a statement of fact those brief words do not in any way accurately tell the love story that had developed between the twenty-two-year-old heiress and the forty-year-old estate worker. It is worth quoting from the *Oban Times*, for it gives a vivid picture of the events of that day:

> In the beautiful Church of St Conan's, picturesquely situated on the shores of Loch Awe, the marriage of Miss Monica Allan of Shuna to Mr Bert [*Robert*] Sutherland, Dunbeath, Caithness took place on Wednesday afternoon. All arrangement for the event were kept private, and neither the church officers of St Conan's nor the inhabitants of the village of Lochawe had the slightest indication of the marriage, until the arrival of the interested parties.[4]

Sutherland was born on 10 July 1896, the illegitimate son of Catherine Ann Sutherland, the daughter of Donald Sutherland and Ann Grant of Latheron, Caithness. Catherine was a General Servant; her father was a shoemaker/crofter. On his marriage certificate Sutherland was described as a "land owner", which at the time of his marriage may have been technically correct: Mickey had purchased the Island of Shuna, off the west coast of Scotland, fourteen miles from Oban, a year before her marriage.

The headlines in the national press were not slow to point out the difference in social status of the bride and groom. They made much of that difference, stating that Sutherland had been a gillie to Mickey's father. Once again the Press were wrong. According to the estate records of Dunbeath Castle, at the time of his marriage Sutherland was an under-keeper.

Mickey had arrived unannounced shortly before the ceremony with her mother Georgie and Charles Tennant. They had lunched at the Loch Awe hotel and then motored to the church where Robert was waiting, accompanied by a friend who unfortunately is not named. The only other persons present were Mickey's chauffeur and maid, again not named.

The marriage was quietly and solemnly performed by [*Mr Adam Anderson, Minister of Glenochry and Inishail*] The bride was given away by her step-father. There were no floral decorations except a vase of red, white and blue flowers.[5]

Not for Mickey a gown of silk and lace: she wore a fawn tailored costume and beige fox fur, with a brown velour hat. She had cream gloves and carried a hand bag, and on her jacket was a delightful corsage.

News of the wedding ceremony had filtered out somehow, for as the newlyweds emerged a small group of locals were there to greet them. The *Oban Times* reports that a number of telegrams were handed to the couple, and as Mickey and Robert entered their car, confetti was thrown. There is a rather sad and poignant end to the story of Mickey's wedding day, for there would be no reception. Instead, Mickey and Robert drove away accompanied only by her maid and the chauffeur. Georgie and Tennant had to wait for a couple of hours before starting their journey back to London. Tennant had given his step-daughter away and both he and Georgie had witnessed the marriage, but that was the end of their involvement in that important day.

Perhaps the last word on her marriage to Sutherland should go to Mickey. She told an inquisitive journalist that she loved the out-door life and had absolutely no interest in the cocktail circuit. She added that she preferred the "*lonely quiet of Shuna to the bustle of Mayfair*".[6]

Mickey and Robert had two daughters, Shuna Anne and Lorna Jane, both born on the Isle of Shuna. Mickey restored the old manor house, bringing in modern plumbing and electricity from a generator, and in many ways it must have been a paradise during the early years of her marriage to Robert. He farmed and supplied the household with most of the produce they needed. Though the summers may have been balmy, the winter storms of the west coast would have tested the resolve of most mainlanders. Mickey and Robert were hardy people and clearly for them the wildness more than compensated for their lack of daily visitors.

A link with the past was broken when in January 1938 Hugh Andrew, the son of Old Andrew of Montreal, died. Hugh had inherited many of the traits of his uncle Sir Hugh, in that he was always ready to embrace new ideas and new challenges. He had married Margaret Elizabeth Rae, and had one daughter, Rachel, born around 1898. He had spent his early years in Boston with his cousin Bryce James. On Sir Montagu's retirement as President and the takeover of the Allan Line by the Canadian Pacific Railway (a decision that Hugh Andrew never came to accept), he left Montreal and conducted the business of the H & A Allan Line from London. Hugh Andrew was the last of the Allan family who could truly be called an outstanding figure in the transatlantic shipping trade. The first love of Sir Hugh and of Hugh Andrew was the same as it had been for Capt Sandy: ships. The younger generation were equally successful in many ways, but they were pursuing other careers.

This was certainly true of Claud's younger son, Bobby; in December 1938, he was unanimously adopted as prospective National Government candidate for the Coatbridge Division of the Unionist Association. Bobby had been a pupil at Harrow where he won the Rothschild Scholarship. He went up to Clare College, Cambridge to read history, and from there he won the Mellon Scholarship to study at Yale, where he obtained his post-doctoral degree. He was a first-class athlete and ran for the university in cross-country races. At the time of his adoption as a future parliamentary candidate he was working for his father's business. In his address to the constituency meeting Bobby showed that he was a young man with a wide knowledge and understanding of the problems the nation faced, saying:

> one vital issue, at the moment was the preservation of democracy, and to-day democracy was faced with so many difficulties, both external and internal ... The only way in which this could be done was by preservation of a really strong National Government. That was the answer to those problems which in other countries, had seen their reply in Fascism and Nazism ... In order that appeasement may not become retreat, the representatives of this country must be in such a strong position that they can not only walk into a conference with the "Iron Men of Europe", but that they can walk out as well.[7]

However, Bobby did not get his wish to become a Member of Parliament for another thirteen years. The war interrupted his plans, as it did for so many other young men.

The rumours that the Royal Northern Yacht Club was to move were finally resolved when the club moved its headquarters from Rothesay to the imposing manor house of Ardenvohr at Rhu before the start of the 1937 season. It did not mean that they had severed all their associations with Bute, as some races would still be held over the old Craigmore courses.

> When the official list of Clyde racing fixtures for this season was drawn up, the time-honoured opening cruise of the Royal Northern and Royal Clyde was abandoned, the Coronation Regatta at Hunter's Quay taking its place. At the same time, the opening fixture of the Royal Northern was confined to matches at Rothesay tomorrow. Within the past few days an alternation has been made and through the generosity of Mr Claud Allan, the Commodore, two special prizes have been provided for cruising races to-day from Rhu to Craigmore.[8]

Claud and the Allan family, both direct descendents and collateral descendents, would all enjoy the delights of Ardenvohr for many decades, enjoying the spectacular scenery of the that wide expanse of the Clyde. Ardenvohr gave them many days of great sailing and many great social occasions.

Henry's death left Claud as the last surviving son of Alexander and Jane, but he had already shown that he was more than capable of taking on the mantle as the head of the wider family. He had also shown that he had inherited some of the socialist characteristics of his brother, JamesA. He may not have gone so far as to join the Independent Labour Party, but he was certainly not one who believed in the strict division of the social classes. A passionate curler, his team was frequently made up of members of his household staff, such as Andrew Aitken, who had been with him for over fifty years, beginning as his coachman and then, when horses gave way to the motor car, as Claud's chauffeur. Two other team members were Dunbar, his head gardener for more than thirty years and Stratton, his handyman.

In a letter written to Bobby in January 1938 Claud chides his son for sending Christmas cards to the staff at Kilmahew but leaving his parents letter and cardless. He gave Bobby news of the Christmas and New Year celebrations at Kilmahew, and the annual entertainment they arranged for the James Allan Trust almshouses in Whiteinch. The film show with which he had hoped to entertain the Kilmahew staff did not go exactly to plan: the films were supposed to be comic talkies, but instead they were shown newsreels of the Coronation of George VI, and of angling for a big fish. The year, however, had begun with a good deal of curling, and he and his team had gone to Edinburgh for an inter-province match (though the result was not as they would have wished: they were relegated to the second division). The journey back to Cardross was not without incident, as he told Bobby:

> We left Edinburgh by the 4.50 train and owing to fog it took us 4 hours to reach Glasgow, at one point we saw our fireman climbing the signal post with a lamp in his hand to see if the signal was in his favour.[9]

As 1938 gave way to 1939 the looming menace of war hung over them and for the next six years there would be little time for pleasure. Just as had happened in 1914, the lamps were going out all over Europe. It would be a long time before a mood of optimism would return.

Adeline was elected a Justice of the Peace in 1939 and an office-bearer for the British Red Cross Association, while in May Claud was appointed Vice-Lord-Lieutenant for the County of Dunbartonshire. They should have been able to look forward to spending their retirement years in tranquil surroundings enjoying the comforts of their beautiful home at Kilmahew, but like all other families the Allans would find the war would bring them worry, anxiety and heartache.

Chapter 25

Their World Changed

Christmas 1938 and the New Year of 1939 were the last really joyous occasions for many years to come. Few people as they gathered round the dining-room tables to celebrate the birth of Christ could imagine what their lives were going to be like for the next six years. It was less than twenty-one years since the guns had grown silent in the last War, and now they stood on the brink of yet another terrible, bloody conflict.

Charlie came home to Kilmahew to spend the festive season with his parents and siblings, but as he was to recount after his return to London in early January his journey home had not been a comfortable experience:

> I left London on one of the midday trains on Friday, December 23. Practically all the seats ... were reserved, so that the company knew fairly accurately how many passengers they were to carry. I settled down in the long coach containing 31 others in the hopes that so many bodies in such a comparatively small space would create adequate warmth, helped by the company's steam heating.[1]

Poor Charlie! Requests to the guard to improve the heating proved fruitless. He then had to suffer a further indignity by not being able to secure a table for lunch. At five o'clock he made his way to the restaurant car for tea only to find that the queue for service was very long, and to add to the passengers' problems with the cold there was also no lighting all the way from London to Carlisle, except for a few odd minutes.

> After standing in this queue for an hour and a half I eventually won a place in the restaurant car, and, a few minutes after sitting down, the attendant came along to say that he was very sorry there would be no tea as they had run out of gas. ... All the bread and butter, toast, &c. had also run out and we were offered a small tin containing a few chocolate biscuits ... I complained bitterly to the attendant, who asked me ... if I would

come along and see the conditions under which they were working. I accepted the invitation, and on reaching the kitchen car I found about four attendants groping about among the shelves, and the only light they had was a dirty old oil lamp borrowed from the guard. ... I arrived at Glasgow nearly two hours late feeling I had had a really "Raw Deal" and no "Square Meal".[2]

Col Bryce had been born in Aros, and had been Laird of Aros for over ten years, but facing the prospect of another world war he took the decision to sell part of the Aros Estate. In June 1939, through the agents Walker, Fraser and Steel, he offered for sale some 3,875 acres including two farms, the island of Calve, and Aros House. The advertisement made clear the sale would be by private treaty, not by auction.

It cannot be known with any certainty why Col Bryce took the decision he did. He loved the island and its people, and the estate had been gifted to him by his father, who had served the people of Tobermory for almost fifty years. On the other hand, the years of the Depression had seen the income from the estate decline rapidly, and this income would in all probability decline even further if there was another war. It was also true that Alastair and his family were unlikely to want to take on the role of Laird of Aros, while Sheila and Bill Sykes on their retirement had made their home at Linndhu House in Tobermory. But whatever Col Bryce's reasons, to the wider Allan family and to the people of Tobermory it must have seemed that their world had indeed begun to die. However, as it turned out, the declaration of war on 3 September ended any hope Col Bryce might have had that he would be able to sell before the return of peace.

As in the previous war the young men were ready to serve their King and Country: Charlie, Bobby and Chris Jennings were among the first of the younger generation into the fray. Dick, farmer and soldier, rejoined his old regiment, and was appointed as ADC to the Scottish Commandant. He should have looked forward to an easy war, but nothing in Dick's life had ever been that simple. He contracted tuberculosis, and spent months in a sanatorium at Tor-na-Dee, Murtle – the same sanatorium where Georgie's father, Rev Dr Alexander Stewart, had so diligently worked half a century earlier to improve the treatment of TB sufferers. Dick made a partial recovery but he was never again fully fit; he returned to his lonely life on his farm. Poor Dick never had much luck either with war service or with pretty girls. He died in 1973 at the age of sixty-five.

Hamish was past the obligatory age of conscription but nevertheless volunteered for service the day after the declaration of war. He was accepted, even though in the previous war he had been refused on medical grounds. He was posted to a Field Ambulance Unit, but a month later he requested a transfer, and was accepted as a member of the British Expeditionary Force (BEF) with the rank of acting major. He could not have known in those first confused months of the war that service with the BEF would prove to be so appalling awful. In May 1940 Hitler ordered the invasion of France. The BEF and the French military were ill-equipped to counter the advancing German military machine and they had no alternative but to retreat.

The retreat from Dunkirk was a humiliation, but a humiliation that was in a sense transformed into a triumph. Under constant bombardment from German guns on land and dive bombers in the air, the story of the "little ships" has earned its place as one of the miracles of the Second World War, focusing particularly on the courage of all involved and the tenacity and seamanship of the crews. The evacuation from the beaches of Dunkirk between 27 May and 4 June 1940 saw an armada of trawlers, yachts and little boats rescuing thousands of British and French troops.

Hamish returned to Dover on 3 June. The next day he was struck off the strength of the BEF and rejoined the Field Ambulance Service as an Officer Commanding, with the rank of Captain.

The war left many of the older men with nothing but loneliness, depression and a sense of bewilderment and hopelessness. They had been told the last war was the war that would end all wars. Now it had all begun again.

Doris Vernon had left Hanbury Hall and her husband Sir George in 1930, refusing him a divorce. He continued to live at the Hall with his secretary/adopted daughter Annie Ruth Horton, but his income was dwindling and he was increasingly unable to manage the Hanbury Estate.

He had accepted the National Trust's offer to take over the management of the estate with the proviso that he and his estranged wife Doris should have the right of occupancy until their deaths. Sir George died by his own hand on 14 June 1940; he bequeathed what was left of his estate to Annie Ruth Horton or Vernon. Among his executors was Donald MacLean Matheson, Secretary of the National Trust. Doris returned to Hanbury Hall, where, drawing on her own inherited wealth and with the assistance of the National Trust, she was able to make essential repairs. She continued to live at the Hall until her own death in March 1962; and in contrast to her late husband, Sir George, her estate at probate was considerable, surely indicating that she had invested her inheritance from her father with more care than Sir George had brought to his own financial affairs.

Charlie, according to all the rules of military enlistment, should not have been recruited at the start of the war. A series of serious accidents while pursuing his passion for point-to-point and National Hunt steeplechasing had left him medically unfit for active service. However, he was a man of action, as his passion for fast horses had shown, and he was determined to serve. Early in the war he joined the North Somerset Yeomanry.

In May 1941 Charlie married Bethia Dundas Jardine, at Devizes, Wiltshire. She was the divorced wife of Jack Greenshield Watherston, a farmer from Timpendean, Jedburgh, and the daughter of Brigadier General James Bruce Jardine of Chesterknowes, Roxburghshire. While her marriage to Waterston had not lasted long, this second marriage was to give both Charlie and Bethia great happiness. There were two children, Gillian and Caroline. In one of those strange twists of fate that happen, Watherston also married again in 1946 and he and his new wife Eildon [Elizabeth McConnell], remained friends with Charlie and Bethia.

If the young men were ready to fight then the Allan women were also not slow in offering their services. Margaret Jennings with her wide experience of motor vehicles drove an ambulance, as her Canadian kinswoman Martha had done in the Great War. Janie, too old for any kind of active service, nevertheless was not prepared to sit out the new war in splendid isolation in the East Lodge Invergloy, well away from any enemy action. She wanted to make a contribution.

> Typical of her readiness to help the underdog, and her unselfishness, was her action over refugees from Hitler's Germany. She turned her house at Invergloy over to refugees and had four or five families living with her for several years.[3]

In Canada, Martha must have viewed the prospect of another war with distress and bitterness. She had seen service in the last war, a war which had taken the lives of all three of her siblings; on her return to Montreal after the war she had been determined that this would not be a return to the world of salons, dancing and husband hunting. She went to Pasadena, California to study the operation and management of repertory theatre; once back in Ravenscrag, she moved out of the big mansion and into the coach-house, where she started the Little Theatre Company. In 1929 her little theatre company became the Montreal Repertory Theatre Company, and its success over the next twelve years could be said to be Martha's legacy to Canada. She believed that the repertory theatre was the best and perhaps the only means of giving young people their first chance of becoming professional actors. There is little doubt that that she succeeded, and that many fine Canadian actors began their careers with the Little Theatre Company and the Montreal Repertory Theatre Company.

Martha had the same strong streak of character that was so evident in Janie. There is a neat thumbnail sketch of Martha which seems to sum her up well:

> Perfectly bilingual ... she was a close cropped blonde, slim of figure, and always very well-tailored. She was also overpowering and very abrupt, though friendly enough in manner, and used all the influence at her command as the daughter of Sir Montagu.[4]

In early 1942, Martha became gravely ill and was advised by her doctors to leave the cold of Montreal and travel to the Pacific coast where hopefully the warmer weather would aid her recovery. To begin with it seems the new location would work, but in March her condition again deteriorated and she was admitted to hospital. Her parents rushed to her bedside, but sadly she died in St Joseph's Hospital, Victoria, British Columbia on Saturday 4 April. She was forty-seven years old. Her body was returned to Montreal and her final resting place was beside her sisters Anna and Gwen and the memorial to her brother Hugh. Her grief-stricken parents were left to face the future without a single one of their children. Montagu died in September 1951, Marguerite in 1957; he was ninety-one, she seventy-four.

The war may have seemed a long way off to those living at Aros, but there were moments of grief: Alastair was away serving with the RNVR, but he was at home on the morning of 4 July 1942, when Col Bryce died suddenly of a coronary thrombosis. Bryce was sixty-eight years old. He had given his life to Aros and the people of Tobermory, and had been feted as the "Young Laird" when his father was alive, but although he had held many public appointments in Argyll he had never been held in the same esteem as his late father. The work and support he had given to the Boy Scout Movement, of which he was such a strong advocate, was perhaps his true legacy to the children of Scotland.

His divorce from Hilda and his marriage to Madge Gough had probably shocked the staunchly conservative Free Kirk folk of Mull; moreover Madge had not been popular with her stepson and daughter-in-law, nor with Sheila and her children. The wealth of Aros had declined following the long years of war and recession, and the Aros Estate had not yet had time to recover. Bryce's Will makes interesting reading; he made the usual small bequest to his servants, providing they had been in his, or his father's, employ for twenty years. He leaves small legacies to Sheila and her children Edward and Elizabeth; the residue of his estate he leaves to his son Alastair. It is the provisions he makes for Madge which are the most interesting; he agrees to honour the terms of his pre-nuptial agreement but his terms for allowing her to remain at Aros are such that she has no real alternative but to leave the island, together with her daughter Barbie. He instructs his executors to invest £2,500 from his estate and pay the interest over to Madge.

Perhaps unsurprisingly, he left nothing to his first wife, not even a mention; but Hilda outlived him by twenty-five years, dying in Edinburgh in 1967 at the age of ninety. It is clear that she and her sister Doris Vernon both came from the same hardy Allan stock; forthright and enduring, courageous and energetic, people who most certainly did not suffer fools gladly.

Sheena had spent a restless kind of existence since the break-up of her marriage to Peter Wilson. In 1932, shortly after the break-up, she had spent a vacation in Montreal with her Allan cousins; in 1938 Claud and Adeline had taken her to New York aboard the *Queen Mary*; but she had still not found a real purpose for her life. The war, for a little, changed all that; she had been very ill with pneumonia and Claud and Adeline persuaded her to leave Shamley Green and return to Scotland. This was a very wise decision: for one thing the south of England by 1941 was not a safe place to bring up two small children. In the event, with her nursing experience and her desire to be useful Sheena became a matron of the Braeholm Nursing Home in East Montrose Street, Helensburgh. The first few months were a busy time preparing the house for its first expectant mothers. The house was not quite large enough for Sheena's plans and she commissioned the building of a wooden bungalow in the gardens of Braeholm to accommodate her nursing staff. Unaware of, or not bothered by, such small matters as planning applications, Sheena was soon in trouble with the Local Authorities: even in a time of war bureaucracy had to be observed to the letter. But Sheena, undaunted, continued with her plans to open her nursing/maternity home, and finally on 13 August, the birthday of her son, Michael, the first babies, twins, were born at Braeholm.

However, nothing was secure: in January 1943 she wrote to her sister-in-law Barbara Wilson, the wife of Canon Harry Broughton, that she feared the Admiralty were about to commandeer Braeholm to house Wrens. She was worried about where she and her children would go if Braeholm was taken by the Admiralty; she feared she could not go to Kilmahew as it had been badly damaged when a landmine exploded close by the house.

Sheena may have viewed the beginning of 1943 with a mixture of sadness and despair, but by the spring she had been introduced to an

English Naval Officer, John (Jack) Parnell Hunt. In April they announced their engagement and were married in Rhu with a reception at Braeholm and a short wartime honeymoon in Luss, on the banks of Loch Lomond, and in Kent. Sheena left Scotland to follow Jack to his naval posting; she found a home in Eastbourne, in what she hoped would be a home for Jack when he managed to get leave. The Admiralty had other ideas and Jack was promoted to Commander and posted to Algiers as Captain of the Dockyard. War is no respecter of lovers, and Algiers was a dangerous posting. On 4 August a German bombing raid set fire to an ammunition ship in the harbour. Jack Hunt realized that if the ship exploded in the harbour not only would the damage to the town be massive but it would also make allied landings difficult for many weeks. He set out to tow the stricken tanker out to sea, an act of exceptional courage by a very brave man indeed. Just as he was about to cut the tow line the ship exploded, killing not only Jack but many crew members on the tow craft.

It is impossible to imagine the misery that Sheena must have felt when she first opened that awful telegram telling her that Jack was "missing in action", a phrase that brought dread to all those who read those three terrible words. On 26 August a brief but poignant announcement was made in the Scottish papers that Jack was "now known to have been killed". Sheena added a note, quoting Psalm 56 verse 11: "In God have I put my trust: I will not be afraid what man can do unto me." She had been hurt too many times, and it may well have seemed there was nothing more that men could take from her, nor was there anything more she could give to them.

Bobby Allan would have been the first to admit he had an interesting, frequently exciting and at times highly dangerous war. He was tall, good-looking, charismatic, indeed the very epitome of the dashing young naval officer. He was a realist: he may once have believed that peace with Hitler was possible, but by May 1939 he knew it was just a forlorn hope and he joined the RNVR, Clyde Division, where his father Claud had served with distinction since its formation. Bobby spent the first couple of years of the war as a member of the Coastal Forces based at Gosport, Hampshire. In June 1942 he was posted to Alexandria, as Commander of a squadron of motor torpedo boats, and his war began in earnest: he was the youngest

Commander in the RNVR and his exceptional flair for leadership, his courage and his ability to assess each situation soon placed him among the very best of his generation. He led the young sailors of his MTB, his MGB (motor gun boat) and his landing craft with all the skill he had learned as a yachtsman, never showing fear, but chasing and harassing the enemy ships across the Mediterranean while the Allies were battling to drive the Germans and the Italians out of North Africa. An example of Bobby Allan's successful tactics is shown in the following quotation:

> Commander Allan kept his course and speed. When the enemy escort group was about three miles away Allan decided that they were aware of the British ships' presence and were determined to engage. Allan was resolved that the battle should be under conditions as propitious to himself as possible, and he accordingly ordered his fleet to steer so they would come across on a parallel course, and to reduce their speed.[5]

The chase and the battle lasted for many hours but finally Bobby returned to his base in Bastia and was able to report that it had been a very successful night's work for his forces. In 1943 he was at an in-shore base at Augusta, Sicily and there was a delightful Press report of what life was like for the land-based seamen.

> On a hill high above Augusta and some miles from the sewer-like smell of that small town, there is a tree from which hangs a cardboard sign with the inscription: "Ward Room." A table and some chairs are all that is added to the shade of the tree to complete the ward room ... It was not until they came to Sicily that these men of the coastal forces set up camp ashore, and they claim this is the first naval camp of the war... Camouflage at sea is an affair of paint, but on shore it is done in terms of nets, which lose their effect when a long row of laundered white shirts and shorts are strung across to dry.[6]

Peace was finally declared in the summer of 1945, and it was a time for rejoicing across the land. At Kilmahew, Claud and Adeline must have said a prayer of thanks that both their sons had survived the war and would come home safely. Adeline had been ill, but with the strain of worrying about her sons now lifted she might have looked forward to enjoying peace, and her retirement. How sad then that in the afternoon of 4 August

Claud should die of pneumonia. He was seventy-four. He and Adeline had been happily married for forty-four years, and their Kilmahew home had been a haven of joy. As with his parents, it had been his faith that had helped him through the years of turmoil. He had been an Elder of the Burns Church, Cardross and a member of the Presbytery of Dumbarton. In many ways he was a quiet man; he did not have the aggressive nature of his uncle Sir Hugh, nor the intolerance of his brother Henry. He had always been his own man.

> [He] abhorred pretence, was shrewd in judgement, wise in counsel and tolerant in debate. A man who reconciled strong conviction with real humanity, tempered zeal with charity, was no more generous openly than in secret and sought never the praise of man but always the glory of God.[7]

Claud had become trustee of both the James Allan Almshouses and the Orphanage at Whiteinch. That task would now pass to the next generation, who would have to live up to Claud's exacting standards of service in respect of both charities.

Kilmahew and Cardross had not escaped damage from German bombing raids; the parish church and a number of houses had been destroyed by incendiary bombs. Kilmahew itself had suffered extensive damage when a land-mine had dropped nearby. Claud's death meant that either the family found sufficient funds – and the enthusiasm – to carry out a major refurbishment, or they would have to sell Kilmahew. A decision was taken to sell. St Peter's Roman Catholic Seminary already owned the nearby Darlieth House, and they moved into Kilmahew in 1948.

Adeline must have left Kilmahew with mixed emotions, it had been her home with Claud for most of their married life. She did not, however, leave Cardross but spent the remainder of her life at Ardardan, where she died in July 1952.

Claud was the last of Alexander and Jane's sons to die, and a few months later, in November 1945, the youngest of Old Andrew's sons, James Bryce

KC, died in Montreal. He had never married. After a very short career as a lawyer, less than fourteen years, he had retired in 1903, shortly after inheriting a sizable fortune on the death of his father. In 1929 he set up a trust fund for his old Oxford college, Oriel; in the trust settlement he makes the point that:

> The income of the Trust Fund shall be applied as the Provost and Fellows of the said College may in their absolute discretion think fit either (a) in making grants to Undergraduate Members of the said College to enable them to travel on the Continent of Europe or (b) for any other purpose whatsoever.[8]

He stipulated that the trust fund should always bear his name. Travel was obviously very much in James Bryce's mind from the moment of his retirement. He spent the first few years touring Europe, but returned to Canada for the duration of the Great War, then he returned to Italy, where he settled until 1938, when he again returned to Montreal to live with his sister Brenda Meredith. His obituary in the *Montreal Star* is a little light on detail regarding his life in Italy, but we can assume that James Bryce would have found many like-minded expatriates and Italians with whom to socialize, enjoying the sunshine a long long way from the biting winters of Quebec.

He is buried in Mount Royal, along with other members of both Sir Hugh's and Old Andrew's families. Sir Montagu and Lady Marguerite were among the mourners, although these two remarkable people were eighty-five and seventy-two respectively at the time of the funeral. The list of mourners was as one would have expected for a member of the Montreal Allans' extensive connection, even though James Bryce had spent much of the last thirty-odd years away from his ancestral home.

Charlie's brother Bobby Allan came home from the war a much decorated hero. He was awarded the DSO for his service off the west coast of Italy, the Croix de Guerre in 1943, and the OBE in the New Years' Honours List of 1944. Also in 1943 he was appointed a Commander of the Legion of Honour. He was mentioned in Despatches five times. Back in the civilian world he fought the General Election of 1945 but lost, and went to Washington as Deputy Chief of Naval Information. In July 1947 Bobby married Maureen Catherine Stuart-Clark at St Saviour's Church, London. They had two children, Alexander and Jane. In 1951 Bobby finally achieved his ambition of becoming a Member of Parliament, winning the London seat of Paddington South for the Conservative Party. He made his maiden speech on 6 March 1952; not surprisingly it was during a debate on Naval Matters, which gave him the chance to reflect on his own wartime experiences. He admitted, as all new Members do, that he was nervous and diffident at addressing them:

> I wish to discuss the subject of the RNVR ... It is well known that before the war there was not a great deal of enthusiasm in the Service for training the RNVR. Before the war I served for 10 days in a destroyer, as a sub-lieutenant, and the commanding officer never once spoke to me. I know that during and immediately following the war that near-hostility has completely vanished, but I do hear, from those whom I know in the RNVR, both officers and men, that something of that feeling is creeping back. I urge ... [that he do] everything he can to try and stop it, because it can be done so easily. Now is the time to do it, because the younger officers, who now command the small ships in which most of the RNVR do their sea-training, have not had first-hand experience of the value of the Reserves in time of war, and they may be a little sceptical.[9]

In Parliamentary terms, Bobby's tenure as the Conservative Member for Paddington South was rewarding but brief, lasting only fifteen years. They were turbulent years, as the nation tried to recover from the war years. He served under four Prime Ministers; Sir Winston Churchill, Sir Anthony Eden, Harold Macmillan and Sir Alex Douglas Home; but it was another Conservative MP elected in the early 1950s, Edward Heath, who became a close friend. They shared, of course, not just the same political principles but a love of yachts and sailing. There is a story told by Lady Maureen Allan that the only time her husband admitted to being scared was when he was sailing with Edward Heath.

The General Election of 1966 saw the return of Harold Wilson's Labour Party, but by then Bobby had already turned away from politics and returned to a business career. Among other banking and commercial interests, he was Chairman of Ladybird Books, a Director of Pearson/Longman, and a Governor of the BBC between 1971 and 1976. In 1973 he was made a Life Peer and took the title Lord Allan of Kilmahew. Bobby died suddenly on a trip to Australia in 1979. It was a short life in terms of the Allan family but a life to be proud of in his exceptional service to his country in both war and peace.

Bobby's and Maureen's wedding was not the only family wedding to take place in 1947; a few months earlier, in Edinburgh [Helen Agnes] Elizabeth Sykes, Sheila's daughter, married John Murray Normand, a colonial administrative officer. They would have three children, two sons (Hugh Alexander and Charles), and a daughter (Rona Margaret Elizabeth). As the wife of a colonial officer, Elizabeth would find her life drawing her away from Scotland: Murray and she were in Kenya at the time of the Mau Mau uprising, and this was followed by a posting to Malaya. Elizabeth had seen service in the war with the WRNS and was posted to the South-East Asia Command; she must have known when she married Murray that her life would be very different from the peaceful, tranquil beauty of Aros. Yet she and her children would return to Linndhu whenever the opportunity presented itself. They still do.

Hamish had spent part of the war in Italy before being posted to India; he had been promoted to the rank of Lieutenant-Colonel, and had more than earned the many decorations he had been awarded. When he finally left the army, he and Lucy and their children moved to Yaldhurst, a rambling mansion house in Pennington, near Lymington. The advent of the National Health Service in 1948 saw Hamish become a partner at the Wisteria Practice, in St Thomas's Street. The partnership would last until his retirement at the age of seventy-two: he was a true family doctor in the real sense of that phrase, and much respected by his patients. He died in January 1993 aged ninety-six.

Jack also returned to Hampshire. After leaving Dartington Hall in 1950 he returned to Bedales as Honorary Secretary and Treasurer of the Bedales Society, a post he held for twenty-four years. He died three years before Hamish, in February 1990.

There have been and still are, many myths and legends associated with members of the Allan families. In trying to distinguish fact from fiction it has been necessary to try and find incontrovertible evidence to support the actual truth. Never has this been more important than in the life of James Bryce Allan, of Wemyss Bay. Poor James Bryce has had so many stories told about him and his life with his French wife Marguerite Jolivet that one begins to wonder if the full truth will ever come to light. According to one source, based on a written report from a relative of Jolivet, James Bryce died in tragic circumstances in Monaco when the car he was tinkering with caught fire and he burned to death. However, according to his English death certificate he died on 12 May 1960 at 20 Devonshire Place, St Marylebone, London. He suffered a massive pulmonary embolism, certified by R Ian Milne, the Coroner for the County of London, after a post-mortem. There was no inquest since the cause of death was not in dispute.

Castles are another source of contention in James Bryce's life; it is true he lived in Ballikinrain Castle in Balfron for a few years. It is equally true that sometime in 1939/1940 he bought Ince Castle in Saltash, Cornwall. It is also true that shortly after James Bryce's sudden and untimely death Marguerite Jolivet, his widow, sold Ince to Viscount Boyd of Merton, whose son still owns the Castle to this day.

It is perhaps fitting that the final tale in this book is of dear old Janie; born on the 28 March 1868, she lived to celebrate her hundredth birthday at Invergloy. She had a party for her family, the villagers, and her friends; the guests included Sir Donald Cameron, Chief of Clan Cameron of Lochiel and former Lord-Lieutenant of Inverness-shire. It must have been a puzzling task for her family and friends to know what to give an old lady who had given so much but had also been surrounded by so much wealth. In the end they made handsome donations to the Guide Dogs for the Blind organization, a gesture that surely delighted her.

Sadly the party was the very last family occasion that Janie would enjoy; she died on 29 April. Her memory lives on in the minds of others;

she was fearless, courageous, determined and energetic even up to the last years of her long life. Only a fall a few years before her death, trying to jump a burn, caused her to reduce her activities.

She was a woman of her time, and an Allan woman to the last. She certainly left the world a better place. Like everyone, after death she keeps her own counsel; but we are still allowed to speculate. At the end of that long life did she sit and remember her childhood, her parents and all the departed Allans, the ships, the travelling, the parties, the family dramas; and did she think about her younger nieces, nephews and cousins who were carrying the name forward? Did she ponder the astonishing social changes she had witnessed? Did she think the trials and tribulations that she and her fellow suffragettes had suffered had been worthwhile? (We must hope so.)

And thankfully we can only wonder what she would have thought about the cruel irony that was soon to follow: the night before her funeral, heartless individuals broke into her home and stole her silver and family heirlooms. They must surely have deserved the harshest sentence the courts could hand down, but had they done this in her lifetime, it would not have been the financial value that she would have most resented losing, but the memories that connected these possessions with her family and her past.

This story of the Allan family began in 1780 with the birth of Capt Sandy in Dundonald, Ayrshire; or perhaps we may prefer to date it from 1806, when he married Jean Crawford in Saltcoats. It ends in 1968, after nearly two centuries of change, with the birthday celebrations and death of Sandy's and Jean's granddaughter in her home near Spean Bridge.

In war and in peace the story has criss-crossed the globe – by sailing-ship, steamship, motor torpedo boat, yacht, liner, glider, rally-car and railway – and now it ends back in Scotland, a mere 130 miles from the little west coast town where Janie's grandfather first went to sea.

Bibliography

APPLETON, THOMAS E, 1974 *Ravenscrag: The Allan Royal Mail Line*. Toronto: McClelland & Stewart Ltd.

JUDD, DENNIS & KEITH SERRIDGE, 2002 *The Boer War*. London: John Murray.

KERR, J LENNOX and DAVIS JONES (editors) 1950 *Wavy Navy: "by some who served"*. London: George G Harrap & Co Ltd.

—— 1957 *The RNVR: "A Record of Achievement"*. London: George G Harrap & Co Ltd.

KINSLEY, JAMES 1968 *The Poems & Songs of Robert Burns*. Oxford: Clarendon Press & Oxford University Press.

LANG, ANDREW (ed) 1896 *The Poems & Songs of Robert Burns*. London: Metheun.

MUNN, CHARLES C 1988 *Clydesdale Bank: "the first one hundred & fifty years"*. Glasgow and London: William Collins Sons & Co Ltd, in association with Clydesdale Bank.

NOCK, O S 1950 *Scottish Railways*. Thomas Nelson & Sons Ltd.

—— 1963 The *Caledonian Railway*. Hersham: Ian Allan Ltd.

—— 1962 *Historic Railway Disasters*. Hersham: Ian Allan Ltd. Revised *BAC*, 1992.

ROLT, T L C 1966 *Red For Danger*. London: Pan Books.

STODDART, ANNA M 1906 *The Life of Isabella Bird*. London: John Murray.

WILSON, CONRAD 1993 *Playing for Scotland: The History of the Scottish National Orchestra*. Glasgow: Harper-Collins.

WILSON, MICHAEL ALLAN 2008 *From Trench to Sky: Letters Home 1915–1918*. Durham: Roundtuit Publishing.

NEWSPAPERS

The Glasgow Herald (The Herald)
Kilmarnock Standard.

The Oban Times
The Scotsman
The Times

WEB-SITES

www.scotlanspeople.gov.uk
www.findmypast.co.uk
www.ancestry.com
www.theshipslist.com
www.shipwrecksofcorkharbour.com
www.spartacus.schoolnet.co.uk

Acknowledgements

It is all difficult to convey in a few words the depth of gratitude I feel to members of the Allan family. I can only name them and trust they will know how much I valued their help and friendship while writing the story of their family.

Michael and Rosemary Wilson, were the very first family members I met and among the most ardent and generous supporters of this project. They were closely followed by, Rona Baker, Hugh Normand, David and Frances Lander, Lorna Clarke, Shuna Marden, Gillian Dalton and her sister Lady Caroline Ure, Lady Maureen Allan, Jane Stedman, Sarah Henderson, Rosalind Urwin, R Glen Allan. If I have missed a family member I truly am sorry.

As with any project of this nature, libraries, museums, archives are an invaluable source of information. Again I can only hope to list a few: the museum at Tobermory, that house so many of the Aros Papers, and a special mention must be made to Jean Whittaker for the help she has given me. The National Library of Scotland, the National Archives at Edinburgh and Kew deserve a special mention, their digital collections have made research a pleasure. Liverpool Libraries and Maritime Museum, also have rendered a service beyond anything I could have expected. If I have not listed those libraries and archives that are mentioned in the source notes.

A special mentioned should be given to the Quebec Family History Society and the Manitoba Genealogical Society Inc; the Shropshire Family History Society, they supplied me with fascinating information.

In conclusion, and I know I have failed to record all those who have assisted me but I must ask for their indulgence. However, there are a few people I must name, Mary Hancox, Bedales School; Martin Williams, Hurstpierpoint School; Christine McLaren: Edwin Atkinson; Tony O'Mahony, Lorna Bryne and James Gibson.

Four other people deserve a very special vote of thanks: my husband Dr James C Borland; Graham Lumsden, typesetter, whose expertise is why the pages of this book are so beautifully designed; Ken Mitchell, printer and designer who has given such an extraordinary degree of service; and Dr Michael Halls, who was always there when I needed him.

I have attempted to locate all copyright holders, but in some cases this has been impossible. I apologise unreservedly to anyone whose copyright I may have infringed.

Maureen Borland

June 2013

Source Notes

PART ONE 1750–1869

Chapter 1 *Old Rome*

1. *Ayrshire Notes* 37, Spring 2009: taken from *The Statistical Account of Scotland:* Drawn up from the communications of ministers of different parishes. W Creech, Edinburgh, 1793, vol. 7.
2. Andrew Jack, letter, 4 October 1886.
3. Thomas Lovell Beddoes, *Dream-Pedlary,* written 1830, published 1851.

Chapter 2 *New Horizon*

1. *Glasgow Herald,* 27 March 1820.
2. C W Jones, *Pioneer Shipowners,* Vol V1, 1935.
3. Ibid.
4. Andrew Jack, letter, 4 October 1886.
5. *Ayrshire Notes,* Spring 2009.
6. Ibid.
7. *Kilmarnock Standard,* 29 April 1905.

Chapter 3 *A Long Voyage*

1. *Albion,* letter, R Glen Allan.
2. Ibid.
3. Ibid.
4. Ibid.
5. Ibid.
6. Ibid.
7. Ibid.

Chapter 4 *Shipping Disasters*

1. *Glasgow Herald,* 8 June 1964.

[2] *Memoirs & Portraits of 100 Glasgow Men*, University of Strathclyde Digital Library. Published by James Maclehose & Sons, Glasgow, 1886

[3] *The Scotsman*, 9 March 1860, p. 2.

[4] *The Scotsman*, 24 June 1861, p. 3.

[5] Ibid.

[6] Ibid.

[7] *The Scotsman*, 11 May 1863, p. 3.

[8] *The Scotsman*, 5 June 1863, p. 3.

[9] *The Scotsman*, 9 March 1864, p. 3.

[10] *The Times,* 25 April 1864, p. 12.

Chapter 5 *Bird & Dunlop*

[1] *The Scotsman*, 16 June 1866, p. 7.

[2] Anna M Stoddart, *The Life of Isabella Bird*, published by John Murray, London, 1906, p. 53.

[3] Ibid.

[4] *Scottish-History* (*History of the Kilt*), on the *Internet*.

[5] Anna M Stoddart.

[6] *TheShipsList.Com.*

[7] Ibid.

[8] Ibid.

[9] Ibid.

[10] Ibid.

[11] Ibid.

PART TWO 1870–1893

Chapter 6 *Politics & Aros*

[1] *The Scotsman*, 6 November 1871, p. 6.

[2] *The Scotsman,* 26 August 1871, p. 6.

[3] Andrew Aird, *Glimpses of Old Glasgow,* published by Aird & Coghill, Glasgow, 1894, p. 399.

[4] *Grieve's Scrapbook of Obituaries*, Mitchell Library, Glasgow.

[5] Ibid.

[6] *The Scotsman*, 8 October 1873, p. 5.

[7] Ibid.

[8] *Glasgow Herald,* 8 October 1873.

[9] *Liverpool Paper,* not identified: Liverpool Library, and Macfie Internet page.

Chapter 7 *Arise Sir Hugh*

[1] *Dictionary of Canadian Biography On-Line Vol X1*, 1881–1890, p. 2.
[2] Ibid.
[3] *The Daily Free Press,* 16 February 1877.
[4] Thomas E Appleton, *Ravenscrag: The Allan Royal Mail Line,* published by McClelland & Stewart Ltd, Toronto, 1974, p. 129.
[5] *Glimpses of Old Glasgow.*
[6] Thereforeinformation.info/quarrierhomes.
[7] *Who's Who in Glasgow in 1909.*

Chapter 8 *Change of Management*

[1] *Dictionary of Canadian Biography On-Line*, p. 8.
[2] Ibid.
[3] Ibid, p. 9.
[4] *The Scotsman*, 18 February 1886, p. 5.
[5] *The Scotsman,* 15 May 1886, p. 8.

Chapter 9 *Love & Loss*

[1] *Memoires & Portraits of 100 Glasgow Men.*
[2] Andrew Jack. Copy of letter in care of James Gibson of the Burns Society.
[3] *Paisley Daily Post*, 28 April 1886.
[4] Ibid.
[5] *The Times*, 6 August 1889, p. 9.
[6] Ibid.
[7] *The People's Friend*, 29 April 1911. Copy also in the Alexander Allan Estate of Aros Papers at the Mull Museum
[8] Aros Estate Papers, 01-025-009.

Chapter 10 *Sadness*

[1] *The Scotsman*, 24 August 1900, p. 9.
[2] Gillian Dalton, *Discourses.*
[3] *The Scotsman*, 4 April 1892, p. 6.
[4] Martin Williams, College Archivist, Hurstpierpoint College, November 2011.
[5] Conrad Wilson, *Playing for Scotland*, published by Harper Collins, 1993, p. 2.
[6] *The Scotsman*, 31 October 1893, p. 5.
[7] Ibid: 7 November 1893, p. 5.
[8] *Montreal Daily Star*, 16 January 1893, p. 6.

9 Ibid.
10 Ibid.
11 *Montreal Daily Star*, 18 January 1893, p. 6.

PART THREE 1894–1914
Chapter 11 *Pleasures*

1 *Oban Times*, 15 June 1895, Aros Estate Papers.
2 Ibid: 29 June 1895, Aros Estate papers.
3 *Glasgow Herald*, 30 January 1892.
4 Ibid.
5 Ibid.
6 Ibid: 16 December 1897.
7 *Scottish Mining Web-Site*.
8 *The Times*, 19 August 1896, p. 5.
9 *Glasgow Herald*, 29 August 1896.
10 *The Times,* 5 June 1896, p. 9.
11 Ibid: 13 January 1898, p. 4.

Chapter 12 *Problems*

1 Aros Estate Papers, 02-025/009.
2 *The Scotsman*, 2 April 1900, p. 10.
3 Ibid.
4 Ibid.
5 *Montreal Daily Star*, 28 June 1901, p. 7.
6 Ibid.
7 *The Scotsman*, 20 June 1901.

Chapter 13 *Janie & Politics*

1 *The Scotsman,* 25 January 1898, p. 8.
2 Ibid.
3 Ibid.
4 *Glasgow Herald*, 5 February 1900.
5 Ibid: 3 November 1900.
6 *The Scotsman*, 19 February 1903, p. 5.
7 Ibid: 7 October 1903, p. 6.
8 Ibid: 7 April 1904, p. 5.
9 Ibid: 27 May 1904, p. 5.
10 Ibid: 18 June 1904, p. 11.
11 Ibid: 15 November 1904, p. 5.
12 Ibid: 30 September 1904, p. 6.
13 Ibid: 5 December 1904, p. 10.

Chapter 14 *Goodbye Old Friends*

[1] *The Scotsman,* 26 December 1904, p. 4.
[2] Ibid: 3 April 1905, p. 8.
[3] Ibid: 15 April 1905, p. 7.
[4] *Kilmarnock Standard*, 29 April 1905.
[6] *The Scotsman*, 7 October 1905.
[7] *Kilmarnock Standard,* December 1999.
[8] *Ancestry.com, Historical Newspapers,* 1851–2003.
[9] *The Scotsman*, 18 February 1902, p. 7.

Chapter 15 *Change of Direction*

[1] *The Scotsman*, 1 July 1909, p. 9.
[2] Ibid: 11 August 1909, p. 9.
[3] Ibid: 14 September 1909, p. 6.
[4] Ibid: 10 November 1909, p. 12.
[5] Ibid: 28 March 1910, p. 9.
[6] Martin Williams, Hurstpierpoint College.
[7] Peter Slowe, *Manny Shinwell*, published by Pluto Press, 1993, p. 38.
[8] *The Herald*, 100 Years Ago, March 2011.
[9] (1) David Marquand, *Ramsay MacDonald*, published by Jonathan Cape, 1977. (2) Green Benches, *Leicester Pioneer*, 9 March 1912.
[10] John Simkin, *Spartacus.school.co.uk.*
[11] Ibid.
[12] Ibid.
[13] *The Scotsman*, 14 March 1913, p. 8.
[14] Ibid.
[15] Ibid.
[16] Ibid.
[17] NLS (ACC4498) Janie Allan Archives.

PART FOUR 1915–1925
Chapter 16 *Lusitania*

[1] *Montreal Star*, 26 September 1951.
[2] *The Scotsman*, 12 February 1915, p. 5.
[3] Ibid: 12 May 1915, p. 10.
[4] Ibid: 16 June 1915, p. 10.
[5] Ibid: 2 July 1915, p. 11.
[6] Ibid: 17 June 1915, p. 8.
[7] Ibid: 19 July 1915, p. 5.

[8] Ibid.
[9] Ibid.

Chapter 17 *Quintinshill*

[1] O S Nock, *The Caledonian Railway,* published by Ian Allan Ltd, 1963.
[2] O S Nock, *Historic Railway Disasters*, published by Ian Allan Ltd, 1966; revised by B K Cooper, published by BAC, 1992.
[3] Ibid: p. 95.
[4] Robert Gilkison Allan's obituary – unnamed Liverpool Paper.
[5] Michael Wilson, *From Trenches to Sky*: *Letters Home 1915–1918,* published by Roundtuit, 2008.

Chapter 18 *Warriors*

[1] The Will of James Alexander Allan.
[2] Tony O'Mahony, *Shipwrecks of Cork Harbour.*
[3] Ibid.
[4] Ibid.
[5] Ibid.
[6] *The Scotsman*, 21 February 1917, p. 4.
[7] Ibid
[8] Ibid
[9] C W Munn, *The History of the Clydesdale Bank,* published by Collins/ Clydesdale Bank, 1988, p. 83.
[10] *The Scotsman*, 11 March 1918, p. 4.
[11] Ibid: 29 April 1918, p. 4.
[12] Ibid: 22 November 1918, p. 3.
[13] Ibid
[14] General Jack Seely, *Warrior: The Amazing Story of a Real War Horse*, re-published by Racing Post Books, 2011, p. 79.
[15] Ibid: p. 131.
[16] *www.WorldHorseWelfare.co.uk.*
[17] *The Scotsman,* 20 March 1919, p. 3.
[18] Ibid: 11 December 1918, p. 7.

Chapter 19 *An Uncertain Future*

[1] *Who's Who in Glasgow*, 1909.
[2] Ibid.
[3] *The Scotsman*, 21 January 1920, p. 8.
[4] Ibid: 7 November 1921, p. 9.
[5] Ibid: 11 July 1923, p. 13.

6 *The Times*, 25 March 1922, p. 9.

7 Ibid.

8 Ibid: 14 November 1922, p. 9.

Chapter 20 *Sayonara*

1 *The Scotsman*, 2 February 1923, p. 7.

2 Ibid: 8 February 1923, p. 4.

3 *The Times*, 21 February 1923.

4 C W Munn, p. 153.

5 *The Times*, 14 February 1924, p. 18.

6 *Miss Cohen's Diary*, privately printed by Charles E Allan, 1926.

7 Ibid.

8 Ibid.

9 Ibid.

10 Ibid.

11 Ibid.

PART FIVE 1926–1955

Chapter 21 *Death of a Laird*

1 *The Times*, 2 July 1925, p. 25.

2 Ibid: 2 December 1929, p. 9.

3 Ibid.

4 *Manitoba Free Press*, 20 March 1926.

5 Aros Estate Papers.

6 Lady Nora Fairfax-Lucy, *Hebridean Childhood*, published Richard Drew Ltd, 1981, p. 89.

7 Ibid: p. 90.

8 *The Scotsman*, December 1927.

Chapter 22 *Fatal Times*

1 *The Times*, 2 November 1926.

2 Ibid: 3 January 1929, p. 7.

3 *The Scotsman*, 3 January 1930, p. 7.

4 Ibid: 6 February 1930, p. 5.

5 Ibid.

6 *The Times*, 13 February 1931, p. 4.

7 Ibid.

Chapter 23 *More Tragedy*

1 *The Scotsman*, 15 February 1932, p. 7.

2 Ibid: 2 February 1933, p. 6.

[3] Ibid.

[4] Martin Williams, Hurstpierpoint College.

[5] *The Times,* 17 August 1928, p. 8.

[6] *The Scotsman,* 6 September 1933, p. 3.

Chapter 24 *Prelude*

[1] *The Times,* 17 March 1930, p. 5.

[2] Ibid: 2 August 1932, p. 11.

[3] Ibid: 7 August 1933.

[4] *The Oban Times*, 22 May 1937.

[5] Ibid.

[6] *The Scotsman*, 20 May 1937, p. 10.

[7] Ibid: 6 December 1939, p. 8.

[8] Ibid: 28 May 1937, p. 7.

[9] Letter from R A Allan, in M A Wilson's Collection.

Chapter 25 *Their World Changed*

[1] *The Times*, Letter to Editor, 7 January 1939, p. 8.

[2] Ibid.

[3] Newspaper cutting M A Wilson.

[4] *Montreal Theatre, 1920–1949, Setting the Stage,* Herbert Whittaker, McGill-Queen's University Press, Montreal.

[5] *The RNVR*, p. 200.

[6] *The Times*, 23 August 1943, p. 3.

[7] Minutes of Dumbarton Presbytery, September 1945, M A Wilson.

[8] Archives, Oriel College, Oxford.

[9] Hansard On-Line, March 1952.

General Index

Allan Male Members

JAMES ALLAN, Dundonald

Sons of James:

Alexander – Capt Sandy, Dundonald, Saltcoats, Greenock, Glasgow

John, Dundonald, Loudoun, Newmilns

Andrew, Dundonald, Loudoun, Galston

James, Dundonald, Mauchline.

CAPT SANDY

Sons of:

James – Capt James

Hugh – Sir Hugh, Montreal

Bryce – Capt Bryce, Liverpool, Aros

Andrew – Old Andrew, Montreal

Alexander, Glasgow

Sons: Robert Smith (RobertS)

James Alexander (JamesA)

Henry

Claud

James AlexanderA

Alexander

Hamish

John (Jack)

CAPT JAMES

Sons of Capt James:

Alexander

Robert Gilkison – RobertG, Liverpool

James Hugh – JamesH, Liverpool, Shrawley Wood
Bryce – Bryce of Wemyss Bay
Son: James Bryce, Ballikinrain
Richard Gilkison – RichardG,
Son: Richard
Grandson: Richard (Dick)

SIR HUGH
Sons of Sir Hugh:
Alexander Rae, Ontario
Son: Hugh Travers
James Bryce of Boston
Hugh Montagu (Sir)
Son: Hugh
Arthur Edward, Montreal

OLD ANDREW
Sons of Old Andrew:
John Smith – JohnS, Montreal
Son: Andrew Hamilton
Andrew Alexander, Montreal
Hugh Andrew, Montreal
James Bryce, QC, Montreal
William Rae, Winnipeg

ALEXANDER of Glasgow
Sons of Alexander:
Robert Smith – RobertS, Glasgow, Hafton
Charles Edward – CharlesE, Belfast
James Alexander – JamesA, Glasgow
Henry, Glasgow
Claud Andrew, Kilmahew

CLAUD
Sons of Claud:
Charles Claud – Charlie
Robert Alexander – Bobby, Lord Allan of Kilmahew

ALEXANDER of Aros
Son of:
Col Bryce of Aros
Grandson: Alastair Hugh